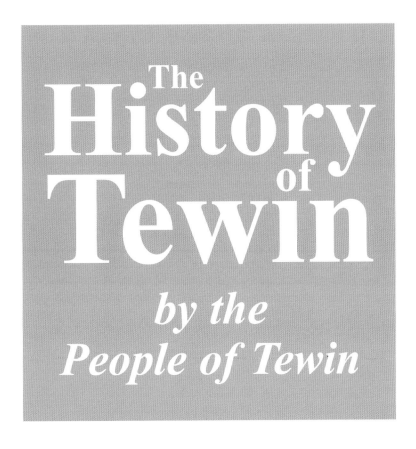

The History of Tewin

by the People of Tewin

TEWIN ORCHARD IN ASSOCIATION WITH THE TEWIN SOCIETY
2009

The History of Tewin by the People of Tewin

Published by **Tewin Orchard** in association with **The Tewin Society History Association**
1 Upper Green Tewin Welwyn Hertfordshire AL6 0LX
ISBN 978-0-9549508-3-6   EAN 9780954950835
Copyright 2009

This book is based on *The History of Tewin Exhibition*, originally held in
Tewin Memorial Hall in 2000 to celebrate the Millennium.
A great deal of research was carried out at that time, and has continued throughout the
preparation of the book. Apart from official sources, including written accounts, the Tewin
History Book Committee has drawn heavily on information given by local people, hence the
full title. Every effort has been made to present the facts as accurately as possible, but we
have learned that official accounts can vary and, with the passage of time, personal
recollections can differ. Therefore, if there are any inaccuracies or misrepresentations, we
sincerely apologise. We are also aware that there may be additional stories not covered in
the book, but hope you will appreciate that it is not possible to include everything. However,
if you have information which you feel should be held in our archives, please contact us at
tewinorchard.co.uk and any original pictures copied will be returned at once.

The History of Tewin by the People of Tewin was completed after three years by a mainly
amateur group of authors. It covers the history of the village from 500,000 BC to the present
day and has been a challenging but enjoyable project. The Book Group members wish to
thank everyone who contributed. We also thank our Editor, Patricia Klijn, who kindly took
on the mammoth task of putting the book together and displayed great patience in coping
with ten authors. Our thanks also go to Emma Pitrakou for her understanding and diligence
in preparing our work for publication.
We are also most grateful to Michael and Anna Clark who, for many months, have
welcomed us all into their home where the book has been put together and prepared for
printing. Special thanks are due to Michael who, with his knowledge as an author and of the
publishing world, has been our guide and adviser throughout.
Finally, we appreciate greatly the interest shown in our project by Viscount Gage and
Lord Laming of Tewin and thank them for their contributions.
The Book Group members: Elizabeth Wilson (Chairman), Linda Adams, Jean Canton,
Michael Clark, Mary Gregg, Patrick Holden, John Lee, Rosemary Nodder,
Ben Roberts, Lilian Southgate. (See full credits on page 260).

Cover: S. Crosbie's *Tewin, 1919* watercolour by kind permission of Pauline & Tom Warehand. (Tom can be seen
as as Tewin schoolboy on page 92).
Front endpaper: Alf Fulford's *Tewin Lower Green, Spring 2009*, exhibited at the Spring Show.
Back endpaper: *Tewin Memorial Hall*, June 2009.

Printed by Times Offset in Malaysia

Foreword

There are many reasons why I have found it daunting to accept the Tewin Society's flattering offer to write a foreword to this admirable and much needed history. Firstly, I am ignorant of so much of the local history and, therefore, a large portion of the content of this book. As a child, Tewin, Welwyn Garden City and the Queen Hoo Hall were all far-off places. The petrol rationing precluded us from driving to them and their distance from Panshanger House was out of walking distance for a nanny and her charges. Hertford was another matter since there was a regular bus route. The most pressing fear in writing this foreword, however, is that it could be pointed out that our family were responsible for the destruction of Panshanger House where my grandparents, the Desboroughs, lived throughout the War.

I went there every holiday and my sister lived there for a while during the latter War years. We continued our visits right up to the death of my grandmother in 1952. My grandfather, who lived downstairs, surrounded by innumerable silver trophies earned on account of his athletic prowess, used to keep a loaded 303 gun under his bed in case he saw a German! He died in 1945, but I remember him chasing us around the parterres with his walking stick and throwing sweets to the local children when they visited Panshanger from local schools. Obviously, I knew my grandmother better since she lived for a further seven years. I remember her playing tennis in thick fur gloves and to the end of her life she held court to the great and the good. Even in the War, Winston Churchill found time to come down to see her when she lay bedridden after a stroke. Ambitious and intimidating socialite she may well once have been, but I remember her as a dear and loving grandmother.

I could draw you every room in the impressive High Victorian mausoleum of a house, which contained the vast collection of the Earl Cowpers. I remember, aged 11, frequently visiting the enormous picture gallery, generally completely deserted, where Rembrandts, Tintorettos, Guardis, Correggios and other priceless Italian and Dutch Masters were hung, one above the other, threatened by the occasional fungus. As children we, and a curious assortment of completely Dickensian retainers, had our meals in the back of the house. We only met our grandparents at lunch or at tea when my grandmother used often to read to us. I remember the locked room where the private possessions of my legendary war hero uncles, killed in the 1914 War, were stored. Had they lived, Panshanger would have been a different story. I also remember the aged gardeners and the overgrown garden paths, loved by the Cowpers, which were much too complex to be maintained by them. I also recall, aged nearly 18, that I had an unfulfilled ambition to find an alleged secret passage behind one of the panels in the state room, but I never succeeded.

Panshanger had an enjoyable but slightly melancholic atmosphere. Now, apart from the derelict Orangery and the stables, nothing whatever remains of the great house. Of course the destruction of the country house is and was endemic. In the 1950s there seemed so little future in great houses and so few building materials with which to maintain them, which I suppose was the case in the early years of the 19th century too, when Tewin House and our own strangely similar, but equally beautiful, Gage property – High Meadow – met similar fates.

One cannot mourn forever. I am immensely grateful to the local historians who have written this learned and instructive book and hope that by their splendid efforts something of the greatness of the Cowpers, and fascinating glimpses of the other areas depicted, can be preserved and passed on to other generations.

Nicolas Gage.

Viscount Gage, Firle Place, Firle, Lewes, East Sussex

Introduction

About a decade ago, just before the turn of the century, a very enthusiastic group of volunteers were busily putting together a History Exhibition of the story of Tewin and its people to mark the millennium. Villagers shared photographs and documents that ensured it was a great success. It generated a vast amount of interest from far and wide. So much so that many thought it would be a huge mistake if the treasures of the history of the village and surroundings were to be lost. As a result a group of volunteers set about a formidable task of serious research, drafting and the preparation of the publication of an authoritative book on the past and present of this community.

For me it is a great honour to make this minor contribution and, much more important, to be given this opportunity to congratulate the authors and to pay a warm tribute to them for their industry, endeavour, determination and now their success. Together they have produced a remarkable publication that does justice to the rich history of this village and its people. There can be few small villages blessed by such a remarkable range of historic buildings and consequently a distinctive variety of occupations and social history. Perhaps one of the most surprising aspects of the village is that it survives as a vibrant community despite its location and easy access to London. It remains a healthy, lively community surrounded by attractive working countryside whilst retaining its engagement with the wider society.

There is so much in this book that casts light on the changing social order, new styles in architecture, developments in education and employment as well as leisure activities. The village benefits greatly by having an active Parish Council, numerous voluntary and special interest groups, sports facilities, public houses and restaurants, a well supported parish church, working farms, energetic wildlife groups, a highly regarded school and village shop run by the community for its benefit. In these days of concern about the anonymity of many housing estates and suburban areas this village remains a beacon of social cohesion engaging all ages.

The fascinating chapters on the historic past are matched by the most informative information on the local wildlife and the variety and richness of the countryside. Farm work may now employ fewer people but it has an important impact on the productiveness and attractiveness of the environment.

The authors of this book deserve warmest congratulations for producing a publication that provides something for everyone. More than that the book is a positive treasure trove of how a community responds to so many changes, affecting every aspect of life, yet not only survives but actually prospers. It is my pleasure on behalf of all readers to congratulate the authors and to thank them for their achievements. Most of all I have no hesitation in commending this book to you. I am sure you will enjoy it.

The Lord Laming of Tewin
June 2009

Contents

Chapter 1

500,000 years ago

500,000 years ago, all life, human, animal and plant, was ruled by the climatic fluctuations of an Ice Age. England was then part of a continuous European land mass.

In what is now East Anglia, a large Ancestral Thames and the Bytham River (since disappeared) made their way across country to join a tributary of the Rhine in a large flat delta in what is now the North Sea.

If Tewin had existed it would have been on the North bank of the Ancestral Thames, which ran from near Henley via St Albans, and through the Ware Valley on its way to its delta.

Also at this time, successive generations of Ancient Man, having migrated over many thousands of years from their place of origin in Africa, reached several locations in what is now England.

The closest locations to Tewin were 50 miles away at High Lodge and Warren Hill by the Bytham River, near present day Mildenhall, Suffolk. There large family groups settled long enough to leave numbers of stone tools as their only trace.

After the Anglian Glaciation

After the Anglian Glaciation ended about 420,000 years ago, the climate continued to fluctuate, and the River Thames developed new tributaries and settled into its present route.

Long periods of intermittent settlement by Ancient Man took place in the South East of England on sites by rivers and lakes. There are two local areas where significant discoveries were made in the period

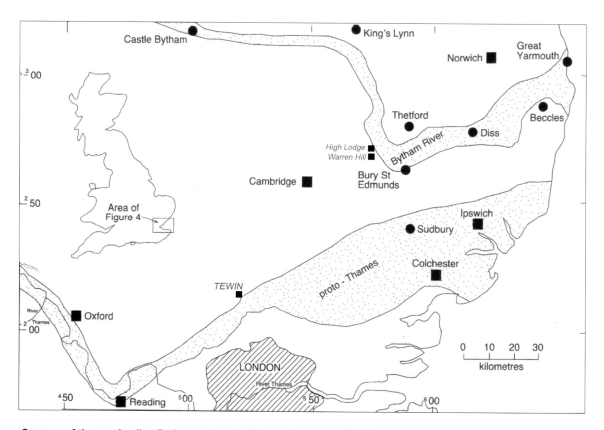

Courses of the pre-Anglian Bytham and proto-Thames rivers, modified from Hamblin & Moorlock (1995) by J B Riding *et al*. High Lodge and Warren Hill are shown in red on the map.

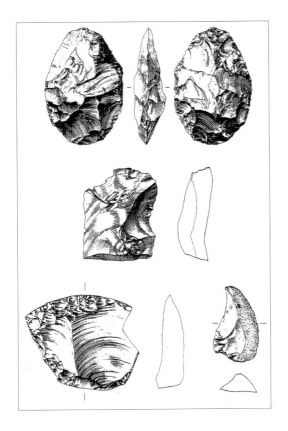
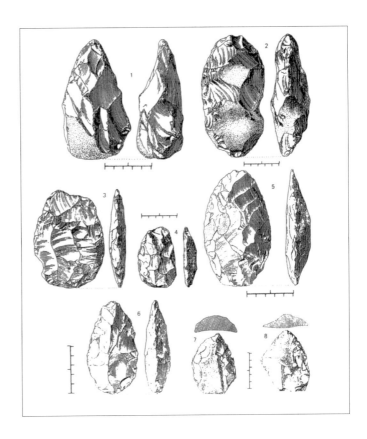

Left: **Examples of Lower Palaeolithic artefacts from High Lodge. High Lodge provides evidence for pre- Anglian human occupancy in Britain, at a location that was subsequently overridden by the Anglian ice sheet.**
Right: **Artefacts from Warren Hill of a similar date to those from High Lodge.**

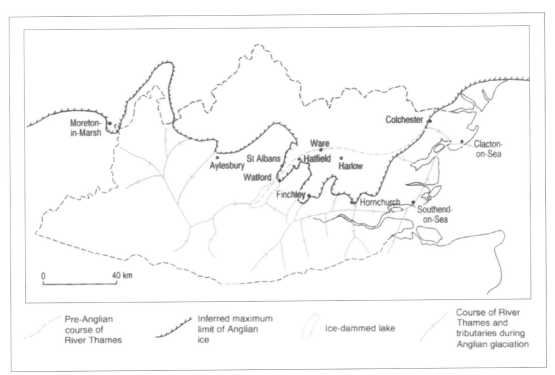

The extent of Anglian glaciation in the region, the blockage of the Vale of St. Albans by Anglian ice, and the diversion of the River Thames.

between the end of the 19th and in the early part of the 20th centuries.

Near the north-west Hertfordshire town of Hitchin, 64 hand axes were found in a lake bed deposit at Jeeves Pit. Implements were found in similar deposits in other Hitchin brickyards and in one at Stevenage, just six miles north of Tewin. Analysis of the deposits gives these implements an age of 250,000 to 350,000 years.

Some of the hand axes are in the Hertford Museum

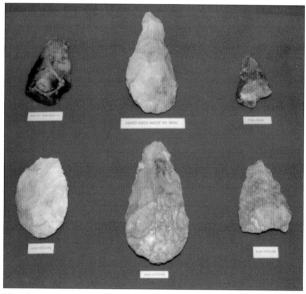

Hand axes on display at Hertford Museum.

and are shown in the photograph above.

Near the village of Caddington, just over the border into Bedfordshire, between Markyate and Luton, sites here on the slopes of the Chilterns have yielded 150 hand axes and over 3,500 flakes. An age in the range of 150,000 to 250,000 years is estimated for these implements.

Pressure caused by the need to survive in long periods of intense cold for over 100,000 years caused Ancient Man to adapt and evolve into a new race in North Western Europe, Neanderthal Man. This happened by about 200,000 years ago.

Neanderthals were the sole inhabitants of our region until about 40,000 years ago when a new immigrant arrived on the scene and, in a period of a few thousand years, modern people had arrived.

Very few finds have been made for the period from 70,000 BC to 20,000 BC, partly due to the Devensian Glaciation.

A selection of flint hand tools found in the vicinity of Hopkyns' Wood and Upper Green, Tewin.

Neolithic Age
6500-4500 years ago

After the old Stone Age intermittent settlement continued in our region. It was a period of hunter-gatherers travelling mainly by boat with temporary settlements on the banks of rivers. This was an age called the Mesolithic. Occasional surface finds have been made. As the river level was eight or nine feet lower it requires excavation to find the traces. Major finds were made during the extension of the GlaxoSmithKline pharmaceutical site at Ware.

As average temperatures rose, water levels increased, flooding the North Sea and making the separation of England from the Continent more permanent.

The change from hunting to farming had already occurred in the Middle East and groups of farming people were migrating across Europe. Their settlement in England led to a change in lifestyle and the evolution of new types of tools suited to tree felling, planting, primitive ploughing and harvesting. This was the Neolithic period. Without major excavations actual living sites are not accessible and we are limited to surface finds in modern ploughed fields. Flint working at this time included the polishing of stone axe heads to make them more efficient and the creation of scythes by glueing small pieces of flint to a wood or bone backing. Some of the flint work was very precise and the illustration on page 9 shows the way Neolithic man made his own kit of small tools.

Ware museum holds a collection of Mesolithic and Neolithic finds.

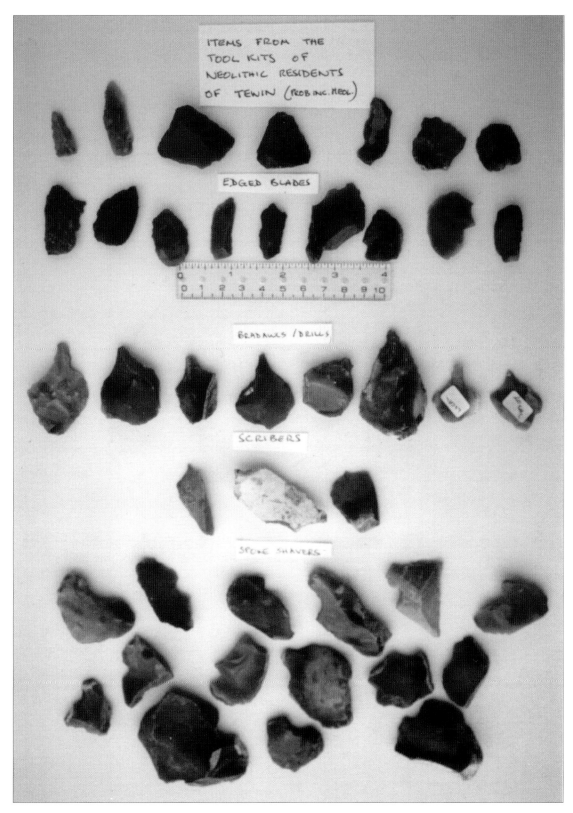

The Neolithic tool kit: from top to bottom; edged blades for cutting; bradawls/drills mainly used to make holes for sewing skins; scribers points used to mark pottery and metal; spoke shaves, which have two uses, making small shafts for arrows and thinning split tendons for sewing.

Bronze Age 4500-2700 years ago

The Bronze Age and Tewin

There is firm evidence from a grave found near the Volunteer range at Tewin that there was Bronze Age activity in our area. A beaker and a spearhead found on the old site of Wimley Bury Manor (Sewells Orchard) and a socketed axe found near Tewin Water confirms this. These finds are pictured here with an example of a bronzesmith's hoard found at Hertford Heath.

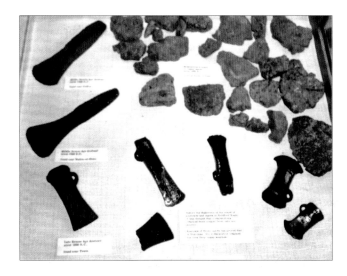

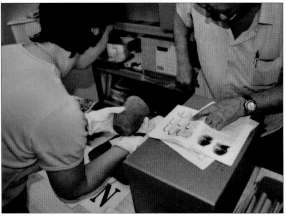

Above left: **The Tewin beaker was found in 1955 in a grave damaged by chalk extraction near the Volunteer Rifle Range. It is Bronze Age of 1900-1700 years BC approximately. Beakers are a form of pottery which reached Britain from Europe about 2000BC and by about 1500BC had been replaced by indigenous items. The beaker is 13cm high and 9.5cm in diameter. Its decoration is by small comb on the neck and by fingernail imprint on the belly. Beakers like this were for domestic use. They are found in single graves with grave goods representing personal belongings. The beaker is currently on display at Mill Green Museum, Hatfield.**
Bottom left: **Confirming identification of the beaker.**
Above right: **The spearhead is 9cm long and dates to the later Bronze Age 1200-800 BC. It was found in 1936 during the building of 106 Orchard Road.**
Above left: **This socket axe-head is 9cm long and dates to the later Bronze Age 1200-800BC.**
Bottom right: **Metal workers hoard of bronze ingots and axe-heads about 1000BC. Found at Hertford Heath.**

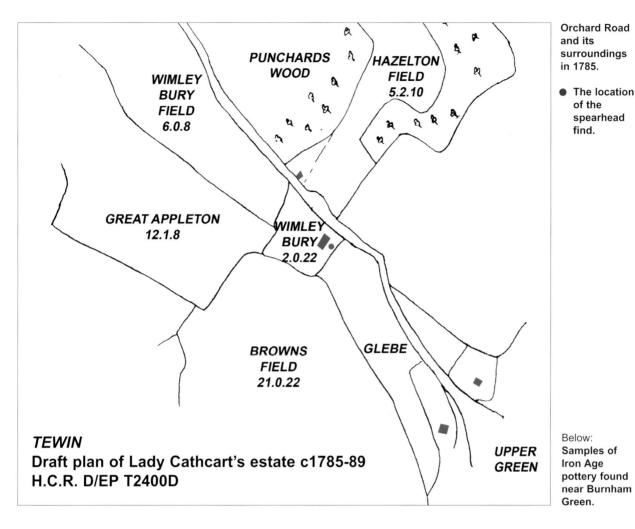

Orchard Road and its surroundings in 1785.

● The location of the spearhead find.

WIMLEY BURY FIELD 6.0.8

PUNCHARDS WOOD

HAZELTON FIELD 5.2.10

GREAT APPLETON 12.1.8

WIMLEY BURY 2.0.22

BROWNS FIELD 21.0.22

GLEBE

UPPER GREEN

TEWIN
Draft plan of Lady Cathcart's estate c1785-89
H.C.R. D/EP T2400D

Below: Samples of Iron Age pottery found near Burnham Green.

Iron Age
2700 -2100 years ago

At nearby Hertford, Welwyn, Braughing and Wheathampstead significant finds have been made. Royal burials have been found at Welwyn and Panshanger. Iron Age pottery has been found at Burnham Green near a major Iron Age farm excavated by local archaeologist Tony Rook.

Romans
BC 55-54, AD 43-410 (approx)

By 50,000BC tribes of Belgae were settling in South East England. In our area the tribe of Catuvellauni settled at nearby Welwyn, Wheathampstead and close to the site of Verulamium.

Local settlements were at Lockley's, Welwyn, with its Roman bath. A manor at Welwyn and Prae Wood near Verulamium were the start of other developments. The area of Tewin would have been used for food crops.

Anglo Saxons
AD 410 - 800

The name 'Tewin'

Much has been written about the origins of the name 'Tewin'. The situation is not helped by the almost complete absence of early Saxon remains in our area.

M J Whittock in *'The Origins of England 410-600'* suggests there was a setback in the early settlement of Essex. It suffered an eclipse in the early 6th century, possibly due to a British revival after the Battle of Badon.

Its ruling dynasty was established in the early 6th century by King Aescwine who probably ruled in the decades after 510AD. He may have established rule in this demoralised region, if not it was done by his father Offa or grandfather Bedca before 500AD.

There are grounds for believing that the ruling dynasty was peculiar. Firstly it claimed descent from Seaxnet, not from Woden. The rejection of Woden was unique. The Kings of Essex claimed descent from the warrior god of the Saxons an older mythology than Woden.

It is stated that in the 4th century a migration of a tribe called the Swaefe occurred. They left East Holstein and Mecklenberg and migrated to the Lower Elbe river near Cuxhaven, Germany. There they united with a local tribe [using a runic symbol '↑' to decorate their pots] and became known as Swaefo Saxons. Pottery with this marking has been found near Norwich.

It is considered by M J Whittock that the cult name 'Tiw' (or 'Tew' the Swaefo Saxon god of war) is preserved in the place names – 'Tewin', and in 'Tuesley' (Surrey). This view is supported by the fact that the Swaefo Saxon dynasty had dominance by the end of the 6th century over 'Greater Essex', an area including Middlesex, London and much of Hertfordshire.

It seems quite probable that a small group from this tribe gave us their name.

Hertford Mint

The Saxon Kings were the first to make silver pennies in England. A piece of silver, weighing one pound, was divided into 240 parts. These were made into pennies and were used for everyday life. For book-keeping, however, the pound was divided into 20 shillings, each worth 12 pennies.

There were few early Saxon mints, where the

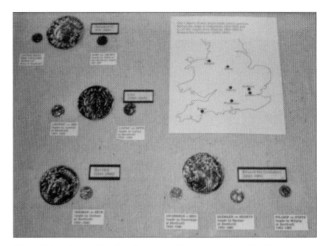

Top: **Coins from the Hertford minters including Godman (1038-1040), Deorrsige (1044-1046), Saemar (1059-1066) and Wilgrip (1062-1065). Location of Mints are shown on the map: Chester, Derby, Oxford, Exeter, Winchester, London and Hertford.**

pennies were made. The number was increased in 924 and by 1066 there were 87 towns where pennies had been made. Only 7 of these towns made pennies during the reign of Aethelstan (924-939) and in all the reigns from Eadwig (955-959) to Edward the Confessor (1042-1066).

Hertford was one of these 7 towns. Coins continued to be made at Hertford until the reign of William II, about 30 years after the Norman Conquest.

A reference to Tewin in an Anglo-Saxon will of 980AD

Aethelgifu declares her will

Aethelgifu was a wealthy widow with Royal connections (Aethelred II 'The Unready') and her properties and interests were in many parts of what are now Hertfordshire and nearby Bedfordshire.

The interest for Tewin is that she left a major part of her estate to a favourite kinsman, Leofsige, and his large inheritance included an estate at Tewin.

'The land at Offley and all that the title deed directs is to be given to Leofsige and the land at Tewin as swine pasture for him on condition that from these two estates he provides for the community of St Albans three days food rent each year (16 measures malt, 3 of meal, 2lbs of honey from Offley, 8 wethers, 6 lambs, 1 bullock for slaughter and 30 cheeses)'.

'Aethelgifu begs the Queen, Emma of Normandy, that the legatee Leofsige is allowed to serve Atheling'.

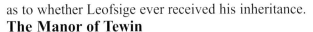

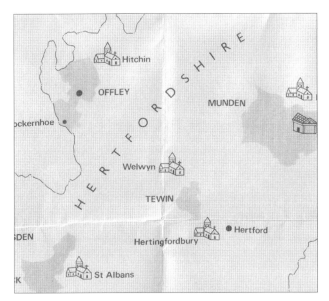

Top: **Extract from map showing Aethelgifu's land and properties.**

Personal bequests in Aethelgifu's will

**Ethelred Unraed
B79-1016**

Aethelgifu

Aethelgifu's 'kirtles' (dresses) and head-dresses were to be left to the ladies of her household and to her female relatives.

Headband, probably richly embroidered and decorated 'mancuses' pieces of gold, to be cut off and distributed to friends and relatives.

Head-dress, Aethelgifu gave her 'best head-dress' to Beornwynn. This may have been linen rather than wool.

Subsequent developments

In 1015, the Atheling, Aethelstan, left land in Tewin to two laymen, Aethelweard the Stammerer, and Lyfmg.

In the Domesday Book, the Abbot of Westminster is recorded as owning a manor in Tewin rated at two and a half hydes. It includes pannage for fifty hogs. This would appear to be the 'land at Tewin'. This raises doubts

as to whether Leofsige ever received his inheritance.

The Manor of Tewin

The written history of Tewin starts with the Domesday Book. This book refers to the ownership of land and its taxable assets and shows that in 1043 Tewin, like most of England, was owned by the King, Edward the Confessor. When he died in 1066 ownership passed to King William who granted the overlordship of the manor to Aldene. By 1166 the rights to these lands had been divided between Godfrey and Brian de Tewin.

Godfrey's grandson - also named Godfrey - granted part of the land to the Prior and convent of St Bartholomew and by 1303 all of it had been passed on to the convent by Godfrey's descendants. Meanwhile the rights to the land held by Brian de Tewin were subdivided. In 1166, part of the land was held by the de Valognes [sic] family, who also owned Bennington [sic] Castle and manor, but by 1323 this had been left to the Priory of St Mary and Little Wymondley. In 1365, records show that some of Brian's land, which in 1377 was now held by the lords of Walkern, had also been passed to the Prior and convent of St Bartholomew. By the middle of the 14th century much of Tewin was held by the church.

This web of overlordships and rights, so difficult to make sense of from our home-owning 21st century perspective, becomes more complicated if we want to understand the geographical history of Tewin. The manor of Tewin as we recognise it today also consisted of four other manors: Marden, Queenhoo [sic] Hall, Tewin House and Wimley Bury.

Around 1050, ownership of the manor of Marden was held by Tova, widow of Wihtric, which after her son's death was passed to the monastery at St Albans. In contrast, it would appear that the church never had possession of the manor of Queenhoo, and that the manor may originally have been classified as part of the manor of Bramfield.

At the time of Domesday Tewin was a part of two Hundreds. The area around Queen Hoo, or Quenildehaga, (Enclosure of a woman called Cwenhild), was in Broadwater Hundred and the rest was in Hertford Hundred. Queen Hoo had 2½ Hides while the rest had 5½ Hides. It appears that a fair sized settlement surrounded Queen Hoo at that time, and in 1334 the tax quota was just under a pound. This assumes at least 24 places or a rule of thumb assessment of a population of about 100 souls. This suggests that Queen Hoo falls into the category of a deserted medieval village. As the present building

OWNERSHIP OF THE MANORS OF TEWIN AND WIMLEY BURY
Since the Norman Conquest

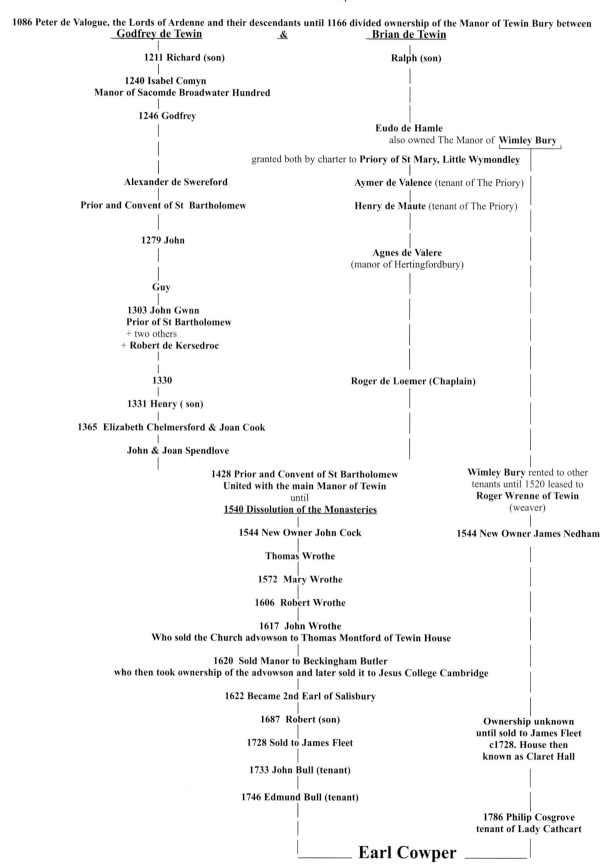

1086 Peter de Valogue, the Lords of Ardenne and their descendants until 1166 divided ownership of the Manor of Tewin Bury between

Godfrey de Tewin	**&**	**Brian de Tewin**

1211 Richard (son)   **Ralph (son)**

1240 Isabel Comyn
Manor of Sacomde Broadwater Hundred

1246 Godfrey

Eudo de Hamle
also owned The Manor of **Wimley Bury**

granted both by charter to **Priory of St Mary, Little Wymondley**

Alexander de Swereford   **Aymer de Valence** (tenant of The Priory)

Prior and Convent of St Bartholomew   **Henry de Maute** (tenant of The Priory)

1279 John

Agnes de Valere
(manor of Hertingfordbury)

Guy

1303 John Gwnn
Prior of St Bartholomew
+ two others
+ **Robert de Kersedroc**

1330   **Roger de Loemer (Chaplain)**

1331 Henry (son)

1365 Elizabeth Chelmersford & Joan Cook

John & Joan Spendlove

1428 Prior and Convent of St Bartholomew
United with the main Manor of Tewin
until
1540 Dissolution of the Monasteries

Wimley Bury rented to other
tenants until 1520 leased to
Roger Wrenne of Tewin
(weaver)

1544 New Owner John Cock   **1544 New Owner James Nedham**

Thomas Wrothe

1572 Mary Wrothe

1606 Robert Wrothe

1617 John Wrothe
Who sold the Church advowson to Thomas Montford of Tewin House

1620 Sold Manor to Beckingham Butler
who then took ownership of the advowson and later sold it to **Jesus College Cambridge**

1622 Became 2nd Earl of Salisbury

1687 Robert (son)

Ownership unknown
until sold to James Fleet
c1728. House then
known as Claret Hall

1728 Sold to James Fleet

1733 John Bull (tenant)

1746 Edmund Bull (tenant)

1786 Philip Cosgrove
tenant of Lady Cathcart

Earl Cowper

was constructed in about 1550 it might be fair to assume that this is the case.

A recorded mention of 'Queenhoo Hall' occurs in 1223-4 when a Richard Hamme of Havering appears to have owned the rights. The manor of Tewin House is only recorded as a separate manor from the beginning of the 17th century when Thomas Montford bought the house from the Lord of the Manor of Tewin.

Before the Reformation and the dissolution of the monasteries, the overlordships of Tewin had largely been passed over to the church. By the middle of the 16th century most of Tewin that had originally been held by Godfrey de Tewin and Brian de Tewin was in the hands of the Prior and convent of St Bartholomew, although some of this land had been subdivided and was held by the manor of Hertingfordbury. This land eventually passed to the Priory of St Mary and Little Wymondley. The manor of Marden had also been passed to the church, but was held by the monastery at St Albans. The manor at Queen Hoo stands out as never having been held by the church, remaining to this day in single family ownerships.

Post Reformation

The dissolution of the Priory of St Bartholomew took place in 1540 when the manor of Tewin was granted to Robert Fuller. Over the next 200 odd years, the manor changed hands 16 times, until George 3rd Earl Cowper became its owner in 1746. The Cowper family consolidated its landholdings, acquiring the manor of Tewin House in 1804 and the manor of Marden in 1877. When Katrine, Countess Cowper died in 1913, Lady Desborough inherited the estate and when she died in 1952 properties and land around Tewin were sold.

Upper Green

From records and maps held by the Records Office in Hertford it is confirmed that the main village of Tewin was for many years a small hamlet based around Upper Green. Houses, shops, a cordwainer (shoe maker), wheelwright, farms, an inn *The Plume of Feathers* and Church land, possibly with a 'parsonage' near the pond, are all recorded.

Back Lane and Dead Lane were well trodden thoroughfares, and the map dated 1785-1803 shows details of the tracks used around Upper Green, one of which remains today. The farm near Piggotts owned by Mr Dean has completely disappeared although the

pond that was in front of those farm buildings was there until the early 1950s when it was filled in. Known by many as Peacocks Pond it was full of all kinds of treasures: frogs, newts and crested newts to name but a few.

Dead Lane it is thought possibly gets its name from the time of the Black Death and perhaps adjacent fields were used as a burial ground.

On the site where the tennis court car park is now built was a well cover and well, similar to the one on Lower Green. The area near this well cover was later used to excavate gravel and possibly bricks were made on the site.

Upper Green as the main village of Tewin declined gradually and by 1700 a few more houses were beginning to be built around the Lower Green.

The road from Burnham Green is obviously a very old communication link and houses such as Piggots and The Cattery are of 17th Century foundation. Wormlybury [sic] Manor where Scwells Orchard now stands is also mentioned in the Records Office.

Lower Green and the Well House

Since about 1650 the village has gradually developed round Lower Green. The oldest house is opposite the Memorial Hall, and *The Rose & Crown* and the Old School House were early buildings.

The Well House was at one time more in the centre of the green over the village well. There were three water pumps, one on each corner of the Green, which remained in use until after the Second World War.

In 1953 the Parish Council, as a way of marking the coronation of Queen Elizabeth II, moved the Well House to its present site. The green was ploughed and re-seeded with grass, the footpaths were put in and the flagpole erected.

Parish Council

In 1894 the Parish Councils came into being. Previously the Church had taken responsibility for managing the country districts and prior to this each area had its own manor known as the Manorial System.

The Local Government Act passed by Mr Gladstone's Government, brought about the Parish Councils. These Councils did not include the Church and were not popular.

Chapter 2

The Mimram and Mill House

The Mimram below the site of Panshanger House. The Panshanger Oak is amongst the trees, top left, the Orangery top centre, stables to rear and lodge at top right. Below: **The Mimram at its source near Whitwell.**

Maran or Mimram

> *What was it like in centuries past*
> *A quiet place of clear waters, fast*
> *Gurgling Maran, springs trickling, otters playing?*

From *Digswell* by Janet Gladwin (1975).

Memeran, the earliest recorded name of our beloved chalk-stream dates from the beginning of the 10th century. Thereafter its name appears as Meran (c.1000), Maeran (c.1100), Mimeran (c.1130), Memeran and Memaran in the 12th and 13th centuries, Marran and Memmarran in the 16th c., Maran from 1728 and Mimram from 1790. The last two were both in popular use as recently as the 1930s. The origin or derivation of the name remains unclear.

The Mimram is one of the eastern group of Hertfordshire's wildlife-rich chalk-streams which drain south-eastwards from the dip-slope of the Chiltern hills to flow into the deeper slower-flowing lowland River Lea at Hertford. Prior to its depletion by water-extraction, the originating source of the river was a series of springs emerging from the Lower Chalk above Kings Walden. Now, in the first decade of the 21st century, the river bed above Whitwell remains dry with much of it having been converted to arable farming. The potential for the river's full recovery was, however, evident during the unusually wet spring of 2000 when water again flowed from the springs above Kings Walden, scouring the original river-bed, and flooding its original course across Lilley Bottom Road near its junction with Church Road, Kings Walden.

The present source of the river is now to be found near Stagenhoe Bottom a mile NW of Whitwell. From there to Welwyn it receives water from a series of small springs, side streams, and from the artesian bores that feed the watercress beds at Whitwell and Kimpton Mill. The accumulation of silt due to the reduction in flows, mainly as a result of the ever increasing demand for water to supply the continuing post-war expansion of the county's towns, has caused much shallowing. Many living residents, including the present writer, remember swimming in depths of four or more feet of water at various points between Digswell and Poplars Green even as recently as the 1970s.

In the hot summer of 2006 the river dried up along its whole length above Digswell. Fortunately, flows from the springs in the Digswell Basin, including those that feed Digswell Lake, were sufficient to maintain a level of water from there downstream although at times the flow almost ceased, and the river took on the character of a linear pond. Within the Parish of Tewin the Mimram is further replenished from springs along the base of the chalk and the artesian bores that supplied the former watercress beds at Tewin Fish Farm and Archers Green.

Some 4,000 years ago, when our area was dominated by Oak-Hornbeam forest, Neolithic people, whose flint instruments are still found in the parish, cultivated a succession of patches in woodland clearings along the valley sides. The Belgae, and the Romans who followed them, progressively farmed our area clearing more of the forest along the Lower Mimram Valley. By 75BC, when the Belgae invaded our area from France, a ford had been established at Welwyn meaning *'at the Willows'*. This, as might be expected, suggests that the wet marshy areas were once dominated by willow woodland. Extensive osier beds, used for making fencing and baskets, had probably existed long before they appeared in the 18th century records. Willows of a variety of species, some spectacularly

The River Mimram at Tewin Water, Tewin Water lake and Alders towards Archers Green.

ancient, together with Alder, still characteristically shade from the riverbank and are a major component of the remnant wildlife-rich wet woodlands at Tewin Water and the Tewin Bury Nature Reserve.

Entering the parish at the west end of Tewin Water, the river presently flows along the north side of its floodplain through Tewin Water. Tewin Bury Farm and its former domestic mill, Tewin Mill House, (the site of the corn mill), demolished in 1911, and Archers Green which is surprisingly not shown as such on Ordnance Survey maps. Along its course it loses height, passing over a number of weirs, eventually leaving our parish at Poplars Green where it enters the Panshanger estate.

The course of the river has been variously altered, but the precise details of some of the changes and when they took place, are unclear. Research into the history of Digswell Lake found that at least from the early Middle Ages the river there ran in two channels with their confluence at Digswell Water. Thence the river followed its present course to Tewin Water Lake, which was created as part of Repton's landscape in 1801, and Tewin Bury Farm. From there, topographical and other evidence strongly suggests that historically the river ran in two channels diverging some 250 metres downstream from Tewin Bury to converge again at Archers Green.

The history of the northern channel of the river is better recorded. At sometime this channel was partly canalised and modified to power the mills at Tewin Bury Farm and Tewin Mill. It is only possible to guess as to when these changes may have taken place. It is known that by 1086 Tewin, one of the earliest Saxon settlements in Hertfordshire, had a corn mill. If it was on the same site as the mill demolished in 1911, then the first changes may even have been made in the late Saxon period.

The valley is largely formed from huge deposits of Glacial Gravel with the soft Upper Chalk surfacing at the base along each side. The high diversity of flowering plants on the floodplain pastures is largely due to the calcareous influence of the river and flows from the chalk which enriches the glaciofluvial alluvium floodplain soils. The brown soils above the valley flood plain are mostly neutral to slightly acid. The valley has been essentially shaped by farming, (dealt with elsewhere, see Chapter 3, page 27), and more recently by the Williams and Barton families at Tewin Bury and Warrengate farms respectively. In particular the botanical richness of the floodplain pastures, some of which are unimproved, i.e. have never been ploughed or dressed with agro-chemicals, is the result of many decades of seasonal grazing by cattle.

Left: **The trout lagoons at the fish farm.** Top: **Operating the water filtration.** Bottom: **Landing a trout. (Kings Bridge is in the background where the cottage shown on p. 22 stood).**

Hertfordshire was once the national centre for cultivating watercress. Within our parish watercress beds existed at Tewin Bury, on the site of Tewin Fish Farm which has been owned by Ivor and Vaughan Williams since 2005, and at Archers Green. Production since before 1836 lasted until 1972 when Mr. Ginger, who farmed the last two sites, sold up and retired.

Originally the fishing rights to the river, once famous for its wild Brown Trout and Grayling, belonged to the Panshanger Estate. When the estate was sold off they were leased to the Tewin Fly Fishing Club who continue to rent and stock the section through Archers Green.

There are still residents who remember the stench from the former Welwyn Garden City Urban District Council's sewage settlement lagoon at Tewin Bury. It has been suggested that the lagoon, and its bypass ditch, were constructed using a former course of the river. Early 19th century maps do not, however, show a watercourse there or, indeed, a second outlet from Tewin Water Lake. When the area's drainage systems were finally connected to the Rye Meads Sewer in 1959 the lagoon, which was still receiving storm water from Black Fan, finally became redundant. The site, which had been rapidly colonised by reed, sallow bushes and other plants of fertile wet habitats, developed a significant wildlife interest. In 1962 it became a nature reserve managed by the Welwyn Natural History Society. Together with the rich diversity of flowers in the adjacent, 'unimproved,' wet grasslands and woodlands it was next designated a Site of Special Scientific Interest (SSSI). In 1996 the management agreement with the Thames Water Authority was conveyed to the Hertfordshire & Middlesex Wildlife Trust. The whole of the SSSI now forms the Trust's Tewin Bury Reserve under the wardenship of Robin Cole.

It is both for the richness of its wildlife and beauty and other qualties of its landscape that our valley is so highly valued. Within the river, with its carpets of white-flowering Water Crowfoot and submerged domes of Water Starwort, fish such as Brown Trout, Miller's Thumbs or Bullheads, and Stone Loaches continue to thrive. Sadly the once abundant native White-clawed Crayfish, which the writer remembers catching and barbecuing, have disappeared. The reason for this appears to be a combination of low flows and the spread of 'crayfish plague' by the increasing abundant non-native Signal Crayfish. Although predatory Mink have penetrated the valley, small numbers of the nationally threatened Water Voles remain, possibly as a result of the former being systematically trapped in Panshanger and at other sites downstream. In recent years there has been evidence of Otters, last resident here in the late 1960s, visiting the valley.

The river supports good populations of Mayfly and other aquatic invertebrates on which two, sometimes

Top: **Robin Cole releasing a newly ringed Kingfisher, (photo by David Laming), Southern Marsh Orchids and Redshank flower, Tewin Bury Nature Reserve.** Left: **Meadow-sweet on the banks of the Mimram, a short way downstream from the bridge and Anti Tank obstacles by Tewin Lodge, seen below.**

three, pairs of resident Grey Wagtails feed their young. In recent years at least two pairs of Kingfishers have bred successfully. Little Grebes and Moorhens also nest along the river.

The lush marginal vegetation comprises a great variety of species including Lesser Skullcap, Mimulus or Monkey Flower, Brooklime, Blue Water Speedwell, Marsh Willowherb, Marsh Marigold, Water Mint and Water Figwort. Watercress and the poisonous Fool's Watercress are commonly found side by side. A fine colony of early flowering

Tewin Bury, about 1956, showing the B1000 before it was widened and the then open sewer lagoon on the left of the picture. When the system was changed to drain to Rye Meads, the area became the valuable nature reserve managed here today.

Butterbur may be seen at Archers Green.

One of the great environmental disasters has been the loss of over 96% of Britain's flower-rich grassland since 1945. We are therefore most fortunate that significant areas of old grassland of high conservation value remain in our part of the Mimram Valley. The pastures at Tewin Bury, Tewin Mill, and Archers Green are ecologically some of the finest in the region. In these are to be found plants such as Marsh Thistles, Lady's Smock or Cuckoo Flower, Meadow-sweet, Meadow Saxifrage, Fen Bedstraw, Ragged Robin, and wonderful displays of Southern Marsh Orchids. In addition there are the fine pastures at Warrengate Farm with their radiant carpets of Meadow Buttercups that flower in late May and early June. There is so much to see in the

Left: **Butterbur on the edge of the Mimram at Archers Green; 1968 views of the river at Tewin Bury Farm where the water wheel straddles the water and cows return to the water meadows after milking. Cattle poaching (i.e. trampling) the river margins significantly increases the diversity of the flora.**

20

Above: **Tewin Lodge, showing the weir as the water flows from Tewin Water lake under the road bridge towards Tewin Bury. (See also page 224).** Left: **The Bridge which originally led to Marden Hill House, at Archers Green. This bridge over the River Mimram was built in 1911 and before that there was a ford here.** Below left: **The view of the river from the little bridge that leads to the dairy, Archers Green.**

valley and so much to enjoy.

The wet Alder woodlands at Tewin Water, have spring carpets of Snowdrops. Tewin Bury and Archers Green also contain important plant communities which include Opposite-leaved Golden Saxifrage, Greater Tussock Sedge, Yellow Iris, and Broad Buckler and Lady Ferns. Here is the natural habitat of the Stinging Nettle so often associated with nitrogen-rich disturbed ground. It is in these Alder woods that wintering flocks of Siskins and Lesser Redpolls are to be found.

As already indicated, the valley also attracts diverse and important bird populations. Tufted Duck, present all year, breed at Tewin Water Lake where Shoveler and Gadwall are occasional winter visitors. Grey Herons fish along the river banks in every month and are joined by Little Egrets, a recent coloniser of Britain, through the winter. The lagoon at the Tewin Bury Reserve, which can be viewed from a public hide, has breeding populations of Reed and Sedge Warblers, and Reed Buntings. The last is now red-listed as a species of high conservation concern by the UK's non-

The original cottage at Kings Bridge by the watercress beds on the river, which were replaced by the trout farm. On the hill, St. Peter's Church can be seen in the background.

Below: **Warrengate Farm House and the B1000 road over-look these water meadows which feature Buttercups and less common species of wild flower. The avenue of Limes,** top right, in the same picture, **shows the position of one of the ancient drives to Marden Hill House.**

governmental bird conservation organisations as a result of the national population declining by more than 50% in the last 25 years. Other species red-listed for the same reason and which are still to be found in the parish are Song Thrush, Starling, House Sparrow, Linnet, Bullfinch, and Yellowhammer.

Our section of the Mimram Valley has long been valued for the beauty of its landscape and its diverse wildlife interest which is of high nature conservation value. The Hertfordshire Natural History Society held regular field meetings around Tewin in the late 19th and early 20th century. In 1886, with the kind permission of George Burnand, they enjoyed *'the pretty woodland walk by the side of the River Mimram'* through Tewin Water Park. In 1889 it was said that no other view in Hertfordshire can vie with that across the pretty Mimram Valley. In 1895 the Earl and Countess of Limerick provided refreshments and accompanied the party to show them some of their trees. Specifically mentioned are fine mature Ash and Beech trees, some of which can still be seen today, and the beautiful Lime-tree avenue leading towards Marden Hill House. In 1947 the Mimram Valley was designated for its high landscape value in the Abercrombie Plan. The designation was cancelled under pressure from the Welwyn Garden City Development Corporation whose published plan of 1949 sought to expand the town northwards and onto the southern slopes of the valley.

Fortunately the valley's landscape is still one of the most beautiful in our county and its wildlife of national conservation value. The nature reserve at Tewin Bury is a statutorily designated SSSI, and the Archers Green Meadows owned by Ivor and Vaughan Williams, and generously designated as Access Land, also satisfy the SSSI criteria. The pastures of golden Buttercups at Warrengate Farm already referred to on page 20, are a designated County Wildlife Site.

At the present time Tewin continues to look fondly down on its beautiful valley and river flowing healthily along its southern boundary towards the Lea. However. with the threat of even more development and increased demand for water, we will need to be vigilant to ensure the conservation of the landscape and wildlife treasures we all love.

The site of Tewin Mill is next to the Mill House in the centre of this early plate camera study taken from the fields of Warrengate Farm around 1910. The B1000 road is in the foreground before it was widened and re-aligned.

Tewin Mill

It is known that as early as 1086 Tewin Mill existed and ground the corn grown in the neighbouring fields. It was a water mill powered by the River Mimram. An ancient bridleway still passes through the site of the Mill leading to the village of Tewin. The local farmers loaded their sacks of corn on to wooden carts and drove their horses down to the river where the corn was unloaded and ground into flour, reloaded into sacks and taken up the hill to the bakery where it was made into bread.

In 1368 it is recorded that there were two mills on the same site, and they were called La Solo, but later in 1544 there was just one. The miller's name was John Cock. This mill worked as a corn mill for another three hundred and sixty seven years.

However, from 1760 - 1803 a change took place. The mill was closed to visitors and used for polishing concave and convex glass for spectacles and other purposes. Robert Gass worked there. The owner was Thomas Righbright, and later Mr Flindall.

After those forty three years it became a corn mill

again and three years later John Carrington mentions the Mill in his diary:

1806 Fryday (June) 20

..went in forenoon with Mr Bell to Tewin Mill to look of some Hay their near the mill as soon as you turn out of the Welwin Road to go up to the Mill my pony took fright at the post that hooks the gate and I had a most dreadful fall, so Mr Bell took me to the Mill and Mrs Cannon drest my bruises and gave me brandy - good Samaritan, so came home without looking at the Hay and sent for Dr Colbeck from Hertford and was blooded.

1806 Thursday (July) 13

..to Tewin Mill one Mr Cannons to carry a fine cod and osters for a present as Mrs Cannon was good to me when I fell from my horse in June last near the Mill. Made kindly welcome.

The Mill continued in the Cannon family until 1854 when Edward Manser took over, followed by James Beal. From 1860 the Hill family ran the mill apart from one year when J. Cannon was the miller. The

23

The Mill and The Mill House painted by Margaret Knight

Mill continued as a corn mill until 1911 when it was pulled down, thus ending an eight hundred and twenty five year history as a working mill. It had been a breast shot mill with a ten foot diameter water wheel.

Part of the sluice gate and part of the mill pond wall and steps remain. There are also several grinding stones, an old bridge over the Mimram and an underground water way leading to a backwater. These are now ornamental features but provide evidence of a working mill that served the community of Tewin for nearly a thousand years.

The Mill is still a peaceful place but in 1996 there was a freak storm in July. The river flooded, and within an hour the water came into the house flooding the ground floor to a depth of seven inches. This does not sound very much but the whole valley disappeared under a raging torrent of filthy water, so fierce that one could not stand in it.

Events proved that in the history of the Mill it could never have happened before.

The consequence of this led to the discovery of many unknown aspects of the house itself that had been hidden for many years.

The walls were mostly built of crudely cut oak beams and other branches of wood, and covered with lathe and horse hair plaster; this soaked up the water like a sponge. All had to be removed, except for the beams. This exposed two hidden doorways and two stone arches.

The damaged floors were all replaced. One revealed Victorian tiles. Two others fell in, one to a depth of three feet which, surprisingly, had been the home of long eared bats who happily escaped unharmed. The other fell to a depth of five feet, at the bottom of which was a stream, completely hidden, running underground from the Mill pond to the Mill backwater, a distance of about one hundred yards from the west side of the house - now no longer a mill pond but a wood - to the east side, where it eventually joins the river.

It was a remarkable disclosure of the whole history of the house, made possible by the storm and due in part to the amount of building on the south side of the valley where water cascaded down as it had nowhere else to go.

The house itself has been built up over the centuries and is now a large, comfortable residence. The grounds are beautiful, enhanced by the river and other water features. There are lovely views from every window of the house, and it is now floodproof.

A bridleway runs from north to south, which in its time was for the horse-drawn carts carrying corn and flour to and from the Mill.

The Mill House faces south. It has a peg tiled roof, a small slate roof, and a wing was added which has

modern tiles. The walls are rendered and painted. Inside are signs of its age: oak beams and Tudor bricks, Victorian additions such as a servants' bellboard still in use, but now no servants. In the grounds is a bothy which is a listed building, and garages which were stables, all under old peg tiles.

It is the river, so imperative at the time of the Mill, that still dominates the scene. It brings life to the garden in every way. It enchants everyone who sees it. It is always there moving through the passage of time, drawing everything towards it.

Above: **The Mill House.** Below right: **The little bridge over the Mimram just past the site of the Mill and the Mill House, where the ancient bridleway, left, leads to emerge on the B 1000 road in the distance.**

The Maran Vale

In the middle of the country, - neither north, south, east, nor west -
Where nothing ever happens to break the wayside rest -
Where the Maran river broadens as it winds towards the Lea -
You shall find a spot worth finding, all as pleasant as can be.

As you stand close by the water and watch its silvery flow
And wonder where it comes from, and whither it will go -
You cannot but remember and recall some Summer's dream,
When you walk beside the Maran - this charming Maran stream.

You remember Tewin Water, and the bend in Digswell Dale,
And the many lofty arches which span the Maran Vale;
You may trace the river's windings as it journeys from the west-
But these wondrous views at Digswell are of many scenes the best.

'Tis the middle of the county, as near as one can guess -
You will find it worth a visit, all clothed in rural dress;
No need to travel further - to the north, south, east, or west;
This middle of the county will reward the rambler's quest.

From: *The Hills and Streams of Hertfordshire*
by Rev. Albert J Treloar (1945) Sometime Rector of Stanstead Abbots.

Chapter 3

Farms

Tewin Hill Farm: a photograph taken for the Millennium Exhibition in 2000.

Farming was a major part of the life of Tewin long before the Romans and Saxons visited our shores. The soil is variable but good for growing crops and rearing animals.

The large houses and estates built in and around the village over the centuries have all had farms, where many people from Tewin were employed. Today, machinery has taken over most of the heavy work but we can all still enjoy and wonder at the beauty of the ripening crops at harvest time and be enthralled by the changes taking place in the fields throughout the year.

Tewin Hill Farm

Little is known about the early history of Tewin Hill Farm. Research material in *HALS*, the Records Office in Hertford is scant, but it is known that Tewin Hill Farm was probably the home of Henry Hill in 1307. Whether he owned it or was a tenant is not

known. If the date is correct, it indicates that a building was on this site possibly as early as 1300 or before, and therefore it is one of the earliest recorded settlements in Tewin.

The present farmhouse is an old building, possibly dating back to 1650. In 1803 Tewin Hill Farm was included in the sale of Tewin House Estate by William Schreiber to the 5th Earl Cowper. In 1810, the farm was mortgaged by the Earl to The Bank of England. The tenant at that time was Charles Cheffins and the rent for the 259 acres and 13 poles was £210 per annum.

In 1919 it was part of the Panshanger Estate lands, sold by Lord Desborough to the Hale family. In the 1930s Mr Walter Hale became the owner. Over the years he developed the farm. New buildings were put up near the farmhouse. However, later in the 1930s Mr Hale moved from the farmhouse to a new property he had built '*Akaroa*', near Queen Hoo Hall.

Top: **Aerial photograph of Tewin Hill Farm which shows the stabling and dressage area on the right of the road.**
Bottom left: **Alan and Rosemary Davis and family outside Tewin Hill Farm House about 1980. Alan was a highly regarded manager there for the Hales.**
Bottom right: **The farm briefly experimented with ostrich farming in the 1990s.**

Facing page: **Roe and Adrian Hill own and manage Tewin Hill Farm with a refreshingly traditional mixture of arable and livestock. There are also many horses stabled and gymkhanas are held here.**

From the mid 1940s a large herd of Friesian cows was kept. There were about 300 in all - 200 milking cows, 4 bulls, yearling heifers, in-calf heifers and calves. The cows were milked twice a day (in the early days by hand) and in the peak milking season three times a day, 4.30 - 6.00am, 2.00 - 3.00pm and 8 - 9.00pm. Ten cowmen were employed. In 1952 the Dairy was built and milking machines were introduced. The milk was put into churns and collected by lorry. In later years, it was collected by a milk tanker.

Arable farming continued too and about 20 people in total were in permanent employment, with extra staff at harvest time. Pigs were kept at Walnut Tree Farm, now 74 Upper Green Road. These were looked after by the pigman, Mr Arthur Baldwin, who lived with his family in one of the eight cottages owned by Mr Hale at the top of Tewin Hill (near the junction with Upper Green Road). The remainder of the cottages were lived in by other staff, mainly the cowmen, including Mr Charles Barker and his family.

In the late 1960s a manager was employed, and when Mr Hale retired in about 1970 and his son, David, took on the farm, the herd of cattle was gradually reduced in size and finally the farm was sold.

Mr Terry Bennison became the owner of Tewin Hill Farm in 1988. By then farming was not as profitable a business as it once was and farmers began to look for other ways to give them a better return on their assets by diversifying. The new owners converted the

Dairy and other farm buildings into units to be rented out as small business premises and others as living accommodation. An equestrian centre was established with stables and grazing for horses. Land which was not used for grazing and haymaking was arable-farmed, mostly by a contractor.

In the 1990s a flock of ostriches became the new addition to Tewin Hill Farm. It was thought at this time that ostrich meat would become popular on our daily menu. This did not happen and finally, in the late 1990s, this project ceased.

The farm was purchased by Adrian and Roe Hill in 2000. The Equestrian Centre has flourished, with up to 80 horses. Arable farming continues as before and over 100 acres are used for hay production. Once again, cattle are seen in the fields and the farm specialises in rare breeds, with a herd of Dexter cattle and a number of Gloucester Old Spot Pigs. Two alpacas and various breeds of poultry are kept near the farmhouse.

Kings Bridge to Archers Green
Watercress Beds

This land was rented by Basil Welch in the 1900s from Panshanger Estate and a small force of local labour was employed to work on the watercress beds, with the produce provided being sent to Covent Garden and Spitalfields Markets in London and Southend in Essex.

Later tenants of the land were Mr Moule and Mr Ginger, but the project was discontinued on the death of Mr Ginger and was superseded by a fish farming enterprise by the Harris family. It finally closed in 2005/6.

Kings Bridge has quite a history, and there is a legend that on the morning of 28th April 1646, three strangers were observed by the River Mimram at Tewin, near a footbridge.

A rumour spread that one of the three men, who appeared to be a groom, was in fact King Charles I in disguise, escaping to Scotland. Whether fact or fiction, we will never know, but it is an interesting story and the footbridge was thereafter known as 'Kings Bridge.' King Charles was later captured and beheaded in Whitehall, London in 1649.

29

Left, large pictures, top and bottom: **The old tithe barn at Archers Green before and after conversion.** Inset: **The twin of this barn at Marden Hill House in its original location where both once stood. It has also been converted.**

The Tithe Barn at Archers Green

The tithe barn at Archers Green was originally at Marden Hill Farm. It was transferred from there to its present site in 1910. Each timber and brick was carefully numbered before being moved and the barn rebuilt exactly as it had been before.

In 1999 the footpath past the barn was diverted to follow a route round the field above and John Barton sold the building, which was later converted into a private dwelling. This particular barn was one of a pair of identical barns at Marden Hill Farm where the other still remains. The Archers Green barn was originally owned by John's father, Cecil J Barton, after the 1950s sale of the Panshanger estates.

Tithe barns were used to house about one tenth of a farm's annual produce from its land and labour, formerly taken as a tax for the support of the Church and clergy.

Tithes first came to England with St. Augustine (d.604) and by the end of the 10th century tithe payments had become compulsory everywhere. The tithe system finished in 1996.

Top: **Land girls in the Second World War cutting kale at Sevenacres Farm.** Left : **Sevenacres in 1933, north-facing aspect.** Below right: **Cyril Duvall Bishop with his livestock.**

Sevenacres

Sevenacres was a small area of land for a farm, but Cyril Duvall Bishop, a dental surgeon from North London, purchased it in 1931. He had a four bedroomed house built - Sevenacres, now No. 49 Upper Green Road. The land covered a wide area from the house to Back Lane on the south side of Upper Green.

Mr Duvall Bishop planned the layout of the land with the purpose of providing most of the food his family would need. With the slump in 1930 he had decided that it was virtually inevitable that a Second World War would take place. 'Self subsistence' was

his philosophy, and while still working in London during the week, he and his family, with a little help, set about putting the seven acres of land to good use. They became almost completely independent in the provision of their own food throughout the war years. There were two cows, a few goats - often to be seen grazing on Upper Green which was common land - pigs, geese, ducks, chickens and rabbits, plus a pony and cart to help with the work. There were areas for vegetables, crops for animal feed, i.e. oats, mangolds, maize, potatoes, marrow, stem kale, and as much hay as could be made for the winter months. After the war, Sevenacres gradually changed and

31

Top: **Crown Farm yard before conversion to private dwellings.** Below left: **The Cowper crest on one of the old buildings.**
Below right: **Crown Farm viewed from Back Lane and showing** *The Rose and Crown* **in the background.**

became a pedigree poultry farm specialising in Rhode Island Red chickens and bantams. By 1953 the farming ceased and Sevenacres was sold.

Crown Farm

Crown Farm was built by the 7th Earl Cowper in 1878 and it is possible that initially it was called Rose Farm. However, the present farmhouse was built much later, probably in the 1930s. It has only a few acres of land and is non commercial.

Two additional farm buildings on the land were converted into living accommodation in circa 2005.

Warrengate Farm
(On the south side of the B1000)

Warrengate Farm was originally known as Tewingate Farm, as mentioned in the Hertford Records Office, circa 1698. The present farmhouse is of a later date, possibly early Georgian, 1740-1750. It was owned by William Schreiber of Tewin House, and was part of that estate sold in 1803 to the 5th Earl Cowper for £1,500. At that time it was let to Mr James Hankin.

According to records held at Warrengate Farm giving details from 1848, Earl Cowper let the farm to various tenants, (shown overleaf, on page 34).

Above: **Warrengate Farmhouse**
Below: **Cattle grazing with Warrengate Farm in the background.**

1848-1852 Mr Manser
1852-1856 Mr Riley at a rent of £125 per annum
1856-1896 On Lady Day 1896, Earl Cowper
           accepted surrender of the farm, which
           was let to Mrs Kate Collerd of
           80 Addison Road, Kensington, London,
           for her son, from Michaelmas
           (old Michaelmas Day 11 October)
           1896 on a yearly tenancy, which ended
           at Michaelmas in 1903.

   The farm was let to Mr William Hill and a year later the tenancy transferred to Mr Alexander Charles Hill, son of William (father of Mrs May Williams and grandfather to Ivor and Vaughan Williams). In 1927 Cecil J Barton moved to Tewin and rented

Warrengate Farm and the dairy at Archers Green. He had run a milk business in North London and saw the opportunity to supply milk to the developing Welwyn Garden City.

   He later purchased Warrengate Farm and the dairy farm from the Panshanger Estates in the 1950s. The dairy, known as 'The Marden Dairy Farm' was the most modern dairy of its time (see 'The Dairy at Archers Green' on the next page).

   A herd of shorthorns, plus three Channel Island cows (to keep the butter fats up) provided the milk which, after processing, was churned or bottled ready for delivery to Welwyn Garden City and, in 1960, to Tewin. Delivery was by horse drawn milk floats, progressing to electric floats.

Top left: **Cecil Barton and his sister pictured in the 1930s.** Below left:
The first combine harvester at Warrengate 1952.
Top right: **Ernie Temple collecting grain from the combine harvester. Ernie worked at Warrengate Farm for forty-two years.**
Bottom right: **John and Zena Barton.**

In 1972/73 the herd was disposed of and the milk brought in by tanker from the Milk Marketing Board. The milk business was sold c1984 to Brazier's Dairies and used as a distribution depot.

After the death of Cecil J Barton in 1974, his son, John, continued to farm Warrengate as an all-arable farm, apart from a few sheep and battery hens - the hens to keep the milk rounds supplied with eggs.

The water meadows at Archers Green, where once the cattle grazed and wandered in the river, was designated a Countryside Heritage Site in 1988 by Hertfordshire County Council.

The Dairy at Archers Green

The Dairy at Archers Green was built in 1910 by Katrine, widow of the 7th Earl Cowper. It was built with bricks brought from Welwyn North Station by horse and cart. The dairy was of a very advanced design and construction, enabling it to function efficiently. The floor was of granite since this

"WAITING TO DELIVER THE GOODS

WE accept the "goods" from the Fostermothers of mankind, without much thought of the care with which they have been bestowed.

Then 'tis well, that we do take care, to receive them, in such a manner that they will become———

WELWYN'S SAFEST MILK

THE MARDEN DAIRY FARM, TEWIN
PHONE: TEWIN DOUBLE THREE

Above: **Inside dairy showing rail track used to remove the soiled straw and the granite flooring can be seen. Note the detailed plaques above each stall showing names and feed details.**
Below left: **Basil Kirkham working at the dairy in 1957.**
Below right: **The last round before the electric floats. Mr. Reed with milk float and horse.**

material, unlike concrete, is not affected or damaged by milk. There was a rail system in the building to carry food and the soiled straw.

The building housed 60 cows and each cow had its own stall and food trough. There was a cesspool of manure and effluent, which went into a pit, and the effluent was pumped out and used as fertilizer on the fields.

The Barto Pig Tether

Cecil Barton developed a harness which enabled pigs to be tethered. His original idea came from the memory of his sisters's pig being tied to the dog kennel. Instead of a collar, the leather harness fastened round the body of the pig. By 1938 this device had become very successful and was sold all over the country. It was known as 'The Barto Pig Tether'.

During 2001/2 the old barn in the farmyard at Warrengate, and two other old buildings on the left of Moneyhole Lane, were converted into living accommodation. They are known as 'North Barn, 'The Old Dairy, and 'South Barn'.

Subsequently John Barton retired from farming, selling the land and farmhouse separately.

Muspatt's Farm

Churchfield Road, Tewin

Situated just off and to the north side of Churchfield Road, Tewin, Muspatt's Farm is of comparatively recent origin. The first mention of the name of 'Musplatts' is on early 19th Century maps and there appears to have been no farm on that site until after that time.

An out-of-scale map produced for Lady Cathcart dated 1785 refers to that area as 'Hunsdons Land' and he was presumably the owner at that time. Interestingly, that map also shows a building just to the left of the present entrance but which has long since disappeared. There is no evidence that this was ever Glebe land as was much of the surrounding area. In later years, the land was part of the property of Tewin House then adjacent to the Parish Church and an area to the west of the present grain store was terraced with fruit trees and vegetable plots to supply the 'big house'. It has been said to have been recorded that a 'pineapple pit' was to the left of the present entrance which may have been part of the building there or after it was demolished. The Earl Cowper later acquired and demolished Tewin House and apart from uneven ground, a brick wall and a cedar tree nothing remains.

Reference is also made to a sandpit which was probably the excavated area where the present farm buildings are situated.

The large farmhouse on the rise above the present farm buildings was built by Charles and Doris Burgess in 1965. Charles was born at nearby Burnham Green in 1914 and took over farming from his father Peter. Charles married Doris (née Muncey) who was born in the Cowper Cottages, Lower Green in 1914.

Charles Burgess took over some wooden buildings at the site of the sandpit, constructing modern cattle sheds and farming extensively in the area on some

Charles and Doris Burgess

650 acres, about 200 of it owned. Arable crops were grown and cattle reared on the very productive land. His 'satellite' farms were at Burnham Green and part of Bacon's Farm at Bramfield.

Charles, who was a County Councillor and

Muspatt's as it is today.

a Magistrate, died in 1977. Their son Brian, continued the farm until it was sold in 1981, much of the land and farm buildings being bought by the Williams brothers at Tewin Bury Farm, who still farm the adjacent land.

Doris Burgess continued to own and live in the house until she died in 1997.

Tewin Bury

There was a ford across the River Mimram in Roman and Saxon times, and it is possible that a settlement existed on this site in 400-600 AD.

1166	The manor of Tewin, Tewinbury, possibly held by Godfrey of Tewin.
1540	Wrothe family. There has probably been a house on or near the site of the present Tewin Bury House since that time. It was well situated close to the River Mimram and adjacent to the Church.
C.16th	George Butler (or Boteler) of Stotfold acquired the Manor of Tewin Bury.

1600 approx	Elizabeth Piggot of Tewin Water married Beckingham Butler (Boteler) of Tewin Bury. This couple also lived at Tewin Water and possibly the two properties were in the same ownership.
C. 17th	Richard Hale and then the 2nd Earl Salisbury.
1728 approx	James Fleet.
1746	Bought by the 3rd Earl Cowper.
1803	The original manor house was demolished by the 5th Earl Cowper and the present farmhouse built. Only the chimneys and fireplaces of the original house remain.
C.1840	Isaac Peart and his son, Robert Peart.
1927	Death of Robert Peart – sometime Church Warden of St Peter's, Tewin.
1931	Herbert Titmus gave up the tenancy and moved to Albury Lodge Farm in Little Hadham near Bishops Stortford. The

Top: **Tewin Bury farmhouse.**
Bottom left: **Tommy Williams and Vaughan 1965.**
Right: **Billy Williams and an evacuee.**

Harvest time at Tewin
Bury Farm in the 1960s.

Williams family had a small farm in Carmarthen, but wanted a larger farm. They had friends in London who were in the milk trade and an older brother, David, who took over a farm in Cuffley called Cattlegate Farm.

1931   Tommy Williams and his brother, Billy Williams, rented Tewin Bury Farm from Lord Desborough for £280 per annum. The acreage was 400 acres, 2 roods and 27 perches, (roughly two thirds of a square mile) and extended from the edge of Tewin village to what is now Sir Frederick Osborn School, and nearly into Digswell village.

The story of how they came to Tewin Bury was not unusual at that time, but people will agree it would not happen today. Having milked the cows in the morning in Carmarthen, they loaded them on to the train and took them off at Welwyn North Station in the evening. They then drove them along the B1000 to Tewin Bury Farm in time for evening milking.

Although tenants of Lord Desborough, the Williams brothers never saw him but dealt only with his Estate Manager. There were many restrictions on the tenancy. For example, they were not allowed to fish or take game, they had to keep the farm free of thistles and weeds, one fifth of the arable land had to be left fallow, and all dung had to be returned to the soil. In addition, they had to look after the farmhouse, cottages and other buildings, and no barbed wire was to be used without the consent of the landlord.

The rent of £280 per annum was payable half-yearly. Tommy and Billy had no idea how they were going to foot this bill but they looked at what resources the farm provided, and realised that the main natural resource was rabbits! So, for three years, they paid Lord Desborough his rent using the proceeds from the sale of rabbits. Apart from Tommy and Billy, their housekeeper, Hannah, lived on the farm and there were five people working on the land.

Most of the farm was made up of small fields, with traditional hedgerows, cultivated by the use of horse and plough. The Suffolk Punch horses were kept in the 250 year old stable by the Mimram River. There were also milking cows, beef cattle, sheep and chickens. They grew cereals - oats, wheat and barley. The milk went to A1 Dairies at Whetstone, North London, in 12 gallon churns, which were picked up at the gate by horse and cart and taken to Welwyn North Station, and then into London by train.

Tommy and Billy sheared sheep and sold the lambs at Hertford Market, next to the Dimsdale Public House, where many farmers gathered on market day to discuss prices. At harvest time, the corn was cut, initially with the use of horses, and later by tractor, and then hand stooked to dry. The stooks were later pitched high with a pitchfork and built into a corn stack. A threshing contractor from Tring, called Ward and Sons, threshed the grain into 2cwt bags, which then went to the local grain merchants, Titmuss, Sherriff and Tooley of Luton.

When World War II was declared, the Government's War Agricultural Committee (known as the 'War-Ag') decreed that every available acre of land had to be ploughed. All War-Ag farms were loaned at least one tractor and Tewin Bury had two Fordsons. They were also helped by a family of Land Army girls. Besides farming, Tommy was in the Home Guard and had to protect the viaduct at Digswell. One of the fields, called the Range Field, was a 1,000 yard stretch, with a chalk mound at one end, and was used for rifle practice. Bomb craters appeared where German bombs fell on their way to Panshanger airfield, mistaken for De Havillands at Hatfield.

After the War, life continued much as before, until 1960 when Tommy's son, Ivor, started work on the farm. Panshanger House had been sold in 1952 and subsequently demolished. The new landlord of Tewin Bury was Julian Salmond, the heir to the estate. Suddenly, in 1960, the Welwyn Garden City Development Corporation compulsorily purchased 280 acres of Tewin Bury Farm from the Salmond Estates in order to build the new Panshanger housing estate. For ten years the Williams family tried to make a living from the remaining 115 acres.

When Tommy died in 1970, Ivor and his brother, Vaughan, had no security of tenure. Their only choice was either to buy the farm or leave. They bought the farm and took out a mortgage. They worked 7 days a week, 16 hours a day to pay it back but 115 acres was still too small so when 50 acres of land came up for sale at Burnham Green - the Barnes Wood Estate - they managed to buy it at an interest rate of 17%.

At this time they were still milking 50 cows in an old antiquated cowshed, which had to be mucked out by hand. There was no living or future in this but the EEC (European Economic Community) were giving farmers with outdated buildings a grant to get out of milk production, as there was a surplus in the EEC. So, sadly, the brothers sold their cows and converted one of their buildings into a farm shop. They increased their potato production to sell in the shop and added fruit, vegetables, cakes, jams and eggs.

This new venture meant they had to rise at 3am to travel into Spitalfields Market to get fresh vegetables to add to their own.

The produce from the farm crops went into Welgar Shredded Wheat in Welwyn Garden City and McVities Digestive biscuits. The barley went for malting at Harrington and Page at Ware, and then into locally brewed beer.

In 1981, Ivor and Vaughan were fortunate in being able to purchase the farm next door when their neighbours, Sue and Brian Burgess, emigrated. This was a dream come true - an extra 258 acres. With it came a house in Tewin. It was an exciting time for farmers as plant breeders were developing new strains of wheat and barley which yielded very well. However, in 1984, as the price of grain had dropped, it was decided to supplement their income further by letting four rooms at the farmhouse as bed and breakfast accommodation.

A new Safeway store killed off the farm shop in the 1990s and so the Williams brothers decided to concentrate on expanding the restaurant and guest accommodation into a hotel and conference centre, as a venue for weddings and other events. Since then, many of the farm buildings have been converted into event spaces where parties, lunches and bazaars are held, as well as many charitable events.

In 2005, land along the Mimram came up for sale and was in danger of being purchased by a developer. Ivor and Vaughan were able to buy this land in order to preserve it and occasionally the Williams' cattle are to be seen grazing there. This was a happy outcome for the whole of Tewin, and is a further indication of the important part played by the Williams family and Tewin Bury Farm in the life of the village.

Linda and Ivor Williams in the fields next to Dawley Wood.

Chapter 4

Queen Hoo Hall

Raphael Tuck's Postcard of Queen Hoo Hall posted in 1905.

An impressive, stately manor house, Queen Hoo Hall stands on high ground about a mile and a half north-east of Tewin Church, and commands extensive views over the Hertfordshire countryside.

During its lifetime it has borne witness to romance, mystery and many changes, as well as giving shelter to numerous distinguished occupants and visitors, not least being Queen Elizabeth I, who would ride from Hatfield House to hunt in the area around Queen Hoo Hall, which she used as a hunting lodge. Intriguingly, a legendary tale maintains that there is a secret passageway which runs between Queen Hoo Hall and Hatfield House. This is not substantiated, and is probably just a romantic notion, but what colourful images it conjures up.

Queen Hoo Hall, as we see it today, was built in the sixteenth century and has retained many of its original features, among them some wonderful wall paintings (see page 47). However, it is likely that this house was preceded by an earlier, much less imposing one, possibly in place since the first

millennium. Research carried out by W.H.H. Van Sickle in August 1987 established that the first reference to occupation on the site appears in the Westminster Domesday Book, circa 1056, where there is mention of 'Quenildehaga' referring to *'enclosure of a woman named Cwenhild'*.

The name appears again in the 13th and 14th centuries as variations of 'Quenhag', 'Quenehawe', and 'Cwenhagh', and later forms include 'Qwenehall' and 'Queenhoo'. The addition of 'Hall' to the name dates to the 18th century at least, at which time the distinguished engraver and antiquarian, Joseph Strutt, wrote a novel of Tudor life entitled 'Queenhoo-Hall'. This was published in 1808 by Sir Walter Scott, who completed the last chapters following the death of Joseph Strutt in 1802 (see page 79).

13th- 16th Century

There is reference to a manor on the site being owned by a Richard Hamme in 1223-26, although the lands in Queenhoo were held at the beginning of the 13th century by Geoffrey de la Lee. Before 1281 the manor came into the possession of Ralph and Catherine de Ardern, and in 1376 Walter de la Lee granted '*land called Quyneshawes*' to Richard Ravensere and others.

The next reference to the manor appeared in 1501 when the property was conveyed by Henry and Elizabeth Hammys to ten people: Sir Reginald Bray, William, the Bishop of Lincoln, William Hody, John Shaa, Hugh Oldom - Clerk, Humphrey Conyngesby - Serjeant-at-Law, Richard Emson, William Cope, John Cutte, and Nicholas Compton.

Sir Reginald Bray, an extremely powerful figure at Court, had been closely involved with putting the Tudors on the throne. He died in the early 1500s and his interests in Queen Hoo were held by his widow and his heir, Lady Margery Sandys. Sir William Sandys and the Sandys family, who owned a great deal of land elsewhere, would not have resided at Queen Hoo and in 1536 they sold the entire manor to John Malt, a merchant tailor in London. He died in 1552, leaving the manor to his two daughters, Brigitte and Mary, with Brigitte subsequently selling her share to John Forster, whose son, Humphrey, conveyed it to Edward Skegges in 1567.

Although it is widely believed that Skegges was responsible for building the Hall we see today, it is more likely that it was built after 1584, the year in which his widow and her son sold the property to John Smyth. John Smyth died within five years of his purchase and, in 1589, his son, James, leased the house and adjacent land to a London Goldsmith, Aphabell Partriche, for a rental of £21 a year.

This Lease, dated 24 February 1589, gives weight to the belief that the house was built after 1584 since it refers to '*the brick mansion house newlie builte*', as well as to extra bricks and timber with which Partriche was authorised to make changes and additions to the house. Research appears to show that Partriche used the extra materials to add the south side bays. He also replaced a small newel stair with a larger staircase, and it is possible that it was he who inserted an additional floor in the two-storey hall, as well as adding a third chimney stack.

17th - 19th Century

In the meantime, Sir Henry Boteler (or 'Butler') of Bramfield, had purchased various lands and interests in the manor, and Partriche in turn sold his interest to Julian Cotton in trust for Henry Boteler's son. Sir

Henry died in 1609 and was succeeded by his son, John, the first Lord Boteler of Bramfield. The Botelers did not live in the house themselves, their main seat being at Bramfield, and it is likely that Queen Hoo was occupied by Sir Henry's youngest son, Ralph. He is believed to have lived at the house until his death in 1644 and is buried in St. Peter's churchyard, Tewin.

Until the 20th century, this appears to be the last date on which a close member of the owning family actually occupied the Hall, although there were several changes of ownership. In 1637 William Boteler, the son of John, took possession, but since he was declared '*an ideott and a foole natural*', custody of the estate was put into the hands of his two brothers-in-law. Provision was made for William, and the rest of the estate was divided between his five surviving sisters and a nephew. When Lord William died in 1647 the title became extinct. However, Ralph Boteler's son, Francis, who lived at Queen Hoo, had been knighted in 1642 for supporting the King against the Commonwealth in the Civil War, and it was he who set up the Boteler Charity, which still exists, with the aim of helping poor widows (see page 253). Today the charity is administered by trustees who, at Christmas time, nominate the recipients of a £50 cheque. The 330 year old documents relating to this are kept at County Records in Hertford. Sir Francis died in 1690 and his estate passed to his daughter, Julia.

However, before this, the daughter of Lord William's eldest sister married George Villiers, Viscount Grandison. He subsequently bought out the interests of the other five heirs and their descendants and by 1684 had re-consolidated Queen Hoo under

Queen Hoo Hall from the south. An 1813 sketch by Buckler now in the British Library.

George Villiers, Viscount Grandison (1617-1699).

single ownership. Viscount Grandison died in 1699, aged 82, but Queen Hoo remained in the family for another 129 years. During this period the Hall was leased to various people and further changes are recorded in 1723, 1782, 1828 and 1836, when among the residents was Captain William Sabine, the second husband of Lady Cathcart of Tewin Water House, and Benjamin Whittenbury who became a central figure in the capture and shooting of the Highwayman, Walter Clibbon (see page 50).

19th - 20th Century

Benjamin Whittenbury continued to live at the Hall until his death in 1801 but, in the meantime, the Grandison title had been raised to an Earldom and the Earl's daughter, Lady Gertrude Amelia Villiers, became sole heir. In 1802 she married Lord Henry Stuart, the fourth son of the Marquis of Bute, and under the terms of the marriage, settlement of Queen Hoo was placed in the hands of trustees. Lord Henry and Lady Gertrude had four children and the estate eventually came into the hands of their eldest son, also called Henry. However, the new Lord Henry Stuart appeared to have been recklessly extravagant and was forced to raise a series of mortgages to

support his debts. Probably as a result of these debts, the Manor, along with Bramfield, was taken over in 1828 by Edward Marjoribanks, Sir Edmund Antrobus, James Lindsay and Alexander Trotter. Some eight years later it changed hands again when it was purchased in 1836, along with Bramfield, by Abel Smith MP.

The various owners of the house over the years had made little change and had allowed Queen Hoo Hall to remain a grand farmhouse. Fittingly, from 1841 to 1903, whilst under the ownership of the Abel Smith family, the house was tenanted by six farming families, the last of which, the Gray family, lived and worked there for 30 years.

After they left, the house was renovated and leased to Canon Henry Charles Beeching and his wife. Canon Beeching was a noted clergyman and man of letters who gave up his role as a country clergyman to become Professor of Pastoral Theology at King's College, London, and Chaplain to Lincoln's Inn. He was appointed a Canon of Westminster Abbey in 1902, Select Preacher at Cambridge in 1903, and Preacher to the Honorable Society of Lincoln's Inn from 1903. Queen Hoo Hall was therefore a perfect location for him, affording reasonable commuting distance from his London based work, whilst allowing his family to enjoy country living.

However, the Beeching family had left Queen Hoo by 1909 when the Hall was leased to Sir Clement Lloyd Hill and Lady Hill, and it is Lady Hill who is credited with the garden layout, which incorporated the old courtyard walls. Clement Lloyd Hill died in 1913 and in 1922 the house was leased to the Misses Egerton, who remained there until 1946 when the house and five acres of land were sold by Thomas Abel Smith, the great-grandson of the MP who had bought the house 110 years earlier.

The new owner was Elizabeth Theresa Hambro, who was later to marry Major Clement Hill, the son of the family who had leased the house in 1909. The story of this purchase is a romantic one. Major Hill had decided to take his future wife (who at the time was still married to John Hambro) to see his childhood home and discovered that the Misses Egerton intended to move and that Thomas Abel Smith was prepared to sell. This fortuitous visit resulted in Elizabeth Hambro subsequently purchasing the house and marked the first time in at least 350 years that the owner had actually resided at Queen Hoo Hall.

Major and Mrs Hill carried out extensive restoration

work, some of the cost of which was alleviated in 1955 when Queen Hoo Hall was given an Historic Buildings Grant of £1,000 for damp repairs. The grant carried a requirement that the house be opened to the public on certain days of the week. This came into force on Good Friday 1960 and during that first weekend it was visited by over 300 people, who each paid an entrance fee of 2s 6d (12½p). The visitors

became a good source of income for Major and Mrs Hill and they supplemented this further by leasing two cottages in the grounds of the house.

In 1966 the house was sold to Denis and Alison Faith Nahum, along with an additional 17½ acres of land originally purchased by Mrs Hill. The land remains with the house, with the exception of approximately half an acre, which has since become

known as 'Faith's Wood'. The Nahums undertook further restoration work in 1966, during which a major fire broke out in the roof, and in 1972 they sold it to Simon Dallas Cairns, Viscount Garmoyle, the eldest son and heir of the Earl Cairns, who extended the kitchen and added a small bathroom.

His ownership continued until 1986 when it was bought by its present owners, Arthur and Anne Mead. By this time Queen Hoo Hall had fallen into a state of disrepair and Mr and Mrs Mead employed the services of an expert architect and a number of craftsmen to carry out extensive renovation. This work, which took three years to complete, included the re-pointing of the entire house, the replacement of 1500 bricks with hand-made Bulmer brick and tile, and rebuilding six pinnacles above the gable ends on the south side. Then, in 1995, a small porch was added to the north side of the house.

21st Century

Today, fully restored to its true magnificence, Queen Hoo Hall stands amid delightful gardens, overlooking the Tewin countryside. It has seen numerous changes of ownership and several dramatic alterations in structure. It has welcomed many notable visitors, has been the subject of a distinguished book, and been associated with a number of romantic stories. Now, however, it is a comfortable home for the owners, who sum up their good fortune by saying they feel privileged to live in such a beautiful house.

The Wall Paintings

Over the years, few internal alterations were made to Queen Hoo Hall so many of the original features remain, the most remarkable of which are the wall paintings in the main bedroom. The mural above the fireplace was mentioned in a book on antiquities in Hertfordshire, published in 1905, which states that the subject was '*apparently the Elizabethan play entitled 'Abraham, Melchizedek, and Lot'*. It is strange that although this particular play appears in almost all French mystery play cycles, in England it formed part of the Chester cycle of mystery plays only, so its connection with Queen Hoo Hall seems tenuous.

Above: **Wall painting above the fireplace in the main bedroom.**

Centre: **Detail from the above mural.**

Below: **Detail from wall frieze.**

Above from top to bottom:
Detail of free-hand drawing of horses, a dragon pursuing a snake and butterfly and bullfinch.

Sundials

Records show that two cast-lead sundials were built into the front and back walls of Queen Hoo Hall at one time but these have been removed. The dial at the back was about 12" (30cm) in diameter and comprised the face of the sun with a very extended nose, forming the gnomon, surrounded by rays, with the hours shown in Roman numerals round the margin. The date '1812' is inscribed under words believed to read *'welcome sunshine synce 12'*. The sundial on the front, which measured approximately 18" x 14" (45cm x 35cm), showed a coach and horses at the top, and below an inscription reading *'Time is flying the coach is going'*, followed by another which is now indecipherable. Unfortunately, the whereabouts of these sundials is not known at the present time.

Above: **Sundial from Queen Hoo Hall.**
Below: **Aerial view showing Queen Hoo Hall taken by Tony Rook and reproduced by kind permission.**

It is not known when the mural was painted but it appears that the fireplace has been 'cut in' to the painting, which would indicate that at least some of the decoration was in place before the addition of the westernmost chimney stack in the late 16th century.

In 1946, during extensive restoration work carried out by Clement Hill, more drawings were discovered, among them a broad painted frieze on two walls. Below one of these friezes is a wonderful free-hand drawing of horses, and another of a butterfly and a bullfinch. In addition a separate panel depicts what appears to be an exotic dragon pursuing a snake. The drawings are somewhat faded, as are the colours in the main wall painting, but it is still possible to appreciate and marvel at their artistry.

Queen Hoo Hall photographed in 2008.

The Walter Clibbon Affair

It was in 1782, when Queen Hoo was occupied by Benjamin Whittenbury, that it was connected to one of the most notorious incidents in the history of Hertfordshire. Benjamin Whittenbury became, unwittingly, a central figure in the capture and shooting of the Highwayman, Walter Clibbon. Diarist, John Carrington, who was aged 56 at the time and knew all the farmers concerned, recorded the events some years later.

Walter Clibbon of Babbs Green, Wareside, was a pieman who used his trade in the local markets to identify potential victims for his other occupation. After dark, he and two of his sons were footpads who preyed on people returning from market. They carried out many robberies, in the worst of which they killed a farmer named Kent, from Benington, and sent his body home in his horse and cart.

On Saturday, 28th December 1782, Walter Clibbon, with his sons, Joseph aged 18 and Samuel aged 16, hid in Canons Wood near Bulls Green on the road from Bramfield. They were wearing dark smocks and had blackened their faces. In the evening, after a long wait, the Clibbons had their first victim. They robbed a young farmer called Whittenbury who was returning from market to his farm in Datchworth by horse and cart. The farmer escaped and headed towards his farm but, just before Bulls Green, he turned left and drove to Queen Hoo Hall, the home of his uncle, Benjamin Whittenbury. Having heard his nephew's story, Benjamin told him that his father and other uncle had just left but said he would follow in order to warn them.

Together with his son, Thomas, 'his man', George North, and his hound, Benjamin set off, armed with a stick and gun - a fowling piece. However, they were too late for by the time they reached the bottom of the road by Oakvale Wood, the Clibbons had stopped Benjamin's two brothers, had robbed one and the other had run off. Seeing no sign of his brothers, Benjamin and his son decided to climb the hill to try to spot them, with the intention of going home if they saw nothing. They had barely started up the hill when the Clibbons charged out of the wood and attacked them, thinking they were also from the market.

A furious fight ensued. Benjamin Whittenbury knocked down Walter Clibbon but was then overpowered so he called for George North, who shot the Highwayman at close range in the chest. John Carrington's account in his diary records that Mr Whittenbury *'called for his mann to shoot, which he Did and killd the old Roogue on the Spott, he shoot him in the Brest for his gun allmost Touched him...'*. According to the diary, the younger of Clibbon's sons ran away but the other, Joseph, was captured.

Left: **Fowling piece which was used to shoot Walter Clibbon, together with a fragment of the original Clibbon's Post shown in display box on the left of photograph.**

Below: **Clibbon's Post in Bramfield Road photographed in 2009.**

Following the shooting, Walter Clibbon's body was placed in an out-building beside '*The Horns*' Public House at Bulls Green, where it was exhibited. On the following Monday a Coroner and Jury arrived to consider the matter of his death. The Jury concluded he had met the fate he deserved. Walter Clibbon was buried where he died at the roadside in Bramfield Road and the spot was marked by a stout post. 'Clibbon's Post' still marks the spot, although it has been renewed several times over the years.

Postcript: In 1783 Joseph Clibbon was tried at Lent Assizes where he was found guilty and hanged at Gallows Hill, Hertford. George North was tried for the murder of Walter Clibbon but acquitted, and Benjamin Whittenbury was subsequently presented with a silver cup by the Lord Lieutenant.

Chapter 5

St. Peter's Church and the Rectories

St. Peter's Church is a fine example of a small rural church which has been loved and cared for by successive generations since the seventh century. Set at a distance from the main village on high ground above the Mimram Valley, its peaceful churchyard is surrounded by fields. The building has been continuously used for worship for 1300 years.

The history of the church begins with the coming of the Saxons in 449. They worshipped the god Tew, the Saxon god of war, from which Tewin received its name. It is thought that the site was chosen for its closeness to the River Mimram and its ancient ford below the church. The site of their shrine became that of the later Christian church after they were converted to Christianity in or about AD 604, shortly after the coming of St. Augustine. It is thought that the existing north wall of the church is part of the north wall of this earlier Saxon church.

FROM THE SOUTH EAST   FROM THE NORTH WEST

1100

1400

1650

1750

1900

An estimate of how the appearance of St. Peter's has changed over the centuries. The small vestry on the south side was added later than 1750. By 1900 it had been removed.

Above: **St. Peter's Church in 1948 showing the hand pumped organ in the chancel (on the left). At this time the church was lit by candles.**

Below left: **The interior of the church today. The organ is now at the rear of the nave.**

The colonnade built to extend the church southwards in c1266.

After the Norman Conquest the Normans restored the ruined church in about AD 1086, the year of the Domesday Book. The nave and chancel were built by Peter de Valoignes, to whom William the Conqueror had granted the castle of Hertford, its estates and the Manor of Tewin. Traces of a blocked up Norman window can be seen both inside and outside, high in the north wall of the nave. It was also at this time that the church was dedicated to St. Peter.

The next changes occurred during the Early English period when the colonnade was built to extend the church southwards in about 1266. These arches, dividing the nave from the south aisle, as well as the lancet windows of the chancel and the south aisle are all Early English. Above the arches the remains of a clerestory window can be seen in what was once the outside wall. The niche in the second pillar would have contained the statue of a saint. It is likely that it would have been of St. Christopher, the patron saint of travellers. The hole underneath was for hanging a lamp below the statue.

It was another century before more changes were made. In the Perpendicular Period (1377-1547) there were many new additions including the east windows of the chancel and aisle, the westernmost window of the south wall of the chancel and the two windows in the north wall. The south porch, with its inner door and holy water stoup, and the tower were also built during this period. At one time the tower had an upstairs balcony and ringing chamber. Two of the original supports can still be seen. On the north wall traces of a 15th century staircase can be seen which probably would have led to a rood but there are no other traces of a rood screen apart from the large stones which would have supported it.

Nothing much is known of the history of the church during the Reformation and the names of Rectors between 1532 and 1632 are not preserved. It was in 1864 that further restoration took place and then, more notably in 1903 when the 7th Earl Cowper, whose memorial can be seen on the south wall of the chancel, paid for extensive work to be done. The roof of the tower and church were repaired, floors were renewed, closed doors were opened up and refitted and a new vestry built. A ducted hot air heating system with coal boiler was installed and the interior fittings were completely renewed with oak pews, pulpit, reading desk and candelabras. The account from the builders came to £2840.

In 1953 electricity was installed. Before that time the early pipe organ in the chancel was hand pumped.

Later it was replaced by an electric valve organ situated at the back of the church. The existing Allen digital organ was installed in the 1990s. During the years 1985-2005 the whole of the outside of the building was renovated; the old Victorian render was removed, exposing the original flints, worn stonework was replaced and the entire roof retiled.

An intriguing feature of the exterior is the ancient graffiti carved near the west door in the 18th century, together with a sundial on the south wall.

Clock and Bells

The clock is on the first floor of the tower. It is believed that it was originally a 30 hour one hand clock and that it was converted to its present 7 day form in 1729. The 'time indicator' is inscribed REPAIRED BY JOHN BRIANT HERTFORD 1780.

In 1799 John Carrington, the diarist of Bacon's Farm, Bramfield, writes that '*John Briant of Hartford.......had 5sh per year to keep the Church Clock in good order Which Gose well*'

The timing chain weight is very old, possibly the original. Much repair and maintenance work was done in 1983 by Mr Pettey and Mr Barnes. The drive mechanism for the hands was refurbished and the bushes replaced. New hands were made by apprentices of the British Aerospace Aircraft Group,

	Diam:	approx weight:	Inscription
Treble	25ins	3cwt	Arthur Coleman Vidler (Rector 1912- 1939) Mears & Stainbank Founder London 1939
No2	27.5ins	4cwt	John Briant Hertford Fecit 1799 T. Dean C.Warden
No3	28ins	6cwt	Anthony Chandler made me 1673
No4	31ins	8cwt	A.C. 1673 Praise ye the Lord
No5	33ins	10cwt	Anthony Chandler made me.
Tenors	37.5ins	11cwt	G.W.N.A. Churchwardens A.C. 1673

Hatfield (formerly called de Havillands) in 1984.

A new clock face was donated by Ivor and Vaughan Williams in memory of their mother, May Williams, in 1996. It was painted by Dennis Carlton. The gold leaf letters were made by students at Bedford College and donated by Patrick and Jennifer Holden.

There are six bells hung for change ringing in a wooden frame. They run on ball bearings, and were quarter turned and re-hung on cast iron headstocks in 1973. They have been 'turned' at least twice before. The present third, fourth, fifth and tenor are as cast in 1673 from the metal of earlier bells. The treble of the 1673 peal of five bells was recast in 1799. John Carrington describes it in his diary:

'Oct 1799...the Treble Bell of Tewin Church, being Crackt, was New Cast by John Briant of Hartford, and the Recasting and fixing cost £10'

This is now the second bell. At this time a new frame was installed with space (pit) for a sixth bell. It was not until 1939 that this pit was filled with the present treble to make a ring of six. It was given by a former Rector, A.C. Vidler. At the same time as this bell was hung the tower was reinforced and the tie bars can be seen in the belfry. It is interesting to note that this bell did not ring for services until the end of the war in 1945.

There has been some doubt as to the weight of the bells and for many years they have been quoted as an 11cwt ring but it is believed that it is actually a $8^{1}/_{4}$cwt ring. Recent measurements from which estimates have been made and the Whitechapel records suggest that the latter weight is nearer the truth. They have not been weighed.

Details of the bells are shown on page 55.

Memorials

Of several interesting memorials in the church, the oldest is a stone in front of the sanctuary to the memory of Walter de Louth who was Rector of Tewin from 1312 to 1356 and died in 1356. In 1610 these words were inscribed on a small brass in the south aisle, now covered by a carpet for protection:

'Here lyeth buried the body of Thomas Pygott gent, whose ancestors have remayned Dwellinge in this town this 300 years and upwards. He died on the 11 of January 1610 and in the 70 yeare of his age and lefte behinde him 2 daughters Rebekah the wife of Henry Bull of Hertforde gent, and Elizabeth the wife of Beckingham Boteler of this towne of Tewinge gent.'

Thomas Pygott is shown in a full length cloak and is wearing a ruff around his neck. Above the figure are the family arms (a shield and three pickaxes). In his will he said *'.....after my decease the messuage or mansion house called the Waterside....to the use of Elizabeth Piggot my wife for the term of her life.'*

The brass of Thomas Pygott in the south aisle.

This refers to Tewin Water House later inherited by his daughter Elizabeth.

Thomas owned a great deal of land in Tewin but there are no historic references to his family having lived *'in this towne this 300 years.'* It is likely that Tewin was the home of either his maternal ancestors or perhaps his father's maternal line.

The large marble memorial in the south porch was originally in the churchyard. It was moved into both the chancel and nave at the request of the family to stop it weathering before finally ending up in the porch which had to be adapted to accommodate it. It is to the memory of the Hon. Joseph Sabine, Major General of the Welsh Fusiliers and a Governor of Gibraltar, who restored and enlarged Tewin House in 1715. The house was situated in the field to the east of the church drive and was demolished in 1807. All that remains is the long brick wall at the east of the churchyard, the cedar tree and traces of foundations in the adjacent field. Joseph Sabine gave the land for the drive to the church but, at the same time, he enclosed the main road from the village to the river to enlarge his garden. You can still see traces of the terracing beyond the wall.

His widow, Mrs. Margaret Sabine, left money in her will for preserving the monument erected to the

Detail from the memorial to Hon. Joseph Sabine who restored and enlarged Tewin House in 1715.

memory of her husband. Details of her bequest can be seen on a board dated 1787 to the left of the south door as you enter the church.

On the north wall of the nave is a memorial tablet to Edward Sabine, born in Dublin in 1788. He spent much of his youth in Tewin and after a successful army career in North America he returned to Ireland to study astronomy, magnetism and other scientific interests. Between 1819-20 Edward Sabine made another Arctic trip where he tested navigational equipment, carrying out experiments on magnetism. A third trip was made in 1823 and, on his return, he devoted himself to the study of magnetism. Edward

Sabine was a pioneer in the observations of the earth's magnetic fields for navigation and shipping. He was President of the Royal Society from 1861 to 1871. He wrote over one hundred scientific papers during his life and received the Royal Society's gold medal. In 1883 Edward died at the age of 94 and is buried in the family vault at St. Peter's.

His older brother, Joseph, also buried at Tewin, practised law until 1808 when he was appointed Inspector General of Taxes. His lifelong interest was in natural history, particularly rare plants and ornithology. He was an original Fellow of the Linnean Society founded in 1788 to which his brother Edward reported twenty-four species of birds observed in Greenland. Joseph was honorary secretary of the Royal Horticultural Society from 1810 to 1830 and treasurer and vice chairman of the Zoological Society of London.

On the south wall of the nave is a memorial to Lady Cathcart of Tewin Water dated 1789. Her story is an intriguing one which is related in the section on Tewin Water House in chapter seven.

James Fleet, her first husband, has a memorial on the south wall of the church. Barely a year after his death she was married to Colonel William Sabine, brother of General Sabine whose memorial is in the porch. This marriage she is reputed to have said was for wealth. After his death in 1738 she married Lord Cathcart, a widower with ten children and not wealthy. She apparently married him for rank. He died in 1741 and she remained a widow for four years. Her last marriage proved disastrous. In 1745 she married Lieutenant-Colonel Hugh Maguire, of Castle Nugent, County Longford, Ireland. The honeymoon was hardly over when Maguire abducted her to Ireland where she remained a virtual prisoner for twenty years. When they did not return friends sent an attorney in pursuit and they were overtaken at Chester but Maguire was prepared and obtained a maidservant to impersonate his wife. She indignantly told the attorney that she was paying a visit to her husband's castle and so he and his wife were able to continue to Ireland where Lady Cathcart was placed in rooms in the castle. According to her own account she had barely the necessities of life during this time whilst her husband was spending her fortune. However, she does not seem to have lost her health and spirit because when Maguire died suddenly in 1766 she returned to England and began various law suits to recover possession of her house and estates. She lived at Tewin Water House for another twenty one years and died in 1787 at the age of ninety seven. A description of her 'spectacular' funeral is given by Evelyn Wright in *A Hertfordshire Family 1555-1923*:

'What her ladyship had to leave she left among her domesticks (domestics) Her body was dressed in linen and laid in a leaden coffin; the outside coffin was covered with velvet trimmed with gold, on which was a gold plate, whereon were engraven the names of her husbands, her age etc. She was carried in a hearse and six, followed by two coaches and six.....to the church of Tewin, where she was buried in a vault near her first husband James Fleet. Hat bands and gloves were given in general to all those who chose to attend and a sumptuous entertainment was provided....'

She is buried beside her first husband James (John) Fleet.

Windows

The oldest glass in the church is some of the plain glass in the north windows dating from the 18th century. The east window was given by George Burnard of Tewin Water in about 1890. The figures are identical to those in the east window of St. Mary's Church, Lapworth Warwickshire. The designer of both windows was Harry Ellis Wooldridge (1845-1917) and both were made by Messrs James Powell & Sons. Wooldridge worked as an assistant to Burne-Jones and Henry Holiday in the

Above: **The east window designed by Harry Ellis Wooldridge (1845-1917)**
Left: **The two Lancet windows in the south aisle designed by Patrick Reyntiens.**

1860s. His work is distinguished by finely drawn classical figures in a restricted but effective range of colours. From 1895-1904 he was Slade Professor of Art and the window in Tewin Church is a fine example of his work.

The window in the south wall of the chancel is in memory of Susan and Richard Hoare of Marden Hill House, Tewin. Mr Hoare was churchwarden at St. Peter's for over thirty years. Fitted in 1903, this window depicts Moses and Enoch and was designed by H. W. Bryans.

The east window in the south aisle depicts the Annunciation with a full length figure of Mary on the left and the Angel Gabriel on the right. They replaced plain glass windows and were dedicated in 1963 to the memory of Dr Cedric Lane-Roberts who lived at the Mill House Tewin before and after the Second World War and created the garden on the River Mimram. They were designed by Patrick Reyntiens and the colours of the glass are various shades of blue, green, grey and amber. The two lancet windows in the south east and south west of the south aisle are

also of his design and depict arrangements of coloured glass in irregular leading. The glass is in yellow, amber, brown, blue, green and indigo.

Panelling and artefacts

The church has received many gifts over the years. The church register records several gifts from Lady Cathcart between 1780 and 1789 including a bible, a *'new pulpit cushion with a cover of crimson velvet and crimson silk tassels'* and *'a crimson damask cloth to the communion table and fine damask linen; likewise three stools cushions and stuff. Damask covers to the cushions in the year of our Lord 1780.'*

The altar and oak panelling was donated by Sir Otto Beit of Tewin Water in 1928. That situated on the north side of the altar bears the coat of arms of the diocese of St. Albans and a shield with gilt crossed keys

Above: **The window in the south wall of the chancel depicting Moses and Enoch designed by H.W. Bryans.**

Left: **The east window in the south aisle depicting the Annunciation designed by Patrick Reyntiens.**

representing St Peter. The panelling on the south side of the altar is decorated with the arms of Sir Otto Beit and of our patrons, Jesus College, Cambridge. The central beech panelling behind the altar was donated in 1998 by Mr Peter Briggs in memory of his wife, Mary Coome Briggs. Matching panelling behind the altar in the south aisle was donated by Isabel Langreche in memory of Lady Florence Isobel Helm and her daughter Grace Ann Brock. The Helm family lived at the Old Rectory for many years.

The cross and candlesticks on the main altar are made of walnut and inlaid with mother of pearl. They were donated by the Misses Egerton of Queen Hoo Hall in 1928. The Miss Egertons also presented the Memorial Book in memory of their brother Lieutenant-Colonel George A. Egerton, 19th Hussars who died of wounds on 13th May 1915.

The font was restored in 1965 with a bequest from Cyril Geeves in memory of Henry John and Eliza Jane Geeves. The original stone bowl and plinth, made of Portland stone (unknown date thought to be 17th century), were cleaned and retained.

A new pedestal of Hoptonwood stone, a copper bowl and wooden cover were made.

The Churchyard
It would be difficult to find a more peaceful last resting place than St. Peter's Churchyard. As in most village churchyards a stroll around will reveal many generations of the same families buried there. There are also some graves of particular historical interest. The earliest known grave is of Ralph Boteler who died aged 63 on 31 Jan 1644. His grave and three others of the Boteler family are under the east window of the church. The family lived at Queen Hoo Manor House from 1663-1682 and are related to those whose memorial slabs are in the sanctuary of the church.

Probably the most visited grave is that of Lady Anne Grimston, the widow of Sir Samuel Grimston, who died in November 1713 at Tewin House. Her

grave is surrounded by railings in the east of the churchyard and is immediately noticeable for the way that trees have broken through the grave and have encased the earlier railings around it. According to church records, the later railings were added in 1870 because the trees had enveloped the original ones to such an extent. Both sets can be clearly seen today.

A legend grew up that Lady Grimston was a Sadducean and therefore did not believe in the Resurrection. It is recorded that on her death bed she said *'If indeed, there is life hereafter trees will render asunder my tomb.'* For over 200 years trees have forced their roots through the grave. Her notes of accounts of money spent putting up her horses when she drove from her home in Gorhambury, St. Albans to St. Peter's each Sunday, show that she was not a Sadducean. She recalls that it is the first day of the week when her Lord and Master rose from the grave.

The legend was not known until 1840 and may be derived from the tomb of Grafin Henriette von Riling, a friend of Frederick the Great, who died in 1782 and is buried in a similar tomb in Trinity Church, Hanover. An inscription translates *'This tomb must not be opened through all eternity'* - an inscription interpreted as defying the truth of the resurrection. The heavy iron cover is, however, broken by the roots of a tree.

The large grave to the west of the south door is that of Mr Alfred Beit. Its inscription reads:
'Write me as one who loves his fellow men'
Alfred Beit was a pioneer with Cecil Rhodes in South Africa and Rhodesia. He died in 1906 and under his will the Beit Railway Trust was established to develop transport communications in Northern and Southern Rhodesia (Zambia and Zimbabwe). It provided funds to build most of the great bridges in Central Africa and also four hundred smaller bridges

Above: **An early postcard showing Lady Anne Grimston's grave.**
Below: **A THACS painting workshop in the churchyard in 2005, (see page 202-203).**
Right: **The ancient sundial carved into the wall on the south east corner of St. Peter's.**

in rural areas. This not only advanced the cause of transport in Africa but also the development of modern bridge building techniques. The Beit Trust still exists and makes grants for social and educational purposes in Zambia, Zimbabwe and Malawi.

Alfred Beit's brother, Sir Otto Beit, who lived at Tewin Water, was responsible for building Tewin Memorial Hall on land given by Lord Desborough of Panshanger. His son, Theodore Beit, died during the First World War and there is a tablet to him on the north wall of the church.

In the centre at the back of the grave is mounted a stone in memory of Lilian Beit, wife of Sir Otto Beit. His memorial tablet is on the right and that of his son, Theodore, on the left.

In the south east corner of the churchyard are the graves of John Carrington, the diarist, of Bacon's Farm, Bramfield and his wife Elizabeth. John Carrington was devoted to his wife and his instructions for his own burial in 1810 explain the fact that their gravestones are touching.

'Digg Down till come to the Side of my Dame's Coffin and no lower and Set my Coffin on the Edge of Hers and no lower'.

It was after Elizabeth's death in 1797 that Carrington started his diary which he continued until ten days before his death. It gives a fascinating view of life in Tewin and Bramfield from 1798-1810. (More can be

The grave of Alfred Beit soon after construction. Initially wire netting was placed over the entrance to deter rabbits. This was later replaced by a wrought iron gate which is no longer there.

found about John Carrington in a separate chapter, 16, pages 232-235).

To the east of the church lie the two de Havilland graves. One headstone is dedicated to John de Havilland 1918-1943 and Geoffrey de Havilland 1910-1946. The other is to their mother Lady Louie de Havilland 1879-1949.

Although the family did not live in Tewin they had strong connections with it. The brothers would often have flown over the village on the flight path to and from the de Havilland factory in Hatfield. Geoffrey also lodged in Tewin during the Second World War at Orchard House, the home of Mr and Mrs. Cole, 47 Upper Green. *The Plume of Feathers* was a favourite haunt for John and Geoffrey and they also lodged there for a while. John died in a mid air collision whilst test flying a Mosquito in 1943 near Hatfield. He collided with another Mosquito flown by his friend and colleague George Gibbins. Geoffrey de Havilland died in 1946 whilst test flying a DH 108 in an attempt to be the first aircraft to fly faster than the speed of sound. This was finally achieved by another de Havilland test pilot, John Derry.

The inscription on the graves reads:

They gave their lives in advancing the science of flight
To strive, to seek, to find, and not to yield.

Replacement headstones were dedicated on 15th January 1998. Five test pilots attended the service including Sir John (Cat's Eyes) Cunningham who was senior test pilot at de Havillands. The new memorial stones are of selected Portland stone with the hand cut inscription and letter style being the same as the original. There is also an additional inscription to the memory of Sir Geoffrey de Havilland. The work was arranged by Hatfield Aviation Association, carried out by J.J. Burgess of Hatfield and sponsored by British Aerospace.

On 25th November 2000 a service of Celebration and Remembrance on the 60th Anniversary of the first flight of the de Havilland DH 98 Mosquito was held in the church. Flowers were laid on the de Havilland Memorials by John Cunningham and Pat Fillingham.

The War Memorial records the names of thirty one men of Tewin who gave their lives in the 1914-1918 war and seven who died in the 1939-1945 war. Its design with the Crusaders' sword and ship was by Sir Herbert Baker who also designed the Memorial Hall. He is known for his work in Delhi and for the India

Left to right: **Peter, John and Geoffrey de Havilland**

House, London. More information about the men whom it commemorates can be found in chapter eight: *The World at War,* page 105.

A detailed survey of the burial registers from 1810-1990 was conducted by Peter Walters, Church Warden of St. Peter's from 1985-2003. There were 1648 names recorded, 42 were prior to 1810 and 26 had no known date. There were 568 known graves and headstones in the Churchyard. His findings paint an interesting picture of how village life has changed in the last 180 years.

Particularly interesting are those relating to infant mortality, (diagram 1, page 65). This figure shows the number of deaths per decade of children under the age of 10 years. Allowing for variations from decade to decade because the sample, i.e. the population of Tewin, is small it does not show any marked reduction until about the 1930s. This continued into the 1940s when the National Health Service came into being together with advances in medicine after the war. The inference is, that these advances greatly increased the expectancy of life, particularly in children, (diagram 2). The second diagram compares the number of deaths per age band per 60 years. The total number of deaths in each 60 years was 590, 499, and 477 respectively. The percentages should be compared but this would not make any significant difference in understanding the

changes. The most striking change, again, is the reduction in the number of deaths of children under ten.

Secondly, there is also a considerable reduction in the number of children and young adults right through from ten to thirty or forty. After forty the shape is much the same, but the numbers in each age band are higher which means that more people were living longer and since then there are three people who managed over one hundred years.

Tewin Families
The lists that follow show names that appear in the burial registers ten times or more. For three of the names - Wilsher, Clark and Hopkins, there appear to be alternative spellings - these are listed all together and also under their separate spellings. The Carrington family is included for interest, because of John Carrington's Diary, (diagram 3).

From the earlier list which goes back to 1559 the following names appear, (diagram 4).

Christian names
Peter Walters also compiled a data base of Christian names which appeared ten times or more. Where alternative spellings occur, such as Ann, Anne, Annie, he listed them together and also separately. It is interesting to note that William and Mary together

FOUR MEN KILLED

Planes Collide in Mid Air

ST. ALBANS INQUEST STORY

WHEN two Mosquito aircraft collided in mid air during test flights near St. Albans, on Monday, the De Havilland Aircraft Company suffered a heavy loss, for the accident caused the deaths of four highly-valued employes:

Mr. John De Havilland (24), a test pilot, of " Lidisdale," Bushey Heath, **Mr. George Victor Gibbins** (34), of " Windrush," Everlasting-lane, St. Albans, also a test pilot; **Mr. Godfrey Jackson Carter** (32), of " Mansard Gables," Tewin Wood, Welwyn, supervisor of the firm's flight shed, and **Mr. John Henry Francis Scrope** (24), of 14, Altham-court, Hatfield, a member of the Aero Dynamics Department.

Mr. Scrope was a passenger in the aircraft piloted by Mr. John De Havilland, and Mr. Carter was observer in that flown by Mr. Gibbins. Mr. Scrope, Mr. Carter and Mr. Gibbins were killed instantaneously and Mr. De Havilland, who landed by parachute, died in the ambulance on the way to hospital.

Mr. J. De Havilland.   Mr. G. V. Gibbins.

Mr. G. J. Carter.   Mr. J. H. F. Scrope.

Top left: **The de Havilland graves in the churchyard.**
Above: **Sir Geoffrey de Havilland, the father of Peter, John and Geoffrey, pictured with Frank Hearle in September 1910.**
Top right: **The newspaper report of John de Havilland's death.**
Bottom right: **John (Cat's Eyes) Cunningham** (right) **with John and Ann Lee after the service of Celebration and Remembrance on the 60th Anniversary of the first flight of the de Havilland DH 98 Mosquito held at St. Peter's Church.**

CHILDREN
Number of deaths per decade
0-10 year old age band

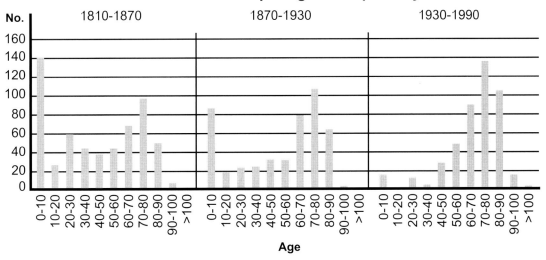

diagram 1

Number of deaths per age band per 60 years

diagram 2

account for 13% of 1580 people and that the top three names in each column, six names in all, account for 31% of all the people.

A 'snapshot' of the Christian names of 115 children in the school in 1992 is included. The sample is not big enough to be statistically significant, but it is nevertheless interesting. The names from 1992 have been noted against the names from the data base. Two of the popular names are Victoria and Mark, neither of which appears in the data base.

Rectors

We have records of the rectors of Tewin from 1312 when Walter de Louth was instituted. There is one earlier name of William de Hereford but no date is

given for his institution. The patron of the living until 1699 was the Priory and Convent of St. Bartholomew's, London. During the Reformation there is a gap in the records between the institution of Edmund Ackeroyd in 1532 who may have been the first priest to read the service in English rather than Latin and the death of Thomas Montford 100 years later in 1632. His son, James Montford, succeeded him and was ejected from the living by the Puritans when Cromwell's Commonwealth marked another turbulent time in the history of the church. The earliest surviving church register covering the dates 1559-1718 enters the baptisms of seven children of James Montford *'parson of Tewinge'* between 1602 and 1610. The first was a boy called John, closely

A survey of the burial registers between 1810 and 1990, and the headstones in St Peter's Churchyard

by Peter Walters 2000

Details taken from burial registers dating back to 1559. They are not such a full record as the registers from 1812.
Another spelling of Wilsher, i.e. Wilcher, is listed.

Name	No	Earliest	Name	No	Earliest
Tyler	1	1574	Archer	20	1597
W/shire	8	1752	Burton	6	1765
(Wilcher)	5	1760	Hopkins/Hopkyns	1	1800
(Wilshire)	2	1804	(Hopkins)	1	1800
(Wiltshire)	1	1752	Chalkley	4	1597
Ward	6	1783	Fordham	7	1655
Watson	9	1763	Carrington	10	1638
Dawes	2	1614			
Clark/Clarke	7	1571			
(Clark)	5	1750			
(Clarke)	2	1571			

diagram 3

This list includes the names that appear 20 times or more. For three names - Wilsher, Clark and Hopkins - there appear to be alternative spellings, so they are listed altogether and also under separate spellings. The Carrington family has been included because of his and his family's close link with Tewin.

Name	No	Earliest	Latest	Name	No	Earliest	Latest
Shadbolt	50	1836	1973	Ephgrave	19	1905	1981
Tyler	41	1811	1973	Archer	18	1820	1891
W/shire	34	1812	1984	Edwards	18	1844	1928
(Wilsher)	16	1875	1984	Burton	17	1814	1938
(Willshire)	9	1817	1862	Hopkins/Hopkyns	17	1816	1967
(Wilshire)	5	1812	1876	(Hopkyns)	9	1876	1967
(Wiltshire)	4	1851	1871	(Hopkins)	8	1816	1904
Ward	31	1814	1943	Chalkley	16	1889	1973
Watson	28	1817	1973	Harding	15	1818	1937
Perry	24	1843	1986	Fordham	14	1825	1965
Dawes	23	1824	1987	Lawrence	14	1833	1935
Brand	23	1839	1950	Wray	12	1815	1948
Clark/Clarke	22	1833	1985	Chambers	11	1845	1926
(Clark)	14	1839	1985	Godfrey	11	1826	1897
(Clarke)	8	1833	1969	Carrington	8	1810	1840

diagram 4

Name	No in list	No in school	Name	No in list	No in school
Mary	98		William	113	2
Ann/Anne/Annie	65		John	100	
(Ann)	47		George	66	1
(Annie)	13		Thomas	54	5
(Anne)	5		James	54	5
Elizabeth	57		Joseph	42	
Sarah	53	5	Charles	34	
Eliza	25		Henry	26	
Jane	24		Robert	24	
Martha	19		Arthur	24	1
Emma	17		Frederick	19	
Hannah	15	3	Richard	19	1
Edith	14		Harold/Harry	14	
Ellen	14		(Harry)	9	
Charlotte	13	2	(Harold)	5	
Maria	12		Edward	14	
Emily	12		David	13	2
Rebecca	11	2	Herbert	13	
Alice	10		Benjamin	12	
			Alfred	12	
			Ernest	11	

diagram 5

The original Portland stone font after restoration in 1965 on the new pedestal of Hoptonwood stone.

followed by Anne, Sarah, another Anne (the first sadly appearing in the burial registers of 1605), Abigail, Susannah and the last child in 1610 whose name is indecipherable. There was a John Montford who, according to Revd. A.C.Vidler, was described as patron of the benefice in 1651 and is buried in the sanctuary. On his memorial slab are the words *Anno Restaurationis 1651.* This was the year when he was restored to his right as patron of the benefice. In that year clergymen were allowed to return to their benefices and use the Prayer Book on condition that they promised to obey the existing government. It was John Montford who first built Tewin House.

In 1699 the living was acquired by Jesus College Cambridge; their archives provide some interesting information about some of the incumbents. From 1702 to 1930 they were all alumni of the college. Charles Proby was the first rector presented by the college in 1702. A document in the church register of that year declares his assent to the Book of Common Prayer. He was preferred to others because of his relationship to the Proby family who were benefactors of the college. The trustees of the Proby Trust purchased the rectory of Tewin in 1698 for £488. The next Rector was Henry Yarborough in 1728. He died in 1774 and in his will gave four copyhold tenements in Tewin for the education of ten poor children of the parish. He also gave the college £500 in trust for building a Rectory house in Tewin.

John Milner who succeeded to the living in 1776 died in 1778 apparently of a dropsy brought on by *'drinking too great quantities of small beer.'*

Several of the incumbents were distinguished scholars. Alexander Nairne, for example, was Regius Professor of Divinity at Cambridge and Professor of Hebrew at King's College, London. He wrote eight books on Theology and at the end of his career was Canon of St. Georges, Windsor.

The last Rector of Tewin was Charles Richard Blamire-Brown who moved to Chipperfield in 1975, after which the parishes of Tewin and Datchworth were united until 1999.

In 2005 Tewin became part of a Team Ministry comprising St. Mary's, Welwyn; St. Michael's, Woolmer Green; All Saints, Datchworth; and St. Peter's, Ayot St. Peter. At that time Tewin Parish welcomed its first woman priest, the Revd. Coralie McCluskey, as Team Vicar.

Above left to right:

Rectors
Alexander Nairne 1894-1912,
Arthur Vidler 1912-1930,
Charles Stebbing 1930-1946 and
Derrick Burke 1946-1958

Left: **The Reverend Coralie McCluskey 2005 to date (photographed in 2009).**

The Rectors of St. Peter's Church, Tewin

Rector	Instituted	Patron Prior & Conv.' of St. Bartolomew's (sic), London
William de Hereford		
Walter de Louth	April 15, 1312	
Richard Malet	Mar. 4, 1356	
John de Prestwold	Oct. 1361	
John le Petit	Nov. 9, 1374	
John Hurthall (or Hurthull)	May 5, 13 79	
William Fordyngton	Nov. 13, 1394	
William Yowdale	Sept. 5, 1397	
John Fraunceys	July 31, 1405	
John West	May 7, 1417	
John Puttenham		
Lawrance Newton	June 21, 1453	
John Cowper	May 27, 1460	
Thomas Mansfield	June 22, 1463	
Thomas Day,	Aug. 14, 1492	
Edward Malherbe	April 10, 1505	
William Marshall	Feb 3, 1506	
Christopher Wilson	Mar. 31, 1508	
Edmund Ackeroyd	Nov. 20, 1532	
Thomas Montfort (d.1632)		
James Montfort (ejected 1643)		
Henry Raynsford (buried Feb.12, 1651)		
Falk Tudor (died 1688)		
George Stanhope	Jan. 21, 1689	**Sir Francis Boteler**, Kt.
Charles Proby	Dec. 29, 1702	Jesus College, Cambridge
Henry Yarborough	Mar. 28, 1728	
John Milner	Feb. 15, 1776	
Arthur Willis	Nov. 5, 1779	
Thomas Newton	Feb. 25, 1797	
Henry James Daubeny	Sept. 12, 1843	
Alexander Nairne	July 12, 1894	
Arthur Vidler	July 11, 1912	
Charles Stebbing	Dec. 8, 1930	
Derrick Burke	Nov. 9, 1946	
Charles Richard Blamire-Brown, M.A.		
licensed Priest-in-Charge	Aug. 1958 to June 1975	
formally inducted Rector	May 9, 1967	
Parishes of Tewin and Datchworth united	1976	
Canon Julian C. Tross	Jan. 6, 1976 (Rector of Datchworth)	
Paul Betts, B.Sc.	Nov. 1979	
Vacancy started	April 1, 1996	
Robert Eardley inaugurated Priest-in-Charge	July 16, 1998	
United benefice dissolved	March 1, 1999	
Robert Eardley formally licensed Priest-in-Charge	April 15, 1999.	
Coralie McCluskey appointed Priest in Charge	Dec 2004	
(Team Ministry formed)	Aug. 1, 2005	
Coralie McCluskey Team Vicar	Aug. 1, 2005	

Left picture: **Charles Blamire-Brown 1958-1975 with his wife, family and the churchwardens.**

Below left: **Canon Julian C. Tross 1976-1979 with (from left to right) Peter Walters, Bob Taylor, Graham Spring, Dilys Applegate, Canon Tross, Audrey Walters, Mrs Tross.**

Below right: **Paul Betts 1979-1996.**

Tom and Janet Gladwin. Tom looked after St. Peter's during the vacancy 1996-1998.

Robert Eardley 1998 - 2005, pictured during a visit to St. Peter's by Christopher, the then Bishop of St. Albans, May 11 2003.

Millennium Kneelers

In 1988 a group of people stitched kneelers for the choir stalls and when it came to discussions about an appropriate way to mark the Millennium it was suggested that a more ambitious project should be attempted. The church is fitted with bench kneelers and the plan was for individual pictures to be made and then sewn together to cover the whole bench. They were mounted on upholstered boards and hinged on to the existing kneelers so that they could be lifted out of the way of dirty shoes. At the same time five of the pictures were formed into a panel to hang in the new library area of Tewin Cowper School. A design was chosen by each participant and the pictures depict scenes of Tewin life, past and present, including the arts, buildings, organisations, countryside and wildlife.

The kneeler end panels alternate MM & 2000 visible along the aisles to give strength and stability to the lengths of the picture panels. The colours of all these end panels are those found in the two front long kneelers, used in different combinations. The greys used in the borders reflect the stonework in the church, the purple, red and yellow the stained glass. The keys of St. Peter are on each length at the far end from MM. Those who worked the keys were encouraged to look at old keys. Consequently, the panels have variations.

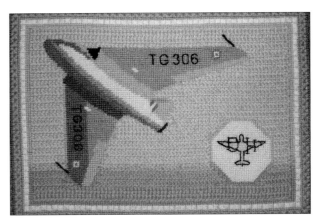

Kneeler 1 is stitched to say

AD 2000 EXULTATE JUBILATE *Hurrah*

Kneeler 2 says

MILLENNIUM 2000

Initially it was hoped to complete the first two pews of the nave but, as more and more people joined the first core of enthusiasts, the project grew. The aim was now to fill the entire church. Over sixty people, both men and women, have now completed a design. The basic design colours and stitching of the surrounds and the management of the project to

maintain consistency was carried out by Elisabeth Buchanan assisted by Audrey Walters. Elisabeth also supplied advice and designs, where needed, to help the participants, many of whom had never undertaken such work before. Revd. Rob Eardley stitched the last panel with an open date of 200 - so there is a deadline to finish by the end of 2009!

The project brings the story of St. Peter's Church up to the present time and illustrates the way in which the people of Tewin have cared for St. Peter's over the centuries. As we have seen, many of their names are known, but just as important are those who have worshipped here and looked after the church through its long history but who have no lasting memorial.

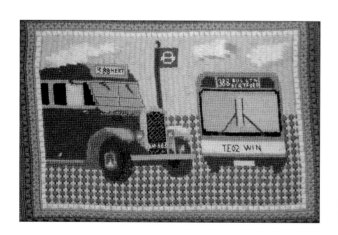

TEWIN CHURCH MAGAZINE.

MAY, 1935.

My Dear Friends,

Our Church looked beautiful at Easter, thanks to the quantities of lovely flowers and the tasteful work of the decorators. We thank them all, and especially Lady Beit for the flowers—not only at festivals but throughout the year. Services were well attended, and the number of Communicants must have been a record again. I appreciate very gratefully the amount and method of disposal of the collections for the day.

The Club General Meeting was held on April 16th, when we were all pleased to see Mr. Bull in the chair. The outgoing officers were re-elected with thanks for their very efficient services in the past, and the new Committee consists of : Mrs. Hollis, and Messrs. A. A. Baldwin, C. Chalkley, C. Geeves, F. A. Hollis, H. G. Mears, A. Quince, A. J. Reeves, C. H. Spratt, R. Taylor, J. J. Wilsher and P. J. Winters. A generous figure was allowed for initial expenditure for a Tennis Club to be organized on similar lines to the Bowls Club. and the distribution of prizes was made by Mrs. Turner.

The great event of this month will be the Silver Jubilee, for which a great deal of preliminary work has already been done. The mugs are already safely to hand, and the order for fireworks has been placed. About a hundred prizes for the sports will doubtless also be ready for display shortly. There will be a celebration of the Holy Communion that morning at 7.45, and I hope that at ten o'clock the Church will be full for the special Thanksgiving Service for the day. This should not take more than half-an-hour of our very full day.

On May 8th our orchestra is competing at the Musical Competition at Hitchin.

On May 10th there will be an open meeting of the Parochial Church Council to divide the various responsibilities for the fête on June 6th. Will anyone therefore who can help beforehand, or on the day, please come to this meeting, so that we can have their help and suggestions.

The Lent Work Parties were better attended than ever this year, and the teas were highly appreciated. The financial result of them is as follows : Donations, £4. 16s. 6d. ; sale of made-up articles, £8. 12s. 11d. ; weekly collections, £2. 3s. 3d. Expenditure on materials amounted to £12. 18s. 9d. So that we start with a well-filled stall of attractive goods, plus a cash balance of £2. 13s. 11d. Excellent.

The Annual Deanery Festival of the Mothers' Union has been fixed for Thursday, July 4th, at Watton, when Canon Meyer is to be the preacher. The annual outing is fixed for Tuesday, June 25th, and as a wish has been expressed that it should be to the sea this year, Mrs. Stebbing is getting quotations for conveyance to Felixstowe or Clacton.

Once again may I say how much the work of the Guild is appreciated in the appearance of the Church. If any of the members would like to have their month of duty altered will they kindly mention it to Miss K. Egerton, so that the list can be revised to date.

C. F. STEBBING,
Rector.

BAPTISMS.

April 19th. Valerie Ephgrave.
 ,,   21st. Ruth Honora Briant.

MARRIAGE.

April 20th. George Edwards and Ethel Winifrid Lyles.

BURIALS.

April 9th. Louisa Tyler, aged 80.
 ,,   20th. James Edwards, aged 74.

A letter from the Parish News of May 1935 mentioning preparations for the Silver Jubilee celebrations of George V and including many local family names.

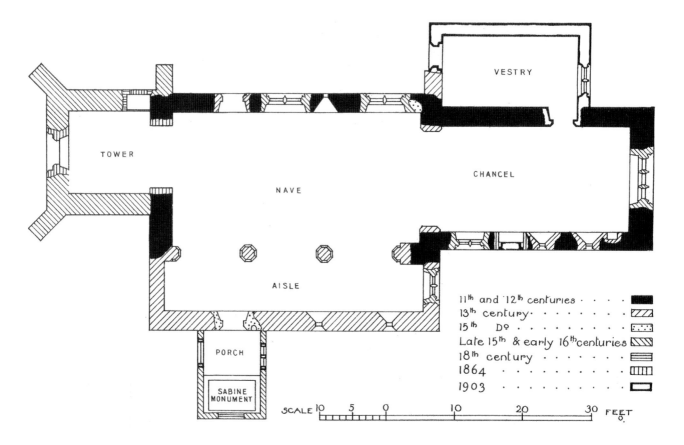

TEWIN CHURCH. PLAN SHEWING DIFFERENT PERIODS.

Drawn by T. D. ATKINSON, Architect, July, 1903.

Top left: **This photograph was taken between 1883 and 1903 before the restoration by Earl Cowper.**
Top right: **A photograph taken in 1914. The alterations made in 1903 can be seen. The small vestry has been removed and windows have been added to the south wall of the chancel.**
Bottom: **Plan of Tewin Church made in 1903 by T. D. Atkinson, the architect at the time of the restoration showing different periods in its history.**

Tewin Rectories

The old Rectory of Tewin is situated opposite the drive to St. Peter's Church. The original house on the present site was built in the seventeenth century. A further house was built *'at his own charge'* by Charles Proby, Rector of Tewin from 1720 to 1728. The present Rectory dates from 1775 following a bequest in the will of Henry Yarborough, Rector from 1728 to 1776. He bequeathed £500 in trust to the Master and Fellows of Jesus College, Cambridge, patrons of the living, to lay out *'in creating and building a House for the Rectors of Tewin for the same to reside in....'*

An even earlier house is mentioned by Sir Henry Chauncy in his book *'Historical Antiquities in Hertfordshire'*. In 1537, the twenty eighth year of Henry VIII's reign, a rectory in Tewin was rated at a value of £14. This, however, may have been a separate building abutting the church.

Dr. Yarborough's successor, John Milner, writing in August 1775 acknowledged receipt of the £500 and described the outcome of a builder's inspection. The house was in a *'very ruinous condition'* and it was agreed that there should be an *'immediate pulling down of the greater part of it'*. A new house would be

Top: **The Old Rectory, built in 1775.**
Below: **The oldest part of the Rectory. The 1775 building can be seen at the top of the picture.**

built to cost *'at least as much as Dr. Yarborough's legacy and the materials of the old house'*. A wing of the original seventeenth century house remains at the east side of the building.

Ten years before the new house was built Dr. Yarborough had experienced an armed robbery at the

Rectory on 3rd September 1765.

'A desperate attack was made upon Rev. Dr. Yarborough of Tewin near Hertford by a young fellow who having left his horse at the gate, entered the parlour where the doctor was, and clapping a pistol to his head demanded his money. The doctor offered him some silver and protested what other money he had was at Hertford, on which the young villain withdrew, saying it was not silver he wanted, took his horse and rode off without further mischief.' (The Gentleman's Magazine)

A report on the house written in 1925 by land agents and surveyors describes it as 'a red brick and tiled Queen Anne Building which has been added to an older Tudor wing, which is Timber, Plaster and Tiled, forming an attractive small Residence which stands back from the road and is approached by a double carriage drive.'

The house had a drawing room, dining room, large kitchen and scullery. Bedrooms consisted of two front bedrooms and dressing room, two side bedrooms over the old portion of the house and two attic bedrooms. In the basement there were no less than four cellars.

The gardens and grounds were described as 'unusually attractive with lawns, shrubberies, fine specimen trees - Scotch, Acacia, Cedar, Large Oak and Small orchard with Meadow at rear.' Outside were 'several outbuildings including a brick and tiled loose box with gardener's Bothy, a timber and thatched Tithe Barn and two tiled pig sties, a brick and tiled coach house and a range of Nag stables.'

There were seven acres of land with the house which was standing 'on high ground, commanding a beautiful view.'

The house is described by successive rectors as a beautiful building but the records of Jesus College are full of correspondence relating to the difficulties of maintaining such a house in a state of good repair. From 1894, when Revd. Nairne was appointed to the living, rectors no longer lived in the rectory but let it to tenants whilst living themselves in the Cottage Rectory on Lower Green.

The rent of the house provided some income for them but they often experienced difficulties over repairs and upkeep. The rector was responsible for exterior or structural repairs and the tenant for the interior. Some of the adjoining glebe land was sold to Lord Desborough in 1887.

In 1911, when Revd. Nairne retired from the living,

A pen and wash drawing of the Tithe Barn c1950s

his tenant in the Rectory, Mr. Grenville-Gray, the church warden, was anxious to remain there or to be able to purchase the house. Revd. Nairne wrote to the college: *'The Rectory is so beautiful that you certainly ought not to part with it lightly'*. However, he also says that the *'difficulty of keeping it fit to use is increasing...not only repairs but the lack of modern convenience. There is no bathroom: the whole arrangement for getting water is curious and inadequate.'* He concludes that, perhaps, if the tenant bought the house for £3000, *'it might be worth while to sell it.'*

The sale did not go ahead and despite the fact that the new Rector, Revd.Vidler, had a family he chose to live in the smaller Cottage Rectory on Lower Green and the tenant remained in the Old Rectory.

In 1913 Revd. Vidler writes to the college to say that the tenant would like to build a further room on the ground floor. He writes that the house is *'at present inconveniently cramped on the ground floor without a third room for a study...'* The college agreed to this.

In 1917 the question of a sale of the house arose again when Mr Otto Beit of Tewin Water sought to purchase *'the house with gardens about two acres and field about 4 acres....as a residence for his agent.'* The Revd. Vidler asks the college for their opinion and explains that, in his opinion *'the present Rectory with its garden, stables etc could only be occupied by a Rector with large private means: that it is of an age which makes it very expensive to keep in repair'* and *'has now been let with the Bishop's consent for 25 years for the reason that it is now considered too much of a burden for an Incumbent's residence.'*

Again, the sale did not go ahead and by 1924 Revd. Vidler is preparing information for the patrons in which he says that the *'foundations, walls and main roof are in a precarious condition.'* In September the tenant was complaining of a crack in the plaster with wet getting through after *'continued rain and winds'*.

It was at this stage that a local builder was called in to give a full estimate of what was needed and the College spent £400 on repairs including a new roof, dormer windows and rebuilding and enlarging of a wing containing bathroom, lavatories and cloakroom. The drainage system was also overhauled. Money was provided from the Proby Fund - a bequest made by Charles Proby, a former rector, from 1702-1728 and finally came to £900. The bursar of Jesus College felt that it would be a mistake to sell the house, *'as it adjoins the church*

most conveniently and is a charming eighteenth century house with a 17th century or earlier wing. It is a house of very considerable character. It has a beautiful garden, not too large, and convenient and picturesque outbuildings. As it is near London it lets well and has been a source of considerable income to the rectors.'

From 1926 the house was rented by Mr and Mrs. Melchior and the interior decoration was completed. They were the first tenants to change the name of the house to the Old Rectory. A letter from Revd. Vidler to the college in 1926 describes the Rectory as *'now*

in a glorious condition of repair and decoration both inside and out.' He writes this on St. Peter's Day and says that *'everything looks very promising for a beautiful day.'*

In 1933 Revd. Vidler retired. His successor, Revd. Stebbing was very keen to live in the Rectory House. In June he made a preliminary visit to Tewin with his wife and wrote of being, *'unspeakably charmed by the Rectory. It is a most delightful <u>small</u> house; not a big one as I feared. We both felt we <u>must</u> live there.'* By July, however, he had realised that with a stipend of £300 per annum and after paying taxes and rates he would not be able to afford to live there. *'It is disappointing as we were so charmed with the Rectory. However, one can't have everything and we are both delighted at the prospect of coming to Tewin.'* Instead, he lived at the Cottage Rectory on Lower Green as Revd. Vidler had done.

In 1932 an offer had been made to buy the rectory. The college was, *'most adverse'* to this proposal, *'on grounds of historical sentiment and present interest.'* Again there is a series of letters discussing the difficulty of its upkeep. The Bishop felt it obvious that no Rector could possibly live in the house unless he was *'possessed of considerable private means.'* He felt that the *'financial strain on the clergy was very great at this time'* and supported a sale, but no sale ensued.

In 1933 a new tenant, Mrs Geddes, took over the house and the college paid for extensive alterations and *'dilapidation work.'* In 1937 she moved to Australia and the house was let to Mr and Mrs Lionel Butler-Henderson. The lease was renewed in 1944. In 1946 the house was occupied by Mr and Mrs Watson. John and Nora Cotton were there from 1951 to 1956 and in 1956 Sir Alexander Knox-Helm and Dame Florence Helm took over the house. They purchased the freehold from St. Alban's Diocese in 1961 thus opening a new era for the house. They stayed until 1967. In the following year the house was sold to Dr. and Mrs. Harold Jory who lived there for nearly forty years. The present residents moved to the house in January 2006, ensuring that the Old Rectory, with its varied history, continues as a family home.

Cottage Rectory

The Cottage Rectory, now demolished, was situated on Lower Green on the site of the present Adams/Huntley houses built in 1968. Nearby was a large barn adjoining Hertford Road.

The Revd. Vidler and his two predecessors did not occupy the Old Rectory but, instead, lived in the Cottage Rectory rented from Lady Desborough for £40 per annum. In 1930, Revd. Vidler does not think that *'this little house'* will continue at £40 per annum:

' I should think it fairly worth £60 with the meadow attached'

The Revd. Stebbings bought the property and lived there from 1930 to 1946. He called it the Cottage Rectory and church fêtes were held in its large garden. During World War II aluminium pots and pans given by villagers for the later manufacture into aeroplanes to help the war effort were stored in the barn and collected periodically.

The Old Cottage Rectory *11 Hertford Road*

After Revd. Stebbings retired this chalet style bungalow, built in the 1930s, was given to the diocese by Lady Beit of Tewin Water as a house for future Rectors of Tewin. It retained the name of Cottage Rectory. Following the retirement of Revd. Blamire-Brown it was sold and is now in private occupancy.

The Old Cottage Rectory

The Cottage Rectory c1910. At one time this was the home of Winifred Lyles. Her mother was in service when the Revd. Nairne occupied the Rectory.

Chapter 7

Tewin Schools

Schooling in Tewin has played an important part in the formation of the village not only in educating the children but also in binding the community together. There have been four schools in Tewin with the addition of pre-school, toddlers, playgroup and even ante-natal classes.

The Strutt Sunday School started about 1789, the Yarborough School 1794-98, the first Cowper School 1847 and the second Cowper School from 1966 onwards.

The Strutt Sunday School

It fell to incomers to start the first school in 1789. They were Joseph Strutt the antiquary, artist, engraver and poet who, to escape his creditors, was lodging with his sons and apprentice at the home of John Carrington, the diarist, at Bacons Farm, and Robert Gass, (Tewin 1760-1804) who worked in the optician's works at Tewin Mill.

W E Hughes' essay on Joseph Strutt records that *'before the school was opened the rector [Rev Willis MA] had been approached and asked to give his sanction and support. The reply was a flat and indignant refusal for the reverend gentleman considered the school to be an impertinent and unnecessary innovation. Strutt, in turn, was indignant and composed some humorous and stinging verses which he chalked...on the wall that enclosed the rector's well'.*

John Carrington notes that there was no support for a school from the local gentry and that the leading family, the Cowpers, who had taken over from old Lady Cathcart as Lords of the Manor, stood aloof.

Carrington further records that despite this lack of support, Strutt, *'was the beginner of it at his own expence'* and Gass proceeded with their own money. They *'Whear the first Beginers of the Sundays School at Tewin which Taught the Children and Braught them to church in 1790'.*

Strutt hired a room from a farmer's widow in which, aided by his sons and Robert Gass, he sought to teach them and *'amend their morals'.*

W E Hughes quotes their success – it was noticed that *'squirrel-hunting and other disorderly sports were no longer indulged on Sundays'*!

The Sunday School was then established in 1792 by Order of the Parish. Further income for the school came from charity sermons.

Carrington records that the first *'was preached at Tewin Church for the benefits of the Sunday School at Tewin which had been established from Mixs (Michaelmas) 1792 by order of the Parish...*

'The sermon was preached by Mr Graham the Curat of Hardfordingbury [NOT Rev Willis – the incumbent Rector!]

'The Churchwarden and overseer collected £21-15-0d'. (A magnificent sum). *'Lord Cowper and his family was their for the first time'.*

Carrington also records each year that such sermons were preached in October and that the collections

Joseph Strutt

were usually about £20 and that he himself gave half a crown! The sermons tailed off and had stopped altogether by the 1820s, as the school itself went into decline.

When Strutt returned to London in 1794, Lord Cowper may at last have given his support.

Tewin Cowper School children photographed in 1900. (Early pictures from *'Two Hundred Years of Tewin School'*, 1995, when Roger Huggins was Chair of the School Governors).

Top: **Tewin Cowper School infant children 1900**
Bottom: **Fire mark on the Yarborough School building 1751 supplied by the Sun Insurance Company.**

Above: **Cowper Endowed School photograph taken in 1913**
Below: **Alfred Brand (Ronald Brand's father and Terry Brand's grandfather) back row, second from right c1920**

School class in the 1920s. Henrietta Shadbolt is in the middle row, 4th girl from the left.
Alfred Ephgrave is in the front row, second from the left.

The Yarborough School

The second Tewin school was the bequest of the Revd. Dr Yarborough DD who was Rector of Tewin from 1728 to his death in 1775. He acquired what is now the Old School House and three cottages nearby in 1758. He bequeathed them in his will, dated 1773, in trust to the Rectors of Tewin and Digswell so that they might provide an education for 10 poor children, both boys and girls. This was an advanced view for his time when girls were thought not to need formal education. These children were to be selected by the incumbent Rector. This was a generous gift to the village and it is unfortunate that Dr Yarborough's name is not better remembered for it.

Between c1769-1789 the Lordship of the Manor was held by Elizabeth, Dowager Lady Cathcart of Tewin Water who had a splendidly colourful life, chronicled in chapter seven. Her memorial tablet in St Peter's Tewin does not record her lively past but includes *'Among her boundless acts of charity in her life time is a perpetual annual gift of £5 to be applied to the schooling of poor children of this parish, secured in 3% East India annuities'*. In fact the 1783 deed, by which this was given, was more specific – it was for coals (then an expensive commodity) to heat the school.

These were two very generous bequests, and it is shameful that there was little immediate enthusiasm to get a school going either among the new gentry or the clergy, who as Trustees presumably just pocketed the income for the next 20 years!

Schoolmaster & Curriculum

The first Yarborough schoolmaster, John Pridmore, was appointed somewhere between 1794 and 1798. We know a little of Pridmore and his family including his predilection for local hostelries and his fine topographical drawings. He taught the three 'R's, biblical instruction and music as well as practical horticulture. Interestingly, he took his choir to Bramfield church rather than St. Peter's, Tewin.

In addition to the 10 free places, to make ends meet he took in not only locals at 1d a week, but boarders from London at 3d a week. 3d was very little even then for a week's board, lodging and tuition. John Carrington (and Pridmore) frequently spent more in

The original Yarborough School on Lower Green now converted to a private residence.

pubs. In one evening session for example, Carrington records he spent 1s 6d (1s at *The Feathers* and 6d at Jack's, *The Rose and Crown*) in one evening in the same week as he records the boarder coming to the School for 3d. Six times more in one evening's entertainment than a whole week's board and tuition for one wretched boy! Indeed Carrington's dearest dinner cost 15 shillings – more than a whole year's fees for this Dickensian boarding school!

It is significant that John Carrington who knew well both Pridmore, the schoolmaster of Tewin, and William Otway, the schoolmaster of Welwyn, sent his own grandchildren to Otway, even though Welwyn was three miles distant.

Pupils

Although there were only around 700 people in Tewin Parish at the turn of the nineteenth century, nevertheless there were at least 40 boys boarding (many from London) at the school in addition to the ten free and other paid for village boys and girls daily and at the Sunday School. Indeed at one of the Cowper weddings in 1805 Carrington records that 87 children claimed to be pupils at the Sunday school or School and thus took part in the wedding feast at the School.

Do not even think about the sanitary arrangements

for 87 boys and girls. There was no water supply. There was only one earth privy as late as 1950. No wonder there were so many epidemics '*Epidemics were an annual event...measles, scarlet fever, whooping cough, diphtheria, mumps, influenza and typhoid. Tragically children sometimes died*'.

Dickensian School

Tewin School was one of the models, along with the famous or infamous Yorkshire Schools, for 'Dotheboys Hall' in '*Nicholas Nickleby*' written by Charles Dickens in 1838. (Dickens was very familiar with this part of Hertfordshire and had active knowledge of these local boarding schools. He visited Yorkshire for only two days taking his illustrator with him).

Pridmore's fees of 3d were pitifully small not only for tuition but also for board for growing boys. Malnutrition must have been rife even with the orchards and gardens and free labour. In a quote from '*Nicholas Nickleby*' headmaster Squeers says, '*Where's the second boy?*' '*Please; sir, he's weeding the garden replied a small voice. 'To be sure,' said Squeers, by no means disconcerted. 'So he is. B-o-t, bot, t-i-n, tin, bottin, n-e-y, ney, bottinney, noun substantive, a knowledge of plants, When he has learned that bottinney means a knowledge of plants, he goes and knows 'em. That's our system, Nickleby: what do you think of it?' 'It's a very useful one, at any rate,' answered Nicholas.'* This 'useful system' was certainly operated by Pridmore in the orchards and gardens of the Yarborough School, and kept going in the first Cowper School.

After the publication of *'Nicholas Nickleby'* in 1838/9 (the 'Dotheboys Hall' episodes appeared in 1838) there was a public outcry about, and interest in such schools.

John Pridmore, a drunkard, left the school in Tewin in 1839 and it was closed in 1840.

The Two Cowper Schools

The third Tewin school was the first Cowper School.

In 1840 Lord Henry Cowper died and left money for the benefit of the Parish School and a Master and Mistress were to be employed. In 1847 the new school was complete - purpose-built with adjoining living accommodation. It was smaller than the Yarborough School and its grounds. It was a day school and no longer took in boarders. He gave an annual Endowment of £78.0.5d. These were very generous gifts to the village.

It does appear, however, that in return the Cowper family quietly annexed the Old School House (which they converted into two houses) and the three cottages plus the gardens with orchards which together were larger and more valuable than the new School. They also 'fined' (a local land tax) the Rectors who were the Trustees, for their own benefit further extortionate sums in 1799, 1845 and 1895. The Cowper family's philanthropy is clouded by their taking so much both in property and cash, from the Trust.

School Log

There is little written history of the School until the 1870 Education Act required the keeping of a school log book. In this log items of interest and significance are recorded and the early years make fascinating reading.

Headteachers (from c1870) and teachers (from 1943) to date

No record exists of the first headmaster in 1847 but a complete list from 1873 can be seen on page 88. There have been a number of long lived headteachers giving stability and direction to the school. To see records of all of the teachers at Tewin since 1943 refer to the School log book.

Above: **The first Cowper Endowed School on Lower Green built in 1847.**

Premises

The school premises which still exist today consisted of a purpose built school house (costing £505) with an attached house for the schoolmaster and his family. Both the Yarborough Old School House and the first Cowper School House have since been converted to family homes, as has the semi-detached headmaster's house. The new school had a playground and grounds for practical gardening. For example Alfred Brand is remembered in a photograph c1926 hoeing the land with other pupils. Indeed, the vegetables etc. that they grew were offered for sale. His son Ronald who was also a pupil in the 1940s remembers tending his patch of ground to produce vegetables which has given him a lifelong interest in gardening. These gardens and playground are now 'The Hazels' housing estate.

The school had an Assembly Room and two classrooms, one for the infants between 5 and 7 and one for the rest whose ages ranged from 8 to 14. Both classrooms had old boiler type heaters and the older boys took turns to keep the fire stoked up with coke. Later additions were a wooden hut, used first for the

Above: **The School gardening club c1926**
Below: **School pupils hoeing the allotments in the 1940s**

Above: **School visit to Richard Hale School in Hertford, about 1950.**
Below: **Football team 1950-51.** Back row, left to right: **Michael Christy, Ian Hay, Derek Pardoe, Mick Ephgrave, Paul Ellis, Alan Hay.** Front row, left to right: **Chris Barker, Dave Ephgrave, David Baldwin, Tony Collins, Roger Temple.**

Tewin Headteachers since 1870

-June 1873	George Wolstenholme
June 1873 - Aug 1873	C.J. Derbyshire *
Sept 1873 - March 1875	Thomas King
April 1875 - Dec 1893	Thomas Brode
Jan 1894 - Aug 1896	G. H. Lander
Oct 1896 - Dec 1910	Miss Rose Watson
Feb 1909 - June 1909	Henry Clavell *
June 1910 - Oct 1910	Clara Berrill *
Oct 1910 - Dec 1910	A.Wentworth Powell *
Jan 1911 - Oct 1925	Geoffrey Lamb
March 1917 - Jan 1919	Amelia Lamb *
Oct 1925 - Oct 1943	Frank Hollis
Oct 1943 - July 1961	Muriel Grant
Sept 1961 - Nov 1973	William Furlong
Nov 1973 - Aug 1974	Brian Elton +
Sept 1974 - Aug 1983	Martin Webster
Sept 1983 - Aug 1987	Roger Green
Sept 1987 - Dec 1987	Paul Edwards +
Jan 1988 - July 1993	Stephen James
Sept 1993 - July 1999	Steve Mellor
Sept 1999 - July 2000	Paul Edwards +
Sept 2000 - Dec 2007	Eileen King
Jan 2008 - March 2008	Nathan Hairon +
April 2008 -	Alison Simpson

* temporary + Acting Head

Headteacher 'Bill' Furlong making a retirement presentation to a member of staff, Mrs Warehand.

Muriel Grant appointed headteacher in 1943 lived in the school house with her family. It was thanks to her, a dedicated and concientious teacher, that this small village school emerged from the war years with the high educational standards that continue today. She was determined that any child with the ability would get a Grammar School place and all children would have as broad an education as possible.

boys' carpentry and girls' needlework and later as the school canteen, and a separate toolshed.

Curriculum
The curriculum was much as one would expect from a village school for 5 to 14 year olds with the emphasis on the practical since most of the children left school at 14 and did not go on to secondary school.

Subjects included reading, writing, mathematics, history, drawing, nature study, and sewing, arithmetic, English and dictation. The girls cooked one day a week and did knitting and sewing and the boys did woodwork in the cedar hut. In addition to the gardening and the vegetables for sale they also kept poultry and bees.

Pre World War I
Apart from the log book there is little other written record of schooling in Tewin until the turn of the century. We are lucky enough to have interviews with some of the older villagers who were at school at that time. For example:-

Ivy Hubbard:
'I started at the school before the first world war. We used slates and chalk instead of paper. There was no uniform. In the playground we played hopscotch, hoops, marbles and football. In the classroom the subjects were reading, writing, maths, history, drawing, nature study and sewing. There were only three rooms and three teachers (Mrs and Mr Lamb and the infant teacher).

In nature study we did bee keeping because Mr Lamb kept bees in his garden. We would tend to the bees while wearing straw hats and using an extractor. Honey would come out of a tap and we would sell it next day.'

Jack Marshall
'The biggest amount of children I can remember in the school was 60. We left school at 14 because there were no secondary schools. We didn't have milk at playtimes, but we had a cup of cocoa. My first teachers were Mr and Mrs Hydum.

One year they spent some of the endowment money on a big new shed. Half of it was for cookery for the

The new Cowper Church of England Primary School built in 1966

Kim Wilde, a former pupil at the school, with Ivy Hubbard (née Quince) and a pupil in 1992.

girls and half for carpentry for the boys. There were four benches with carpentry tools on them. That was there for a long time. When they stopped using it as a shed it became a canteen. That was the only canteen there for dinners until they came to the new building. They also had a garden shed that had spades, rakes, and hoes in it. They were all brand new. We played all sorts of games including football and cricket on the Baker's field. The bakery is now the village shop, but then the shop was at no. 7 Lower Green.'

Rose Dawes

'In school we could not see out of the windows because they were too high up. There was no heating in school like today - we only had a black stove in the middle of the school. In lessons we had to be interested or we would be punished. The subjects we did were Arithmetic, English and Dictation. If someone did something wrong and no one owned up we would all be punished with the cane. As well as the cane you could get lines (lots of them!). Mrs Smith got the cane for forgetting the school motto.

The girls cooked one day a week and did knitting and sewing, and the boys had woodwork. The boys also had a garden where The Hazels is now. They sold vegetables to make money. They did a lot of practical work. Also they kept poultry and bees.

Instead of getting taken and picked up fom school we had to walk, even if it was far away. The sports we played were the drill (P.E.), country dancing and netball. We did not go out on outings like today, but

once a year we went to Lord and Lady Desborough's house for tea. The whole school went and we had to walk there! The school colours were green and white.

At breaktime we played hopscotch, skipping and general ball games. Instead of leaving the school at 11 we left at 14 and didn't go to secondary school. There were 95 children between 3 teachers so the classes were quite crowded. The district nurse came once a week to check up on the children. We were allowed packed lunches but most went home for lunches.'

Continuity

The school records (as alas, do the War Memorials) show several generations of families many of whom still live in the village today and are still sending their children to Tewin Cowper School to be educated. These families include Baldwin, Brand, Chalkley, Ephgrave, Perry, Shadbolt, Tebbutt, Tyler and Wilsher (see Chapter 14).

The 'New' School: Tewin Cowper Church of England Primary School

The fourth village school was purpose built on land near Cannons Meadow and completed in 1966.

Architecture and Premises

The school was designed by the Hertfordshire County Council's well regarded team of designers, in the then modern style with square lines, flat roof and a lot of glass and light.

The premises consist of a main hall used for assembly, PE and serving lunch, plus three main and two smaller classrooms. In addition there is the Millennium Room built as an extension to commemorate the year 2000, a technology area and a computer suite and library.

Outdoor Sports & Activities

Outside activities are catered for by a games field, a hard netball court and hard play area, a soft play area and the swimming pool largely financed by village initiatives. With the vast improvements in transport since World War II, visits to school camps are famous amongst the school children. These include Cuffley Camp for years 3 & 4, Wicken House and longer visits to Norfolk (Aylemerton) and Stone Farm in Devon for years 5 & 6. The outdoor sports include netball, football, rounders, cricket, cross country and athletics with coaching available for badminton and rugby.

Two July 1981 School photographs: Top row: **Lee Wakefield, Sarah Davis, David Tebbutt, Duncan Burles, Samantha Colison, Pippa Bailey, Justine Rogers, Claire Hart, Ian Hampson, Jonathan Davis.** Middle row: **Stuart Bird, John Hopkins, Toby Langton, Douglas James, Richard Melling, Pippa Garwood, Leisha Summers, Katherine Lewis, Maxine Porter, Chris Sharpe, Mike Bennett, Derek Mackey, (Deputy Head).** Bottom row: **Michelle Ford, Sharon Tebbutt, Annabelle St Pier, Leonie Parsley, Rachel Baldwin, Bernice Herd, Darren Kevis, Robert Holden, Russell Davis, Sally Brett, Stuart Pollard, Shaun Preston.**

Top row: **Dawn Pamphlett, Peter Scriven, Zelda Pearson, Gemma Coulcher, Susan Benton, Andrew Lewis, Tracy Moore, Nicholas Drew, Kimberley Knight.** Middle row: **Paul Benton, Emma Woodward, James Parsley, Vicki Bullock, Stephen Hiscott, Christopher Tyler, Dominic Sharman, Tim Poole, Graham Loaks.** Bottom row: **Paul Day, Suzanne Clark, Nicholas Errington, Hannah Short, Tammy Wheeler, Mark Jackson, Susannah Turner, Gillian Webster.**

Curriculum

Were John Pridmore to fast forward 200 years he would not be surprised with the core and foundation subjects of English, maths, history, geography, art, except for design & technology although he would recognise the sewing and other handicrafts. He would be pleased with the religious education and particularly with the music but he would be amazed at the fourteen internet linked computers in the computer area and the interactive white boards linked to the teachers' computers and able to illustrate subjects in class from them.

Music & Dancing

John would have been pleased to hear the teaching of ocarinas, recorders and the flute. While, of course, he would have not understood the computer music generation nor indeed the competitions for them, he would be delighted at the continued progress with music from the school. Remember that he took his choir to other parishes and would be pleased to learn that the then Deputy Head, Paul Edwards, had taken the school as a choir both to Castle Hall at Hertford and to the Royal Albert Hall with the children singing both as a chorus but also with narrators and soloists. Eileen King, the Head at the time, taught free form dance, a modern version of the earlier country dancing. Eileen has now been succeeded by Alison Simpson.

Staff, Parents and Pupils

John Pridmore would be envious of the numbers of staff at fifteen with a Headteacher, five full time, one part-time teacher and three teaching assistants with a secretary, cleaner and three dinner ladies now known as 'midday supervisors'.

Above: **Jimmy Perry and Tom Warehand.** Right: **The four girls in the rehearsal for** *Oliver!* **are L to R: Susannah Turner, Debbie Loakes, Kathryn Halstead and Charlotte St Pier.**

There is a strong tradition of help from parents who give their time voluntarily to assist in the classrooms and outside. The parents have always been active with the school in post war years with a strong PTA. They and the swimming pool committee help with activities and funds for the school for example with an annual fête, bonfire night, quizzes, dances, concerts, a BBQ, even a ladies' pampering night!

A major example of parents' help is the swimming pool which was built in 1968/9 by the PTA of the time. Don Edwards produced the plans and borrowed the JCB plus driver from his employers and Bill Taylor, a local builder who lived in The Old School House, was able to get the materials at cost price. They and other parents helped in the construction of the pool which has been in use ever since. Diane Hagger (Don Edwards' daughter) recalls that Bill Furlong the Headmaster at the time took swimming lessons after class.

The pupils come from a wide catchment area, not only from Tewin. The numbers have been over 100 for several years with the current 130 about to drop to around 110. There are five classes for the ages of 4 to 11. One of the other sources for the catchment include the Mums & Toddlers in Tewin and the Under Fives.

The pupils progress, aged 11, to secondary schools. These cover a surprisingly wide range not only in Welwyn Garden City, Hertford and Ware but also further afield including private schools. In one year leavers went to 16 different schools!

Management & Funding

The School is now run by a Board of Governors some of whom were parents, and includes a number of current parents. The vicar is an ex-officio Governor to emphasise the strong links between the school and the Church of England. Indeed, she holds

Opposite page: **Various school activities: 'first day' in 1981; music and dance; rehearsal for Oliver! with Joyce Turner**
Above: **The planting of the Hundred Year Wood was organised by a sub committee of the Parish Council and the Tewin Society and involved pupils from Tewin Cowper School, 1995.**
Below: **Commemorative mug.**

an assembly weekly for all the children.

The school's funding comes from the Local Authority based on pupil numbers given in the January return.

Current Progress

It is interesting to compare a current report for March 2006 in the 21st Century with the log book in the late 19th Century:-

March was an incredibly busy month for Tewin Cowper School.

On 1 March, Year 6 pupils took part in the Junior

93

Citizenship Programme. They learnt what to do in emergencies such as fire and river accidents and the day involved seeing representatives from the Police, Fire Brigade, Ambulance and Building Industry.

Class Assemblies continued this term, when parents/carers and friends watched the children perform a short piece on topics they have covered in class.

Class 3 told us about eating a healthy diet and explained with a human model the different parts of the body!

Class 4 told us about Fraction Fairy explaining the many different ways to multiply numbers and also performed the Rama and Sita story.

Class 5 told us how to resolve conflict situations with role play and showed us pastel sketches of their leaders.

After many rehearsals, the Hertford & Ware District Primary Music Festival finally arrived on the evening of 15ᵗʰ March. Our choir of Year 5 and 6 children performed with six other schools at Castle Hall. The theme was 'Moses' and Tewin Cowper School performed two extra songs during the show. A huge well done to all our singers - what a show!

On 18ᵗʰ March our netball team entered the Small Schools Netball Tournament at Sele School.

On 21ˢᵗ March we held a musical assembly where our flautists performed pieces they had learnt this year. All our musicians played wonderfully.

On 22ⁿᵈ March the pupils from Classes, 4 and 5 were visited by an Indian Workshop who talked to the children about Indian dance as part of their Geography Curriculum.

The children then performed a dance to the whole school, demonstrating many expressive movements.

Throughout March, Years 3, 4, 5 and 6 had rugby training and Year 4 enjoyed some badminton coaching after school.

On 22ⁿᵈ March our boys took part in the District Football Tournament and again well done to all our players. The football team also participated in the Hope Cup and secured a place in the final. This competition is for all schools in the district, large or small.

On 29ᵗʰ March pupils from Years 4, 5 and 6 were chosen to represent the school at Hartham Pool in the Swimming Fun Gala. All had a wonderful time!

Tewin Cowper's Talent Show was held on 30ᵗʰ March and we were wowed not only by the amazing and original acts, but also by the courage shown by all our children in being confident enough to perform in

front of such a large audience! This was one of the ideas from our School Council and turned out to be a huge success - very well done to everyone involved.

The term ended with a whole school visit to St. Peter's Church on 31ˢᵗ March for our Easter Service. Each class performed a short piece relating to Easter in front of parents, carers and friends, who filled the Church to the rafters!

Report from Eileen King Head Teacher
March 2006

In the 19ᵗʰ Century the Headmaster had to contend with warring parents (in 1889) on the school premises, while in 2006 the P. A. (Parents' Association), is strong and parents help in the classrooms. And a plaintive note for 11ᵗʰ June 1890 *'the school was examined today by Her Majesty's Inspectors T W Danby, Esq and Mr Hayward. I am afraid the result will be disappointing'.*

This is to be compared with May 2006 where in one week the school was examined by each of OFSTED (the updated HMI), the Diocesan Inspection (the links with the school and St Peter's Church are still strong) and the School's Audit.

All three inspections were passed with flying colours showing that the school despite being small and lessening in numbers (from 130 to 110) continues in good spirit at the heart of the village.

The Tewin Cowper School name is attractively welded into the gates at the entrance in Cannons Meadow.

Chapter 7

Tewin Water House

'..... *a new and handsome house*' (in 1819) was the description of Tewin Water House in Nikolaus Pevsner's Architectural Guide, (1953). No longer new, but certainly still handsome, this elegant building is still as pleasing to the eye as it was when Pevsner first saw it. However, the house built in 1799 was not the original Tewin Water House.

It is known that the Tewin Water estate was owned from the 13ᵗʰ century to the Dissolution of the Monasteries in 1540 by the Priory of St Bartholomew, Smithfield, and in 1544 was in the ownership of Sir Thomas and Mary Wrothe and their family, who probably lived on the estate. In 1620 the manor was sold to Beckington Butler (Boteler) from whom it was passed to Mr Richard Hale during the reign of Queen Elizabeth I. For a time, it became the property of William Cecil, the 2ⁿᵈ Earl of Salisbury, and then descended to his younger son, William Cecil.

The first recorded house was built in 1689 by Squire James Fleet who purchased it from William Cecil in 1713. James Fleet was the son of John Fleet, a wealthy merchant who became Lord Mayor of London in 1692, MP for the City of London, and a

Governor of the East India Company, who died in 1712. It is understood that during James Fleet's ownership the house saw a number of improvements. On his death in 1733, James Fleet bequeathed the estate to his widow (later to become Lady Cathcart) during her lifetime and, since there were no children of the marriage, it then passed to Squire Fleet's nephews on her death.

Before that time, however, during Lady Cathcart's ownership, the house was witness to some of the most dramatic events in its history.

Lady Cathcart

Lady Elizabeth Cathcart was born in 1691, the second daughter of Mr Thomas Maylin, a Battersea brewer. A great beauty, she is believed to have taken three more husbands following the death of John (James) Fleet, although the number of marriages is not certain. Her wedding ring was inscribed with the words *'If I survive I'll make it five'*, reputedly referring to her husbands, but reports vary and the general belief is that she married only four times, and it was the fourth of these marriages which was to bring her great grief and misery.

Tewin Water House taken from Humphry Repton's Red Book of 1799. As in other Red Books, Repton (1752-1818) shows himself painting the scene, lower left. All the pictures from Repton's Red Books are reproduced by kind permission of Hertfordshire Achives & Local Studies (credited HALS elsewhere), see acknowledgements p.261.

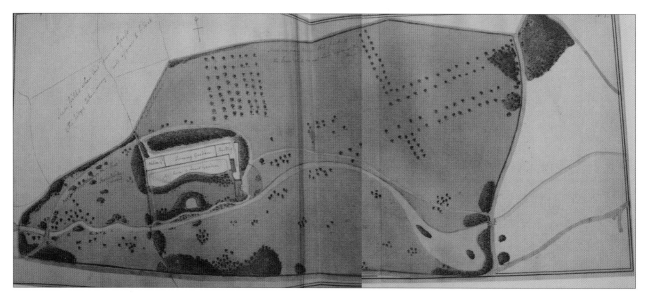

Repton's design and layout for Tewin Water House and grounds from his Red Book. This shows the River Mimram and the design for Tewin Water Lake.

She was known to have said that she married her first husband, James Fleet, for love, her second, Colonel William Sabine (who was killed in battle), for wealth, her third, Charles 8th Baronet Cathcart, (who died at sea), for rank, and her fourth, Hugh Maguire, *'at the instigation of the devil'*! She married Hugh Maguire on the 18th May 1745. She was aged 54 and Hugh Maguire was a 40 year old Irish adventurer, who was commonly known as *'the wicked colonel'*. He became notorious for his appalling treatment of Lady Cathcart, whom he terrorised in an effort to persuade her to hand over her jewels and the deeds of Tewin Water House. Having adamantly refused to succumb to his demands, Lady Cathcart was taken to Ireland by her husband and imprisoned in his family home at Tempo Manor. She was locked up for many years in what later became an out-building, where she remained until his death.

In John Carrington's Diary, the colourful story of Lady Cathcart's kidnapping is recorded. Then aged just 15, John Carrington was given the job of Under Gardener at Tewin Water, and was witness to the events of the day in 1746 when Colonel Maguire persuaded his wife to take a coach ride to Brocket Hall in Lemsford, near Welwyn, for an airing. Accompanied by his brother and a fellow Irishman, they set off at 2 o'clock, with Maguire ordering two geese for dinner at home that evening. But they did not return and, according to John Carrington, he and the other servants ate the dinner! The first news they had of Lady Cathcart came when two of Colonel

Maguire's servants returned to strip the house of its best furniture and china. He told the servants that her Ladyship had given permission since she had gone to Oxford to visit the dying mother of the Colonel. In fact, she had been transported to Ireland, not to return for 21 years.

Her treatment became legendary, but the manner of Hugh Maguire's death is still a matter of dispute. One story suggests that, having been unsuccessful in persuading his wife to reveal the hiding place of her

Tewin Water House c1790.

jewellery and title deeds, Hugh Maguire went to look for them in a cupboard high in the walls of Tewin Water. Whilst climbing the ladder it slipped and he fell and broke his neck.

Another report suggests he broke his neck in Ireland whilst out hunting and it was said that when Lady Cathcart looked out of the window of the room in which she was confined and saw his lifeless body being brought back into the house, she was overcome with feelings of relief and joy.

Yet a third version records that, having emerged from her imprisonment as a ragged, half-starved, largely deranged woman, by then well over 70 years of age, Lady Cathcart gave a different account of the circumstances of her husband's death. She said that having eventually forced her to reveal the hiding place in Tewin Water House, Hugh Maguire hurried to the estate to claim her fortune. Knowing this was stored in a secret compartment behind some panelling, he stood on a table to reach the hidden door. When the rusty lock on the door resisted his efforts, he impatiently attacked it with a jack-knife, but the knife slipped and badly cut his hand. As a result, lockjaw set in and he is said to have died in agony soon afterwards.

After his death Lady Cathcart returned to Tewin. According to John Carrington, she found Tewin Water House occupied by a Squire Steel who, for the previous 21 years, had taken it on lease from Colonel Maguire. However, this arrangement ceased on the Colonel's death and Lady Cathcart was able to resume residence. She initially had difficulty retrieving her money but everything was finally returned to her and she lived at Tewin Water House for a further 21 years. During this time she demonstrated great kindness and charity to the poor, and when she died in August 1789 at the age of 98, she was well loved by all who knew her. She was buried with her husband, James Fleet, in St. Peter's churchyard.

The colourful story of her fourth marriage formed the basis of a chapter in *'Castle Rackrent'*, a novel by Maria Edgeworth.

The Cowper Family
By that time, however, Tewin Water House had been bought by the 3rd Earl Cowper, who acquired it in 1785 when the estate was sold to cover mortgages taken out by Edmund Bull, believed to be James Fleet's great nephew, who had been in possession since 1746. Earl Cowper died in Florence in 1789 and it is reported that under the direction of his trustees the house was pulled down and another built on the same site.

When the house was finished, it was let to Lord John Townsend, who was related by marriage to Earl

Repton's design showing Tewin Water House and the River Mimram.

Cowper, and he occupied the house from 1791-97. In 1798, Henry Cowper, the fifth Earl, and a cousin of the first Earl Cowper, and Clerk to the House of Lords, demolished the house because the design was not to his liking. He then commissioned a house to be built *'in a nobler style'* and after its completion a reference in *Carrington's Diary* records that Henry Cowper held a great feast at Tewin Water for the men working on the new house, stating that it was attended by 130 people, who had a *'Good Dinner & 3 Barrels of Bear'* (sic).

Designed by John Groves and remodelled in a fashionable neo-Greek style, it is this elegant house we see today standing in a beautiful, tranquil setting, framed by mature trees and shrubs. Situated in the Mimram Valley, Tewin Water House sits in such close harmony with its surroundings, it is difficult for today's visitor to visualise any other structure in its place.

The design for its landscaped grounds and parkland (which had previously been a deer park) were drawn up by Humphrey Repton, at the request of the 5th Earl Cowper. This formed part of the plans for landscaping the whole of the Mimram Valley from Digswell to Hertford, including Panshanger. Having been approached by Earl Cowper, Humphrey Repton visited Tewin in May 1799 and his plans for the Tewin Water House Estate, completed in July, are preserved for posterity in *'The Red Book'*, a red leather-bound book now held in the Hertford Records Office. Apart from detailed descriptions for Tewin Water, the book also contains a series of pictures of the house.

The River Mimram was dammed below the house to create a lake with tree covered islets, woodland was planted along the northern shore and the grounds were landscaped. The main approach to the house is via the east of the estate, just north of the bridge on Tewin Road, by what was then the newly constructed Tewin Lodge. In 1798 the road from Welwyn to Hertford ran close to Tewin Water House and so Humphrey Repton decided it should be moved to its present site (now the B1000).

After Henry Cowper's death in 1840, Tewin Water House boasted a number of distinguished tenants, The Earl of Uxbridge from 1840-54, The Marquis of Anglesey 1854-58, and Mr George Burnand (from 1862 until his death in 1891), a wealthy London stockbroker, who was the cousin of Sir Francis Cowley Burnand, a poet and playwright who was the Editor of *Punch* from 1880. In 1892 the tenancy was taken by William Hale Charles Pery, the Third Earl of Limerick, Lord in Waiting to Queen Victoria and Chief Whip to the House of Lords. He died suddenly in 1896, reportedly at Tewin Water House, and is buried in Digswell. In addition, Mr John Currie occupied the house from 1856-61 and Mr Herbert Arthur Trower from 1892-1902.

The Beit Family

From 1902 to 1950 the house became the country retreat of the Beit family when it was acquired on a furnished lease by Alfred Beit. He was born in Hamburg, Germany, in 1853 and although Alfred and

1909

his brother Otto were of Jewish descent, they were members of the Lutheran Church. They are both buried in St. Peter's churchyard in Tewin. Alfred proved to be a genius with figures and, having spent time studying the diamond market in Amsterdam, emigrated to South Africa in 1875 during the 'diamond rush'. There he developed the Kimberley mines and the Rand gold fields. He became Life-Governor of the De Beers diamond mine, as well as holding directorships of many other companies, among which were the British South Africa Company and Rhodesia Railways. He amassed a considerable fortune, reportedly eleven million pounds, and was said to be the richest man in the world. Alfred was a generous philanthropist, one beneficiary of his munificence being Cecil Rhodes, a great friend to whom he gave support in a number of business ventures.

Alfred Beit also founded a chair for Colonial History at Oxford University and bequeathed a great deal of money for university education and research in South Africa, Rhodesia, Britain and Germany. In fact, being concerned about the quality of education in Great Britain, he made a significant donation towards the foundation of the Imperial College of Science and Technology, which gesture was recognised by the erection of the large Alfred Beit memorial which flanks the entrance to the college.

Alfred was a shy man who never married, but it is reported that after giving a ball for 400 people where every lady guest received the gift of a diamond, he was inundated with offers of marriage! However, he remained a bachelor without heirs, so following his death in 1906, Tewin Water House was inherited by his brother, Otto Beit, a financier and, like his brother, a great philanthropist.

The house became the country estate of Otto and his wife, Lilian. Knighted in 1924, it was Sir Otto who had the greatest impact on the village of Tewin. In 1922 he built the Memorial Hall on Lower Green, on land provided by Lord Desborough, as a tribute to the men in the village who had died in the First World War. (See chapter 8, page 110, Memorial Hall.)

Following Alfred's death, Sir Otto and Lady Beit took out a new tenancy of Tewin Water House and later purchased it from the Cowper family heirs. They had two sons and two daughters, but it was the eldest son, Theodore. who was to cause them great sadness. Having entered the army, and become a Second Lieutenant, Theodore was thought to be enjoying his military life, but subsequent events proved otherwise. Aged only 18, he became the victim of a practical joke which caused him such distress, he was later found dying in his room with a sporting rifle by his side. An enquiry revealed that he had been expected to join in a game of 'Cub-Hunting' with other young officers. When he failed to turn up, they entered his room and made an 'apple pie' bed as well as dumping the contents of drawers on the floor. Theodore, a very sensitive young man, who already believed that his German surname was a handicap, felt this 'ragging' represented a rebuke, and in an extract from a letter addressed to his father he wrote:-

' *My dearest family - this is all a great mistake, but I did not hear anything about the fox hunting tonight and so unfortunately went to the pictures. The result is that everybody was extremely angry that I was not in the mess and so my room was all wrecked. I cannot stand all this. It will get about, and what will everybody think of it? Besides I shall have to go through hell another night so I think the best thing for me to do is end my life. It is nobody's fault except that other fellows my age do not seem to like me'.*

Alfred Beit (1853-1906).

99

Sir Otto and Lady Lilian Beit.

A subsequent enquiry into events found that Theodore was well liked and on excellent terms with his brother officers. In his summing up at the enquiry, the Coroner concluded that Theodore Beit was of a sensitive disposition, and it appeared *'the privation of Friday night had taken his nerve'.*

Throughout his lifetime, Sir Otto maintained his brother Alfred's links with Imperial College, and also founded the Beit Memorial Fellowship for medical research in his memory. As a director of Rhodesian Railways Limited, Sir Otto also set up the Beit Railway Trust and there is now a Beit Bridge over Africa's River Limpopo.

An ex resident of Tewin, Gerald Edwards, who was evacuated to the village during World War II, has provided the following fascinating account of Sir Otto Beit's generosity:

'My grandfather worked as an ostler on the farm and lived in a 'tied cottage' - Churchfield Cottages housed members of the workforce (gamekeeper, garage hand, chauffeur, butler etc.). There were 8 houses in all. The houses were very well appointed for the time they were built, (c1909), having electric lighting downstairs (candles upstairs!) and mains sewerage, albeit in a room behind the wash house and not in the house itself.

'There were two instances of generosity from Sir Otto to his staff which I remember my mother talking about. One year he gave every member of his staff, from the lowliest (stable lad?) to the highest (butler?) £100. This must have been the best part of a year's wages. My grandfather didn't know what to do with it so put it into a bank account and there it stayed. When the estate was broken up years after Beit's death my grandparents were given the option of buying as sitting tenants or leaving. This is where the £100 came into its own as they were able to use it as a down payment and with my mother's help, purchase the house - No 3 Churchfield Cottages, for about £950 (as I recall).

'The second instance was when he gave all the staff a gift of some diamonds. My grandfather received 10

Pewter Tankard awarded to the winner of the Falcon Motor Club race during speed trials at Tewin Water, 18th June 1950. One entrant at the event was Lotus founder and motor racing pioneer, Colin Chapman, who drove a Lotus Mk 2.

Top: **Early photographs of the Vinery at Tewin Water House and pineapples growing during Otto Beit's occupancy.**

diamonds, which were made into a brooch for my grandmother. On her mother's death, my mother had the brooch re-made into a tie pin for me and a smaller brooch for my sister.'

Sir Otto died in 1930 and his remaining son, Alfred, inherited Tewin Water House, together with the baronetcy. He continued to reside at Tewin Water with his widowed mother and regularly flew his own plane around the country, taking off from an airstrip in the grounds. He enjoyed a very busy social life and Tewin Water House was visited by many well-known people from the film world, including Greta Garbo.

Otto Beit and his son, Sir Alfred, also maintained an efficient estate fire brigade at Tewin Water, its facilities consisting of a steam pump, and escape and hose cart. In addition to providing a fire service to the estate, the brigade's protection was extended to surrounding villages, whose fire brigades were not so well equipped.

After declaration of the Second World War, Sir Alfred was commissioned into the RAF, and in 1939 he married Clementine Mitford, a cousin of the celebrated Mitford sisters. Sir Alfred and Lady Clementine Beit were said to be *'the most handsome couple in London'*. Great art lovers, they accumulated one of the greatest private art collections in Britain, and took this with them when they later moved to Ireland. Such was the value of their collection it became the target of three robberies in Ireland, one of which subsequently became the subject of a book and several films (e.g. John Boorman's *'The General'* 1998). Sir Alfred died in Ireland in 1994, aged 91, and Lady Clementine Beit died in 2005, aged 89.

Among the eminent people who visited Tewin Water House was General de Gaulle who, during the War years, stayed at the house for many months as the guest of Sir Alfred's mother, Lady Lilian Beit. His great pleasure was to go horse riding around the parkland and by the River Mimram. However, in 1945, before the end of the War, Lady Lilian Beit decided to move to her London home in Belgravia. Before she left Tewin, all her staff gathered on Lower

101

Left: **Lady Clementine Beit (née Mitford) with the Dowager Lady Airlie. 1939.** Right: **Sir Alfred Beit. In 1976, the Beits created the Alfred Beit Foundation to preserve Russborough, their home in Ireland, and its art collection for the future enjoyment of the Irish people.**

Green and she visited them there to say her farewells. She died in 1946 and is buried with her husband and son in the Beit family grave in St Peter's Church, Tewin.

The Concrete Path

The footpath or track which runs from just south of Churchfield Cottages, Churchfield Road, Tewin to Digswell, has always been known locally as 'The Concrete Path'.

Its origin is not entirely clear but it is believed it was constructed under the auspices of Sir Otto Beit of Tewin Water House. There are various thoughts about its construction, one view being that it was built before the First World War, whereas another suggests a later date - 1929. It is said that the path was built by Italian Prisoners of War, but before the 1914-18 War there were no prisoners, and in that War we fought alongside Italy.

The path follows the edge of the Tewin Water parkland and continues along the side of the avenue of lime trees planted by Humphry Repton. It is a continuation of the route from Marden Hill via the Churchyard.

Some say that the path's construction came about in order to allow the staff at Tewin Water to get to work without getting muddy and wet. However, this idea loses credibility when it appears that the onward journey from the path to the house then entailed the negotiation of an unmade track and a steep slope to the house.

Another theory is that Sir Otto did not like an already established path which ran from a gateway further down Churchfield Road and along the side of his house to Digswell. He therefore came to an agreement with the Parish Council that if this path were closed, he would create a concrete path which would be much more acceptable to people walking to Welwyn, Digswell or Welwyn North Station.

The path when first constructed was believed to be 4ft wide in the Parish of Tewin and 3ft wide in the Parish of Digswell. However, although it has been used regularly over the years, and has been a significant feature in the Tewin countryside, the true facts about its construction are still open for debate!

Change of Purpose

For a short period of time following the death of Lady Lilian Beit, Tewin Water House became a Country Club, but the house, park and gardens were then sold to a Mr A. H. Adey. A Mrs Drapers also lived at the house, and sold much of the timber planted by Humphry Repton.

Great changes were to follow when, in 1953, following a compulsory purchase order by Hertfordshire County Council, the house became a school for children with hearing problems. Soon after, the remaining 1,000 acres were sold and the woods felled. A tarmac playground was built across the formal garden and classrooms and out-buildings were constructed in the walled garden area. A boiler house with a brick chimney was added to the north of

An early postcard view of the house and grounds to the rear of Tewin Water House.

the main entrance elevation and alterations were also made to provide kitchens and classrooms for the school. Many people still living in Tewin today were employed at the school. In 1997 a new school was built adjacent to the Monk's Walk School and the Tewin Water School was transferred to the new building. Fortunately, there had always been strong links with Monk's Walk and children from Tewin Water had in the past joined some lessons at the school. This practice continues and students are able to attend the specialist school, now called Knightsfield, as well as the Monk's Walk mainstream school.

In the years following, Tewin Water House was allowed to fall into a state of disrepair. Then, in 2000, plans were submitted for the renovation of the house and other buildings and it was restored to its former glory, albeit now divided into several apartments and privately owned by its residents.

Tewin Water remains the *'noble'* house envisaged by Henry Cowper in 1798. And despite seeing many changes in structure, tenancy and purpose since first built, its fascinating history and peaceful location amid lovely gardens alongside the River Mimram, surely make it one of the most interesting, as well as one of the most elegant houses in Hertfordshire.

**Extracts from a poem
by Mary Caroline Ward**

Taking Leave of Tewin Water - May 12ᵗʰ 1826
*'Grace be upon thee, Tewin
Sweet silvery stream Farewell.
May Peace and Health around thy borders dwell
With thee I'll leave the Christian's parting prayer
The farewell look shall say 'The Lord be
there'...........*

*'Flow on sweet Mimram on thy peaceful bed May
Grace attend who 'er these banks shall tread But
Chief thy honoured owner, till in Love His Lord
shall call him to his home above.'*

The Chinese bridge over the River Mimram in the grounds of Tewin Water House. The artificial rocks still exist there.

103

Top: **Tewin Water House, south side, taken in 2009.**
Left: **An early nineteenth century pencil drawing of Tewin Water House.**
Below: **Tewin Water House, also pictured in 2009.**

Chapter 8

The World at War

Tewin in a Century of Conflict 1901 - 1999

Signal section of Hertfordshire Royal Field Artillery at Thetford, Norfolk, November 1915 prior to proceeding to Egypt via Southampton, Marseilles and Alexandria with the 54th Division. Bottom right of photograph **Harold James Roberts, father of Ben Roberts pictured on page 123.**

The twentieth century opened with Queen Victoria still on the throne and in the sixty third year of her reign. None could have foreseen however, that, before the century had passed, devastating World Wars would ravish much of the world, with unimaginable losses and the social and political life of the country would be changed forever.

The Boer War in South Africa had been in progress since 1899 and was to last until the 31st May 1902 and by then the old Queen would have died and King Edward VII enthroned.

After the Napoleonic Wars in the early part of the 19th Century, Great Britain, like other European powers, had been intent upon Empire Building until large areas of the world had been absorbed. The Boer War, however, came as a lesson for the future, that the pacification of these Empires was only temporary and, eventually, those nations would seek self-determination, hastened by the world conflicts that were yet to come.

With the abandonment of the Militia in the 1870s, to be replaced by Volunteers, many local men served with the Hertfordshire Regiment and Royal Field

Artillery in South Africa. These men had willingly given up their harsh lives of endless toil, mostly as agricultural labourers, for the security of regular food and lodging and payments with a small after-service pension.

Although involved in the sieges of Ladysmith, Kimberley and Mafeking, their losses through diseases, an unhealthy climate and a lack of medical services, greatly exceeded those from the conflict. Nevertheless, those returning had served their country well.

After a few years of peace, the consolidation of power groups in Europe, ambitious politicians, dictators and rulers cast envious eyes on their neighbours with increasing hostility, seeking any excuse for aggression and thus leading to the raising of armies and weapons. The United Kingdom, prudently, instituted volunteer Territorial and Home Service Battalions with Military training.

We may now wonder why and how the incident of an assassination in Sarajevo of an Austrian Duke, (Archduke Franz Ferdinand), should have led to the most terrible First World War. Many millions from

Tented camp of Hertfordshire Royal Field Artillery, 4th East Anglian Brigade, 54th Division, Egypt March 1916.

all parts of the world slaughtered each other in their tens of thousands with the most evil weapons and brought untold misery upon whole nations.

Upon the outset of War in August 1914, nevertheless, men, in their thousands, many from Tewin and the surrounding villages, willingly answered the call to serve King and Country. Many registered and were given the *'King's Shilling'* at the Territorial Army Headquarters in St Andrew's Street in Hertford, and were rapidly directed to Army and Royal Navy, and later, to Royal Flying Corps establishments for training. Large numbers served in the Hertfordshire, the Hertfordshire & Bedfordshire and Royal Field Artillery Regiments and the East Anglian Brigade (54th Division), and trained in local areas of Huntingdon, Peterborough, Kings Langley, Ashridge Park and Thetford.

With the War that was expected to *'be all over by Christmas'*, men cheerfully marched off, never expecting the four long years of bloody conflict that was to follow. Tewin men also served in the fiercest battles in the Ypres salient and at Albert, where they were to suffer great losses in the static trench warfare. Inhuman conditions, merciless enemy fire and pointless attacks in the face of enemy machine guns, secure behind massive fields of barbed wire, were endured. All for the sake of gaining a few yards of devastated and shell holed muddy ground.

By the summer of 1916, those eager volunteers had been decimated and conscription was introduced for the very first time. A number of Regiments with a large proportion of men from Hertfordshire were moved from France to Egypt to recover the Middle East from Turkish control after that country joined the conflict on the side of Austria and Germany. After reforming around Alexandria and close to the pyramids, they advanced through the Sinai Desert into Palestine taking part in all three Battles of Gaza. Slowly advancing northwards, capturing Beersheba and Jerusalem they entered Damascus with General Allenby on the 31st October 1918.

The Great War brought so many changes. Women most successfully took over their menfolk's occupations and worked in their millions in munitions factories. On the Home Front, the civilian population experienced severe food rationing, the threat of a new menace of bombardment by Zeppelin airships and Gotha bombers and almost every home mourned the loss of a son, brother, father or a friend. *'Keeping the home fires burning'* became a sacred duty.

On the 11th November 1918, the 'Central Powers' of Germany, Austria and Turkey surrendered. The Armistice terms were harsh, involving the allied occupation of the Rhineland, severe reparations and led to the collapse of the economy and social order in Germany.

All levels of British society suffered losses, rich and poor alike. Many who survived the terrible losses came home physically and mentally scarred from their experiences. The Tewin War Memorial honours the names of thirty one men from the then, small village of Tewin, who gave their lives for King and Country:

James Winterbourne
Wilfred Grenville-Grey.
Walter Shadbolt.
William Lovell.
Charles Wilsher.
Charles Perry.
William Wilshire.
Bert Shadbolt.
Harry Perry.
Herbert Tyler.
Bert Sutton.
George Egerton.
William Halliday.
Arthur Dawes.
Tom Lawrence.
Theodore Hamilton-Beit.

Wilfred Shadbolt.
Walter Perry.
John Masson.
Frederick Wray.
Ernest Gay.
Ernest Tyler.
Cecil Shadbolt.
Cecil Lyles.
Arthur Woodrow.
Arthur Bagnall.
Cecil Parker.
Lewis Cole.
George Chalkley.
George Ward.
Henry Halliday.

Although not inscribed on the Tewin War Memorial, two of the three sons of William Henry Grenfell and his wife Ethel, (née Fanc), were killed in action in Flanders within a few weeks of each other. Captain, the Honourable Julian Henry Francis Grenfell on the 26th May 1915 and his brother Lieutenant the Honourable Gerald (Billy) William Grenfell on the 30th July 1915. Gerald has no known grave. Julian, amongst his other achievements was an accomplished poet and is well remembered for his *'Into Battle'*, (see Chapter 9, page 144).

Unfortunately, the hoped for *'Homes for Heroes'* to which so many aspired, was as far away as ever, and so many returned to their former hard graft as agricultural labourers.

Compared with the political turmoil on the mainland of Europe however, there was so much to be grateful for and life slowly improved in spite of the General Strike, 1926, and the Wall Street Crash, 1929, which had severe ramifications in the United Kingdom.

The unjust and harshly imposed Armistice Terms on Germany and the resulting severe economic and social disorder would inevitably lead to renewed conflict and in spite of all attempts to placate the rising dictatorship of Adolf Hitler and his ultra nationalistic National Socialist Party, from 1933 onwards, it was increasingly obvious that, sooner or later, the conflict would be renewed. The *'1914-1918 War to end War'* proved to be just a dream.

For the United Kingdom, the Second World War commenced on the 3rd September 1939, when, with France, and in accordance with their treaties with Poland (which had been attacked by Germany on the

Above: **Land army girls working on Tewin Bury farm.**

1st September), war was declared on Germany. Few would then have believed that, before it was over six years later, the whole world would have been involved. On the enemy side would be Germany, Italy and Japan, and on the allied side, Britain, with its Commonwealth and Empire, France, Russia and the United States of America.

Unlike previous conflicts, the 1939-1945 War

would find civilians in *'the front line'* and under enemy attack. Total War and a Peoples' War, would involve the whole population. Again, conscription for the armed services took men and women from every walk of life to serve all over the World.

It became the duty of every person to serve in any available capacity. From growing own vegetables, keeping livestock, salvaging metal, paper, bones, glass for the war industries, to serving in the Auxiliary Fire Service, as Air Raid Wardens in the Medical and Rescue Services, as Firewatchers, keeping evacuees from bombed cities, or helping at Forces canteens. These voluntary services were done after long hours in factories producing war munitions. Everyone was required to serve and they did so willingly almost to exhaustion. Playing fields and every scrap of unused land was turned to growing food crops.

As men were called up for the armed services, women took their places; the Women's Land Army worked very long back-breaking hours in all weathers and were a common sight on the local farms, also producing charcoal for explosives manufacture in Bramfield Forest. Later in the War, these would be joined by Italian and German Prisoners of War. A Canadian Forestry Unit felled the fir trees in Tewin Wood for pitprops for coalmines and to replace the loss of imports.

Whole industries were rapidly changed to producing war material in unused buildings and even in small garages machinery was installed. There was never sufficient labour

Top left: **Spigot mortar base off White Horse Lane, Burnham Green.**
Middle: **'Pillbox' Dane End.**
Bottom: **Anti Tank obstacles, Harmer Green Lane.**

and most factories worked non-stop seven days a week. Plenty of well-paid work with overtime payments gave a degree of financial independence that had not been experienced before. All were encouraged to save and to avoid unnecessary travel.

There would be no petrol for private motoring. Everyone was aware that Merchant Seamen gave their lives in torpedoed tankers to bring fuel and other vital supplies.

In May 1940 after the evacuation of British and French forces from the beaches of Dunkirk and when invasion threatened, the Foreign Secretary, Anthony Eden, broadcast for volunteers to form a citizens' army. Hundreds of thousands volunteered, the majority being men who served in the First World War. Given the title of Home Guard and, initially armed with outdated equipment, they patrolled the countryside, guarded bridges, railway lines and other vulnerable key installations at night and at weekends. Training with units of the Regular Army, and gradually re-equipped with modern weapons, they became a formidable defence force and released men and women for service in the Armed Forces. Youths over the age of 16 were encouraged to join and thus gained valuable experience prior to their call up to the Armed Forces upon reaching the age of 18 years. Tewin had a thirty plus platoon with 'strong-points' at the junction with the B1000, in New Road, Burnham Green, and at the Digswell viaduct. Into the 21st Century, the concrete tank obstacles were still to be seen at those locations.

After the initial *'phoney war'*, the huge and well trained German armies occupied most of Europe and North Africa. Dunkirk, the Battle of Britain, disasters in the Mediterranean, and the declaration of War by Japan were anxious days. Gradually the tide turned, Alamein, Stalingrad, Burma, the Pacific Islands, Sicily, Italy, 'D' Day and the Allied invasion of Northwest Europe, finally led to victory in Europe by the Unconditional Surrender of Germany on the 8th May 1945, followed by that of Japan on the 2nd September 1945.

Once again, servicemen and servicewomen returned from all parts of the world, most having gained by the responsibilities and travel they had experienced. Socially, it was a better world to return to than that from the previous World War. Sadly, once again, so many gave their lives in the service of their Country and the names of those from Tewin are engraved on the War Memorial:

W. Pennycuik Sampson.	Walter E. King.
Kenneth Wright	Walter A. Trundle.
Geoffrey H Thompson.	Frederick P. Thompson.
Frederick E. Noxon.	

Most of the evacuees had long returned to their homes in the cities. A total of 106 were found safety in Tewin and Queen Elizabeth, later the Queen Mother, sent this message:-

Buckingham Palace

'I wish to mark by this personal message my appreciation of the service you have rendered to your country in 1939. In the early days of the War you opened your doors to strangers who were in need of shelter and offered to share your homes with them. I know that to this unselfish task you have sacrificed your own comfort, and that it would not have been achieved without the loyal co-operation of all your households. By your sympathy you have earned the gratitude of those to whom you have shown hospitality, and by your readiness to serve you have helped that State in a work of great national importance'.

ELIZABETH R

Sir Herbert Baker's War Memorial in the grounds of St. Peter's Church, Tewin. He also designed the Memorial Hall on Lower Green in the village. His *'Father Time'* weather-vane, high over the clock tower at Lord's Cricket Ground, is known throughout the world as a symbol for the home of cricket. He presented it as a gift following the completion of his Grandstand in 1926, (replaced in 1996).

Tewin Memorial Hall (Shown above in 1922)

This is the inscription on the dedication plaque in the entrance passage of the Hall:

**THIS
BUILDING
IS ERECTED BY
SIR OTTO BEIT** KCMG
**ON A SITE PRESENTED BY
THE RT. HON. LORD DESBOROUGH** KCVO
**TO COMMEMORATE
THE SERVICES RENDERED BY
MEN AND WOMEN
OF THIS PARISH OF TEWIN
AND IN
EVER LIVING AND GRATEFUL MEMORY
OF THOSE WHO GAVE THEIR LIVES
FOR KING AND COUNTRY
IN THE
GREAT WAR 1914-1919
OPENED ON 23**RD **JAN 1922**

Sir Otto set up a Trust which owns the Hall and which has an endowment intended to cover the insurance and the local taxes of the building. This Trust leases the Hall to the Management Committee. The original Minute Book and the first accounts are still held by the Trustees.

Both of the benefactors, like so very many families in the Country, lost their sons, amongst the appalling casualties and with the dreadful conditions of trench warfare in France in the Great War 1914-1918. (The above inscription gives the date 1919 as the end of the War as casualties continued).

For those who came home, many physically and mentally wounded, they found not the promised *'homes for heroes'*, but returned to their former drab pre-war occupations. Little social welfare assisted them to settle back into their towns and villages and for most, little had changed, and the hard grind, particularly for the huge numbers of agricultural labourers was to continue for some years to come.

In the first two years of the Great War, men from every walk of life in spite of the harshness of so many of their working lives, volunteered in their hundreds of thousands to serve King and Country. Only after the terrible losses in Flanders was conscription introduced. We may well wonder at their loyalty to their King and Country after the harsh life so many had experienced.

Opposite: **Tewin Memorial Hall when it was first built in 1922.**
Above: **Photographs showing the huge hanging lamps and the open fireplaces at each end of the Hall, the piano, the games tables and folding wooden chairs, also in 1922 when the building was opened.**

The cast of a performance in Tewin Memorial Hall in the 1920s.

Tewin was a very much smaller village then, with very little entertainment. The public houses where many still brewed their own ale were the only outlet. With no cinemas or television and very few radios, the lack of bus services confined people to their locality. There were a few proud owners of 'wireless sets' that received programmes via an aerial strung between two high posts in their back gardens but many still twiddled a 'cat's whisker' on their 'crystal sets' to obtain a faint sound.

Designed by the architect Sir Herbert Baker, the provision of a Village Hall for the use of the inhabitants of Tewin, Burnham Green and the surrounding areas changed life so much for the better and for so many people. A place where all ages could meet, play table games, darts, cards or just chat to friends and neighbours.

Originally, there was a wall, level with the present large stage, and a door to the right led to the 'The Ladies Room'. Here was a large kitchen and ladies only meeting area with a toilet to the right. A further door led from this area to the hallway.

The small 'Kimberley Room' reminds us of the association of Sir Otto Beit with his diamond mines in South Africa which provided him with a vast fortune.

The 'Parish Room' was specially built for the use of the Rector of the Parish of Tewin. The whole building was managed by a committee of an elected chairman and secretary, and one member from each of the organisations using the Hall; football, cricket, horticulture, bowls, Girl Guides, Boy Scouts, Mothers Union, Women's Institute and others.

The photographs, (page 111), show huge hanging lamps, an open fireplace at each end of the main hall, a piano, games tables and folding wooden chairs.

It is recorded that some 90% of villagers belonged and paid an annual membership fee of five shillings. The Football Club ran a dance six times each year and other organisations two or three so that there was at least one dance each month. Crowds of up to 170 were quite usual with the entrance fee of 1/6d or 2/- (7.5 or 10p) and live bands played on Friday nights from 8pm until after midnight.

In the 1930s the Memorial Hall had a paid resident Club Steward who, with his wife assisting, lived rent and maintenance free, ran the licensed bar in the 'Mens' Room' which was equipped with tables for cards and dominoes, and frequently obtained a licence to run the bar until 2am for a dance but only to midnight on a Saturday. The bar was located where the present ladies restroom is situated.

In the Main Hall were darts boards, a billiard table and a radiogram for dancing and most evenings of the week there would be about 30 people using the facilities with up to 80 or 90 at weekends.

Members could take friends for the payment of 3d (1.4p) each and were required to sign the Visitors' Book. The 'Club' was well supported by all classes of society and it is recorded how friendly it was and that everyone knew everyone by their first names. The community was quite stable in the years prior to the Second World War and most families remained in the village when they married.

As the 1930s came to a close it was clear that sooner or later Europe would be engulfed once again in conflict. An early sign was the use of the Hall for the fitting of civilian gas masks in September 1938 and, as war approached, it became the centre for the various emergency organisations.

Shortly after the commencement of hostilities, children from the nearby school were given a hot midday meal, prepared and served by volunteers, and this released and enabled mothers to work in the many nearby factories engaged in munitions and other war work. Dances were held for servicemen stationed at the nearby airfield, RAF Panshanger, at the RAF Vehicle Reserve Pool in Marden Hill woods, the RA searchlight near Warrengate Farm and the RAOC Ordnance sites opposite Welwyn North Station and in Welwyn, and of course, attended by the many Land Army girls working on the local farms.

At the rear of the Hall, salvage bins and containers were located in which villagers deposited tins, scrap metal, glass, paper, bones and other useful raw material for the 'war effort'.

The Tewin Women's Institute used the Hall as the centre for their many activities including the sorting of garments for evacuees and others in need. They knitted large quantities of gloves, socks, scarves and other warming garments for Servicemen and Servicewomen, evacuees and wherever needed.

The provision of so much more entertainment, radios, cinemas at Hatfield, Welwyn, Welwyn Garden City, Hertford and two at Stevenage by the end of the Second World War resulted in much less use of the Memorial Hall, hastened by the Catering Wages Act that put the cost of the Bar Steward beyond reach and the closure of that facility.

In the early 1960s the decision was taken by the Management Committee to raise funds for vital improvements and an appeal was launched for funds to modernise the Hall. This was made possible by the generous donation in 1967 by Mrs Angela Bull, a daughter of Sir Otto Beit. The wall between the main hall and the Ladies Room was altered and the present stage built. The kitchen, bar and toilets were

Fiftieth Anniversary commemoration of VE Day in Tewin Memorial Hall, 8th May 1995, (see pages 121 and 244).

113

relocated and. modern lighting and heating installed. The new facilities were opened in 1972.

Both the Trusts which own the Hall and the Management Committee are now Registered Charities. The Trustees of the first Trust are Villagers and Management Committee Members. Originally, it was specified that 'the Rector' of the Church should be a Trustee, but this is a function that no longer exists. The Trustees of the second Trust are all Management Committee Members. The Endowment, which was a large sum of money in 1922, does not now cover 5% of the insurance costs.

In the late 1990s, it became clear that a further refurbishment was required to bring the Hall up to present day requirements not least being the new Health and Safety legislation and the obligation to provide Disabled Persons facilities. The amount of work required was daunting, but with the most generous and practical support of a small group of unpaid volunteers, a vast amount of refurbishment has been undertaken. Much of this work required starting at the roof by replacing broken tiles, working downwards, repairing leaks, guttering replacements, rewiring, altering lighting, and completely overhauling the structure. The two large lamps, at the entrance gates were completely refurbished from their rust covered and dilapidated condition and other exterior safety lighting installed.

With grants from Awards for All (part of the Lottery) and the East Hertfordshire District Council, disabled toilets were installed together with the necessary ramps and safety rail. The Kimberley Room was redecorated by volunteers and part funded by the Friends of Tewin. Volunteers also scraped and cleaned off the old green paint from the doors, this taking some weeks, to reveal their natural wood. The corridor was repainted by volunteers and new large doormats donated. The main Hall was redecorated. The height of the ceiling and the necessary scaffolding required professional attention and, finally, new curtains were chosen and hung. These projects involved very considerable expense, but this was helped by a grant from the Tewin Parish Council.

By the very careful control by the Management Committee of its finances, the success of the fêtes, jumble sales and other events, of donations made by local Societies and the Parish Council, the success of the reinvented '200 Club' (now called Supporters Club) and the claiming of Gift Aid on donations, the village now has a sound financial, stable and well maintained facility. The Management Committee are now trying to increase the use of this splendid and much improved Memorial Hall.

Sir Herbert Baker, designer of both the War Memorial and Tewin Memorial Hall

Tewin is very fortunate to have had one of the most famous architects of his day, Sir Herbert Baker KCIE, DCL Oxon, RA, to design its village hall and war memorial. Sir Otto Beit KCMG and Lady Beit of Tewin Water House, who, like the Cowpers of Panshanger, had lost their son and first heir in World

Detail of the Tewin War Memorial at St Peter's Church.

War I, joined with the Cowpers to create a spacious, beautifully constructed Memorial Hall to remember all who gave their lives for their country.

The most productive years of Baker's career were spent in South Africa. Many churches, St George's Cathedral in Cape Town, St George's Grammar School, fine houses and the Rhodes Building for de Beers were produced. Living in South Africa at the time, Sir Otto Beit would have been very familiar with Baker's work.

Few people in Tewin are aware that the architect of their village hall was also the architect for the Bank of England, Winchester College War Memorial Cloisters (regarded by him as his best work of the period), an apse to the school chapel at Haileybury, South Africa house in Trafalgar Square, India House in Aldwych, and the mansion of Port Lympne in Kent, to name but a few of his accomplishments in Britain. How many cricket lovers know he designed the famous weather vane in the shape of Father Time and presented it to the MCC when he completed one of the grandstands at Lord's Cricket ground c1926 (see page 109).

Baker had been born on a farm as one of ten (some biographies say nine) children to Thomas Henry Baker JP and Frances Georgina Davis in Kent and loved to walk and explore the historic ruins of his neighbourhood around Cobham. He was articled to a church architect uncle with a practice in Kensington, but later joined his brother who had started a fruit farm in South Africa in 1891.

He went on to become the most famous architect in that country. He also met Cecil Rhodes and built private and public houses for him in Rhodesia.

'In his early work in the Cape, with great patience and energy, Baker brought the building crafts of South Africa to a high standard', writes A. Smart Gray in 1986, in his major work *Edwardian Architecture*. Gray also describes Baker's early love of visiting the English countryside, cycling, walking and sketching architecture with fellow pupils of Sir Ernest George RA, including Edwin Lutyens. Baker maintained a correspondence with Lutyens through much of his life.

Following an invitation to Lutyens to join Baker in the Transvaal, (where Lutyens designed the War Memorial and Art Gallery in Johannesburg), they both went on to design the famous Delhi government buildings in India.

After 12 years dedicated to the work in Delhi, Baker returned to England to complete his career with what Gray describes as a formidable list of commissions ranging from the Bank of England in the City of London to Winchester College War Memorial Cloisters. He designed an apse to the School Chapel at Haileybury, India House and numerous other projects. He received the Royal Medal for Architecture in 1927 and was made RA in 1932. Just as Lutyens had worked with the great garden designer Gertrude Jekyll, Baker also collaborated with her for the South African World War I Memorial at Delville Wood in Northern France.

Baker's Tewin Memorial Hall is a gem of his later period and was completed by the Beits on land donated by Lord Desborough KCVO off Lower Green in 1921 to be officially opened on 23rd January 1922 as their gift to the people of Tewin (see the full dedication on page 110).

Digswell Home Guard in World War II. Among the group are Tewin residents of the day, Arthur Edward Quince (4th from left, middle row, arms folded) and Bob Cole (6th from right , middle row).

German 250kg bomb crater in the front garden of Piggotts, Upper Green, Tewin 9th October 1940s. Mr Jackson is seen standing with the spade.

Enemy and other wartime incidents in Tewin and vicinity

Every road or group of houses in every town or village had an appointed air raid warden, supported by fire, ambulance, rescue, emergency shelter and feeding volunteers.

The simple stirrup pump, thousands of which were issued free, were provided for dealing with fires caused by incendiary bombs, although often, a more effective means was to smother the bomb with a sandbag. All attics were required by law to be cleared of inflammable material.

Air raid sirens were sited at Lower Green and at the junction of Desborough Drive and Cowpers Way, Tewin Wood. First aid posts were also located in Tewin village at 'Sevenacres', the home of Cyril Bishop and in Tewin Wood at 'Journey's End' at the junction of West and East Riding, the home of Molly Roche.

Almost all the 'conventional' incidents at Tewin or in the immediate vicinity, were the random unloading of bombs from German aircraft either due to anti-aircraft or night fighter damage, shortage of fuel or being unable to penetrate the London anti-aircraft defences.

Little or no activity was experienced during the *'phoney war'* from the 3rd September 1939 until the attack upon France and the Low Countries in May 1940 and the subsequent evacuation of British and some French forces from the beaches at Dunkirk.

Upon the surrender of France, the German Luftwaffe quickly occupied and extended the airfields in Northern France, Belgium, Holland, Denmark and Norway, as Germany turned its attention to an invasion and defeat of the United Kingdom.

The furious Battle of Britain commenced in mid August, reaching its peak in late September 1940 and lasted until the spring of 1941, by which time the German Luftwaffe was soundly defeated and the air activity much reduced as Hitler turned his attention to the attack on Russia in June. Until the arrival of the V1 and V2 weapons in June 1944, only very sporadic and ineffective enemy action was reported locally.

The following are the principal local incidents throughout the Second World War in Official Records.

11 July 1940	11 HE (high explosive) and several incendiary bombs at **Tewin**. One haystack burned; water main, power cables, and telegraph wires out of use, water in road, 1 man slightly wounded.
30 August 1940	12 HE bombs in Watton at Stone. Road blocked, no casualties. Bomber crashed at Whitwell, 1 crew killed, 2 injured, 1 unhurt. All captured.
17 September 1940	6 HE bombs between Datchworth and Bragbury End. No casualties or damage.
20 September 1940	3 HE bombs fell at Watton at Stone. No casualties or damage.
22 September 1940	12 HE bombs near **Tewin**. No casualties or damage.
30 September 1940	1 Oil incendiary bomb at Place Farm, Bramfield. No casualties or damage.
3 October 1940	5 HE Bombs hit the De Havilland Aircraft factory at Hatfield. Sheet metal shop destroyed, 18 men killed and 33 injured. Nearby streets machine gunned. The German bomber responsible was hit by anti-aircraft fire and crashed at Eastend Farm, Letty Green. All four crew members captured unhurt. The same day another aircraft machine gunned 7 men working in **Tewin** fields but no casualties although there was some damage to nearby roofs and furniture.
4 October 1940	Incendiary bombs at **Tewin** and 4 HE bombs near Westend Cottage, Bramfield. No casualties or damage.
6 October 1940	3 HE bombs near Burrs Green Farm, Watton at Stone. No casualties or damage.
7 October 1940	1 Incendiary bomb at Datchworth and 2 HE bombs at Letty Green. No casualties or damage.
8 October 1940	3 HE and 1 large oil incendiary bomb at Woolmer Green. No casualties or damage.
9 October 1940	2 HE and 1 large oil incendiary bomb between **Lower and Upper Green Tewin**. 5 houses damaged. 1 slight casualty.
10 October 1940	1 HE bomb fell at **Shankeys Wood, Tewin**. 1 House demolished and a child slightly injured.
12 October 1940	1 HE bomb at **Tewin** and an unexploded anti-aircraft shell fell at Bramfield. No casualties or damage.
13 October 1940	1 HE bomb at Mill Yard, Watton at Stone. 2 cottages demolished and three badly damaged. 2 persons killed and 6 wounded. 2 HE bombs at **Panshanger.** No casualties or damage.
16 October 1940	4 HE bombs at Watkins Hall Farm, Datchworth. Some damage to farmhouse but no casualties. 1 HE bomb at **Queen Hoo, Tewin**. No casualties or damage.
17 October 1940	5 Incendiary bombs fell at **Tewin**. No casualties or damage.
21 October 1940	3 HE bombs at Broom Hall Farm and Woodhall Park, Watton at Stone. 3 in **Panshanger Park** and 1 near Bramfield House.

117

	No casualties or damage.
8 November 1940	1 HE bomb near Datchworth Rectory. No casualties or damage.
15 November 1940	1 HE bomb in **Tewin Wood,** 6 near Bramfield, 6 near **Tewin** and 6 at Birch Green. No casualties or damage.
21 November 1940	2 HE bombs near **Tewin Hill Farm.** No casualties or damage.
4 December 1940	13 bombs at Paynters Green, Datchworth. Slight damage to one house but no casualties.
30 January 1941	2 bombs at **Attimore Hall Farm, Tewin.** No casualties or damage. (Parish extended to here at that time).
8 April 1941	German Heinkel 111 bomber hit by anti-aircraft fire crashed near Bendish House. 2 crew members killed and 3 wounded and captured.
10 April 1941	German Junkers 88 bomber hit by anti-aircraft fire and crashed at Frogmore, Stagenhoe Park. Crew of four captured.
14 April 1941	Red Cross Train stabled at Langley sidings, south of Stevenage machine-gunned. Slight damage to train but no casualties. Passenger train at Knebworth machine-gunned. 3 service and two civilian casualties.

For the next three years following the defeat of the Luftwaffe, and the German attack upon Russia in June 1941, little enemy aircraft activity was recorded in the area. Early in 1944 enemy attention returned in attempts to disrupt the allied build-up for 'D' Day on the 6th June 1944. This period, and until the end of hostilities on the 8th May 1945, announced the arrival of Hitler's 'terror weapons'.

19 February 1944	4 HE, 1 large phosphorus and many incendiary bombs around Bramfield without casualties or damage.

	Many incendiary bombs, many unexploded, around **Attimore Hall Farm, Tewin.** Two haystacks burned but no casualties.
14 March 1944	1 HE bomb in Lane Field, Bacons Farm and approximately 1,200 incendiary bombs in open ground **north east of Tewin** without casualties or damage.
21 July 1944	A V1 Flying bomb fell at Monks Green, demolished 'Woodside Cottage' and killed 1 woman, with 1 man and 2 children seriously injured and 3 others slightly injured.
22 July 1944	A V1 Flying bomb at Marden Park, Bramfield. No casualties but damage to a house nearly one mile away.
22 July 1944.	A V1 Flying bomb fell in open country 1 mile east of Watton at Stone. No casualties but some damage to roofs of houses.
24 July 1944	A V1 Flying bomb fell in the garden of a house in Burnham Green Road, Bulls Green. 25 Houses, up to one mile away with considerable damage. 3 men, 4 women and 2 children injured.
26 August 1944	Two Eighth US Air Force B17 bombers, flying in a large formation on a bombing mission to U Boat 'pens' and port facilities at Brest, France, collided in mid-air. Both crashed around Friends Green, Weston. Of the 17 crew members, 14 were killed and of the three who parachuted, one was seriously and the other two lightly injured. Unprimed bombs fell over an area;- one crashed through the roof of a house

	killing a woman and her young child.
2 January 1945	The first V2 long range rocket fell in a small wood south of Bulls Green. Slight blast damage to 13 houses but no casualties.
8 January 1945	A US Air Force lorry loaded with bombs exploded as a result of a collision with two others at Offley. A farmhouse and other houses were badly damaged. A bus travelling in the opposite direction received the full blast of the explosion and 3 passengers were killed with 18 injured.
13 January 1945	A V2 Rocket fell on allotments in High Street, Watton at Stone. Ten houses badly damaged and about 50 others slightly. Four light injuries.
27 January 1945	A V2 Rocket fell in fields 300 yards south of Datchworth Green. Slight damage but 4 slight casualties.
5 February 1945	A V2 Rocket fell near Watkins Hall, Watton at Stone. Damage to 12 houses but no casualties.
3 March 1945	A V1 Flying bomb fell near Perry Wood Farm with slight damage to farm buildings.
22 March 1945	A V1 Flying bomb fell between Bulls Green and Datchworth. No casualties or damage. Official records state this was the last 'V1' (flying bomb) weapon used against the United Kingdom during the 1939 -1945 Second World War. Forty seven days later, on the 8 May 1945, Germany unconditionally surrendered.
23 March 1945	A V2 Rocket exploded in the air over Bulls Mill, Stapleford without casualties or damage.

Panshanger Aerodrome

This grassed airfield to the west of Welwyn Garden City was, from the early 1930s, a private flying club known as Holwell Hyde.

Shortly after the commencement of the Second World War it was taken over by the Royal Air Force and used as an additional landing ground for the Hatfield based No.1 Elementary & Reserve Flying Training School. In the mid 1940s it was converted to a decoy field by the construction of 'dummy' timber and hessian hangars and assembly buildings with mock aircraft dotted around the site. The purpose of this was to detract the attention of enemy aircraft from the De Havilland aircraft factory at Hatfield busily engaged on the war production of fighter aircraft, particularly the outstanding fighter-bomber, the DH Mosquito.

By the summer of 1941 the airfield returned to its former use and in September 1942 the No.1 Elementary & Reserve Flying Training School moved back from Hatfield with a large complement of the famous Tiger Moth training biplanes. With its official change of title from Holwell Hyde to R.A.F. Panshanger, the Training School was fully occupied on grading courses for volunteer pilots and teaching

Second World War RAF Messroom and NAAFI on Panshanger Aerodrome. Photograph taken in 1995.

basic skills. With the later introduction of more sophisticated and faster aircraft, higher standards of pilot training were introduced. A detachment of the 8th US Army Air Force was also at this site operating homing beacons for bombers returning from raids on mainland Europe and some were accommodated in civilian housing in Tewin.

In May 1947 the airfield was redesignated as No. 1 Reserve Training School and remained so until it was finally disbanded in March 1953.

Many Tewin residents were gainfully employed in civilian tasks at R.A.F. Panshanger.

119

Above: **Holwell Hyde private flying club Panshanger c1930s.** Below left: **R.A.F. Blister Hangar.** Below right: **R.A.F. Nissen Hut used as the north entrance guardroom.**

Reverting to a private Flying Club, some spectacular air shows were staged in the 1960s and a war film *'The one that got away'* was partially made there.

Employees of De Havilland Aircraft Company at Hatfield were able to take subsidised private flying lessons on Tiger Moth biplanes at £1 an hour.

In the 1980s the airfield was abandoned and rapidly became derelict. However, in the mid 1990s private flying was resumed and the airfield and some buildings partially restored and it is once again in active use and welcomes training and visitors.

The Moneyhole Lane bridleway that ran across part of the site was closed by wartime emergency measures, but was not re-opened after the cessation of hostilities.

Many of the former wartime buildings may still be seen, including 'Blister' and 'C' type hangars, transport office, motor workshops, messrooms, guardroom, the NAAFI (Forces Welfare Canteen), and air raid shelters. Some of the original 'Nissen' huts at Bericot Green behind Warrengate Farm off the B1000, are still, (in 2009), occupied by families.

Uncle Sam pays us a visit.
The Americans in Tewin

For roughly three years during the Second World War Tewin played host to a small detachment of the American 8th Airforce. About nine in number, they were stationed at a small radio listening post near the Panshanger Airfield where they helped triangulate the position of damaged bombers returning from missions over enemy territory. Amongst them were, Earl Brooks, Shelly Russell, Reuben Timms, (Native American) and De Otis Davis, better known as Tex or Pete. Pete later married a local girl, Vera Shadbolt, and some of the family still live nearby. Some lodged with the Neale family at Meadow View in Upper Green Road while Pete stayed with the Owens at number 42 Upper Green Road.

Another flier who found lodgings in the village was a flight lieutenant/navigator who was stationed at Bassingbourn and lodged at Sevenacres in Tewin, the home of the local dentist.

Memories of Tewin in 1939-1945
Second World War

In May 1995, to celebrate the fiftieth anniversary of the end of the 1939-1945 Second World War in Europe, an Exhibition was held in the Memorial Hall with memorabilia and records of that long conflict from the 3rd September 1939 to the 8th May 1945. (The War in the Far East against Japan did not end until August 1945).

People of Tewin who lived throughout those years were asked to record their memories and these are some of their comments:-

'Cream and red coloured 'Birch Buses' ran from Welwyn North Station to Bedford via Codicote and Hitchin and were a very convenient way to attend the larger shops and the large Wednesday market at Hitchin'.

'The blue paper bags that the grocers put sugar etc. in and neatly folded down the top and quite secure'.

'Many homes had 'Anderson' shelters in their gardens. There was a slit-trench for the children by the side of the school'.

'There was a 'Lion Head' pump on Lower Green where some people obtained their water supply and children could take a drink whilst playing or watching rounders, cricket or football'.

'One day five airmen who had landed at Panshanger Aerodrome came to South Lodge where we lived and asked my mother to cook them a roast dinner. They gave her a large joint of beef and vegetables. While they were there they wrote their names in my Bible'.

'Arnhem. One day we saw a whole lot of planes going over the village. They were towing gliders. They flew from west to east. The sky was full of them. We watched until they had all gone'.

'The Rifle Range at Dawley Wood was used by the Home Guard'.

'During the War there were German and Italian prisoners of war working on Mr Barton's farm'.

'Newspapers, silver paper and tins were collected and stored in the Summer House at the back of the Memorial Hall'.

'A bomb fell in a field at the back of Tewin Garage in 1941. Besides blowing in various windows and doors, it killed Mrs Munn's chickens and goats, and all the sparrows that nested in the nearby hedges'.

'The grounds of Marden Hill were used as a Vehicle Depot by the R.A.F. For a short time soldiers were based on Upper Green and in the grounds of Panshanger House'.

'Early in 1940, Panshanger Aerodrome was made into a decoy airfield for the De Havilland's factory at Hatfield. Later it became No.1 R.A.F Reserve Flying School'.

'You could buy very hard rock cakes at the 'Plume of Feathers' on Saturdays.'

'On V.E. Day in the evening I went to the party on Lower Green. I smoked a packet of 'Capstan' cigarettes, very sick'.

'The terrible smell from the sausage skin factory at Burnham Green'.

'Italian prisoners of war worked on farms in and around Tewin. They were based in a camp at Baldock but many did not return to their camp at night and slept in outhouses and sheds. They seemed to have considerable freedom whilst here and besides their

work they befriended the children, played games and made toys by carving wood and using decorative burnt poker work. These toys included puppets, trains and toy animals'.

'In the evening of V.E. Day, the village celebrated by having a large party on Lower Green with a huge bonfire. An effigy of Hitler had been made and before burning it on the fire it was placed on the road outside Forge Cottage and was run over by a Morris 8 car.'

'Tewin Garage, which Mr Ambrose owned only had one workshop. People regularly took their accumulators (batteries) for their wireless sets to be re-charged.
There were few cars on the road but Mr Ambrose ran a limited taxi service. Petrol was sold only to those who had coupons. A new Hercules bicycle was purchased from Mr Ambrose for £3. 7s. 6d'.

'There was a dug-out in Dead Lane'.

'An anti-aircraft gun was placed by the A1000 opposite Tewinbury Farm'.

'The Blackout'.

'There were two First Aid Posts. One in the village and one in Tewin Wood'.

'There were two sisters,- the Misses Munn. One kept a smallholding, the other taught music and ran the Girl Guides. They lived at 23 Upper Green Road'.

'Christmas decorations made from larch twigs and painted'.

'From 1943, Air Cadets would attend RAF Panshanger for a week at a time. They used to fly with a pilot in the Tiger Moth planes all over Tewin'.

'On V.E. Day I came to Tewin for the first time. I was in the Forces and I had been given two days leave. I came with a friend of mine to visit his aunt. We came on the 388 bus from Hertford and arrived in Tewin at 4pm. There was a party taking place on Lower Green. There was plenty of beer, a 40 gallon barrel. At 5 o'clock in the morning we sat by the dying embers of the bonfire talking'.

'Canadian Forestry Corps cut down the fir trees in Tewin Wood for the War Effort'.

'Women's Land Army girls produced charcoal in Bramfield Forest. It was conveyed to Welwyn North Station, loaded into railway wagons and despatched to factories making explosives. Later, some Italian prisoners of war were also employed there'.

'United States Army Air Force crews based at Bassingbourn, Nuthampstead and Steeple Morden on the Hertfordshire- Cambridgeshire borders, came to Tewin for rest periods between bombing raids on Germany. They stayed with various families in Tewin and greatly appreciated the hospitality and kindness of the village. Other USAAF personnel worked at Panshanger Aerodrome and either lived on the Aerodrome or with families in the village. All these young men were very popular with the young women of the village and the Land Army girls. Nylons, chewing gum, plenty of money and tins of food of all kinds. When the USAAF left Tewin there was only one G.I. bride who made her way to the United States. These young men left many photographs of

Sqd leader/navigator Gerry Moberg 8th USAAF (1943/44) flew B17 Flying Fortress bombers from Bassingbourn and would dip his wings to show his safe return as he flew over Sevenacres, Tewin, where stayed between bombing raids.

Left: **Well House on Upper Green showing the water pumping mechanism. The structure was removed after the War. The house in the background is Orchard House, (see pages 62 and 123).** Right: **Ben Roberts and Linda Crawford, with many others, regularly attend the Remembrance Sunday services to lay wreaths beside Sir Herbert Baker's War Memorial at St. Peter's. Linda Crawford chairs** *Friends of Tewin* **which grew out of the Millennium Committee (see pp 246-247 and 255).**

themselves and expressions of thanks to the people of Tewin and many memories'.

'A shelter on Upper Green housed a water pumping mechanism into a well, for use if the water mains were bombed. It was never used'.

'Food and Cooking. Tewin villagers were fortunate compared with some parts of the country. Everything was rationed but the village had a good supply of poultry, rabbits, eggs, milk, vegetables and fruit. Recipes included chocolate cake made with liquid paraffin- delicious apparently! Pastry was made from the fat from tinned corned beef and tinned sausage meat. Eggs were pickled in isinglass. Dried egg and potato scones were very good. Chickens formed a major part of the diet and rabbits made tasty casseroles. Plucking chickens and skinning rabbits was a skill soon developed by many folk. Many a Christmas party was enjoyed by the children in the school assembly hall and there was food provided by parents and the school cooks'.

'There were a number of evacuees in Tewin. Some children came with their mothers to live in the safety of the countryside. In 1941, further evacuees came from Hastings arriving by coach. Sad and frightened children with labels, gas masks and a few personal belongings. They were sent to various folk who had
volunteered to take them in. Major Johnson of Crown Farm was the Allocation Officer. Each household who took in evacuees was issued with one new blanket for their new lodger. The children stayed for about two years, some for shorter periods and then returned home.
With this group of children came their teacher to help with the sudden increase in numbers in the village school. This meant that the assembly hall had to become three additional classrooms divided simply by curtains and for the sole use of the evacuees'.

'The Women's Institute made jam, bottled tomatoes and fruit, gathered herbs and collected rose-hips for syrup. Most of the women in the village made garments for the evacuated children and for those in the bombed areas of the country. Everyone knitted and for the Forces they made;- 46 pairs of stockings, 360 pairs of socks, 426 pullovers, 84 balaclava helmets, 288 scarves and 289 pairs of gloves. These were mostly distributed to the Herts & Beds Regiment, the RAF, Merchant Navy and to Russia and occupied countries. Between 200 and 300 toys were made and sold in aid of the Red Cross'.

The last Tewin bomb to be exploded?

In the 1980s the occupants of the Old School House were having works done in the cellar. One of the decorators found a World War II incendiary bomb lodged in the cellar ceiling. Presumably believing it to be a replica he threw it to his partner.

When the householder returned home, the painters told him that they had put 'the bomb' on the billiard table in the cellar. Mystified, he found it there and, white-faced, carried it upstairs and outside to the Green. He informed the police who called in Bomb Disposal from Kent. The Royal Engineer Captain and Sergeant carefully placed the bomb in a safe container for transport. This was duly photographed (from a safe distance) by the local paper.

The decorator who found the bomb asked to be photographed with the two Royal Engineer officers and the bomb in its container; the photographer obliged and the photo appeared in the local paper. The decorator asked Tewin Stores to send six copies of the paper to his home address...

The Royal Engineers phoned to say that the bomb, the last Tewin bomb we hope, was safely destroyed.

The volunteer rifle range

Sited in a beautiful dry valley on the border of Tewin Parish is a 1000 yard rifle range. It was built at his own expense by Charles Willes Wilshire of The Frythe, Welwyn. With the growth of Volunteer Regiments in the county, by the 1870s a need existed for a permanent facility for training near Welwyn.

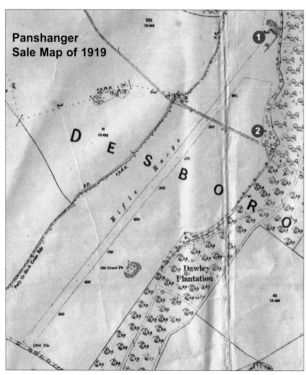

Above: **1000 yd Rifle range showing ❶ location of bullets at the chalk butts end and ❷ location of beaker.**
Right: **Example of bullets found by John Lee.**

Wilshire, a Lieutenant in the 14th Herts Rifle Brigade, installed a modern facility. Its great length (it was the longest north of London) was needed to train soldiers with the new breech loading rifles which were coming on the scene.

The butts (targets) were backed by a bank of chalk to prevent stray shots escaping from the range area. In keeping with the latest ideas, the bank was fronted by a large, deep trench, which provided protected accommodation for equipment to hoist and lower the canvas targets, and for the target markers who operated it.

The range was opened on Thursday, 15th November 1877. The first shots were fired by Lt Col Radcliffe of the 29th Middlesex, who achieved a near maximum score. A Martini-Henry competition was then held for 8 volunteers, shooting at 800, 900 and 1000 yards. On Saturday 17th November, the Welwyn Volunteer Company had its first private use of the range.

Since that time the range has had much use, particularly in the last two World Wars. From time to time it was necessary to renew the chalk bank. The last time led, a few years later in 1955, to the discovery of a partially destroyed Bronze Age grave containing a fine beaker dated to 2500-1200BC, a photograph of which can be seen on page 10.

Tewin resident, John Lee, field-walked this valley for many years since it contains worked flints of Neolithic origin. In September 1977 he found some damaged lead bullets not far from the original butt area. They were identified as Snider bullets.

At a later date he was near the same place and found more damaged Snider bullets, as well as two different bullets of the same weight, but smaller bore, and identified as Martini-Henry bullets. It was a nice coincidence that all these bullets were of an age and type that they could have been fired on the very day the range was opened.

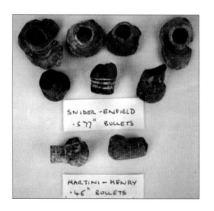

Chapter 9

Panshanger House and Estate
The Cowper and Desborough Families

The entrance to Panshanger House c1904

In the 19th century the Panshanger Estate and the Cowper family who lived there, played an important part in the lives of the people of Tewin and the development of the village as we know it today.

Early records of Panshanger are a little unclear. It was not mentioned in the Domesday Book, but there is a record that Geoffrey Runeville *'held one hide in Blakemere of Geoffrey de Beck'* and it is thought that Panshanger was possibly part of the Manor of Blakemere. Later, in 1198, there is reference to *'Pansangra'* – the first syllable is thought to mean *'Wooden or Wooded Slope'*. In the Middle Ages, it belonged to the Prior and Convent of St Bartholomew in Smithfield, London. In the 14th century the estate was held by various people: Agnes de Valence, John Darcy le Cosyn and William de Melkiscope, who also possessed the right of freewarren in Digswell, Datchworth and Ludwick. In 1446 Walter Cheveli was Lord of the Manor of Panshanger and Blakemere.

In the time of Henry VIII (when a farmhouse was built on the later site of Panshanger House) the Manor was, in part, owned by Gertrude, Marchioness of Exeter, who also owned Mardleybury and Woolmer Green. Later Panshanger reverted to the Crown and soon afterwards it was granted to Sir Nicholas Throckmorton, English diplomat and politician, who was Ambassador to France and played a key role in the relationship between Elizabeth I and Mary Queen of Scots.

From 1587 Panshanger Estate belonged to various people, and finally came into the ownership of the 1st Earl Cowper, possibly in about 1704.

The 1st Earl Cowper (1665-1723) was the son of Sir William Cowper, 2nd Baronet, who was the first member of the Cowper family to live in Hertfordshire and was MP for the borough. At one time, he lived in Hertford Castle. The 1st Earl was educated at St Albans School and was then called to the bar. He had a distinguished career, was made Lord Chancellor by Queen Anne, and again by King George I, who created him Viscount

William 1st Earl Cowper

125

Engraving of Cole Green House c1790. The house was demolished 1801-02.

Fordwich (hence Fordwich Rise, near Sele Farm in Hertford), and Earl Cowper.

The Panshanger Estate was purchased and Cole Green House was built adjacent to Cole Green Village in the early part of the 18th Century. It was a fine brick-built property overlooking the attractive parkland. It was not until 1756 that the 2nd Earl Cowper commissioned Capability Brown, the famous landscape gardener, to *'improve and flatten parts of the surrounding park'*.

The 1st Earl was married to Judith, daughter and heiress of Sir Robert Booth and, secondly, in 1706, to Mary Clavering, who was at one time Lady of the Bedchamber to Caroline Alspach when she was Princess of Wales. The 1st Earl Cowper died in 1723 at Cole Green House. He left two sons and two daughters by his second wife. The elder son, William, inherited his titles. Interestingly, the 1st Earl was the grandfather of William Cowper, the poet.

The 2nd Earl Cowper was married to Henrietta Grantham and it seems they lived for some of the year at Cole Green House. From 1733-1747 he was a Lord of the Bedchamber to King George II and was also Lord Lieutenant of Hertfordshire. He died at Cole Green House in 1764.

The work of the Cowpers in Hertfordshire continued with the 3rd Earl, George Nassau Clavering Cowper, who was MP for Hertford from 1759-1761. However, on the death of his father, and on succeeding to the title and family estates, he lived mainly in Europe and spent most of his later life in Italy, living in Florence. Through the influence of the Grand Duke Leopold of Tuscany, in 1785 he was created a Prince of the Roman Empire by the Emperor Joseph II. Cole Green House at that time it seems was neglected and began to fall into disrepair.

George Nassau was a connoisseur of paintings and it was he who amassed a great number, together with other works of art which were later displayed by the 5th Earl Cowper at Panshanger House. The 3rd Earl, who was married to Anne Gore, died in Florence in 1789. The title went to his son, George Augustus Clavering. The estate was held in trust until he reached the age of 21 but he died unmarried following an accident at the age of 22.

Peter Leopold Lewis Francis, the second son of the

Count John of Nassau-Sigen and his family 1634, Dutch forebears of the Earl of Grantham, father-in-law of the 1st Earl Cowper, painted by Sir Anthony Van Dyke (1599-1641). The canvas measures 9ft. 6ins. by 8ft. 6ins. and is now on display at Firle Place, Sussex.

126

A detail of a painting of George, 3ʳᵈ Earl Cowper, standing, and the Gore family by Johann Zoffany,
George married Anne Gore standing left, in 1775. The original painting is in the Yale Center for British Art, Yale, USA.

3ʳᵈ Earl, inherited the title in 1799 and became the 5ᵗʰ Earl Cowper. He is known, both in the history of Hertfordshire and his family, for the fact that he pulled down Cole Green House and other large houses in the area. He was known particularly to the people of Tewin and surrounding areas for his purchase of Tewin House (a famous and beautiful building adjacent to St Peter's Church to the east side of the Church drive, see page 176) and then razing it to the ground. Carrington recorded in his diary, dated June 1807, how Lord Cowper *'had begun to pull down Tewin Great House by the Church having previously pulled down the various offices of that great house'* - it seems for no apparent reason.

It was the 5ᵗʰ Earl who was responsible for the building of Panshanger House, the planning of which began in 1801. It was to be built on the north side of the park and was to incorporate the Tudor farmhouse, which had from time to time been used by members of the Cowper family. At this time the 5ᵗʰ Earl employed Humphrey Repton to virtually landscape the Mimram Valley between Welwyn and Hertford. Repton had shown his Red Book (now in the Hertford Archives) of Tewin Water House. The procedure was repeated for Panshanger - again Repton presented a Red Book (also in the Archives). The first design for the new house was not adopted and finally a second design by Repton and his son, John Adey Repton, was carried out in Gothic Revival style, facing south, and set in an imposing position with wide views down a gentle slope overlooking the River Mimram. It was not until 1806 that the building work finally commenced. It was a brick building (the bricks being made on site) and then rendered with a new material from Italy called concrete. It seems that two new architects, William Atkins and Samuel Wyatt, were put in charge of the building of the house.

127

Top: **The design for Panshanger House by Humphrey Repton, in the Gothic Revival style before later modifications were made for the 5th Earl Cowper.**
Below: **Panshanger House c1870. The final design showing the southern aspect and the art gallery at the east (right) end of the building.**

The building of the house and its offices, including the Orangery to the western end of the house (the remains of which still stand, see page 141), continued for some time and it is said that the lead from the roof of Tewin House, and other materials, were used in the building of Panshanger. Finally, in 1822 the large *'top lit Art Gallery'* was added to the east end of the house to accommodate the great paintings from the 3rd Earl's collection. Added to these were the Dutch and English paintings and French furniture of the finest quality, which the 5th Earl himself collected.

Inside the building there was a long corridor hung with more paintings from the art collection, with

Lady Katrine, wife of the 7th Earl Cowper, in her sitting room at Panshanger c1891

some of the living rooms off this corridor facing south. There were doors leading out of the house so the Cowpers and their guests could walk out and enjoy the south facing aspect and the lovely views across the Mimram Valley and the lake that had been

Panshanger stables

constructed by Repton. There was a terrace which ran along the south of the house, with a formal garden at the east end of the house near the Art Gallery. There was another garden facing south near the western end of the terrace.

On the north side, the driveway swept round to the front door, and nearby, but separate from the main house, was the red brick stable block. This stands today and houses the offices of Lafarge Aggregates.

When the house was first built, a great deal of the 5th Earl Cowper's attention was given to establishing and planning the whole area of the estate. Initially the drive left the Welwyn-Hertford Road, which ran along the Mimram Valley, at Poplars Green. However, Repton suggested that this road, now the B1000, should be diverted to turn sharp left and up an incline round the border of the estate and to the right up Brocket Hill to the present road - the A414. It seems that in the early 19th century minimal permission was needed and decisions were made by the wealthy land-owners.

The main gateway to the house remained at Poplars Green where a Lodge was built but, in later years, certainly when Lord and Lady Desborough were in residence during the War years, the drive which was mainly used went into the estate via the North Lodge. How much the other two entrances were used, one at Cole Green and one in Old Thieves Lane near Hertingfordbury, is not known. The latter was probably used a good deal as it would have given close access to Hertford and Hertingfordbury, where the Cowpers attended church.

To accommodate the needs of the household the large walled garden was used. Possibly this garden was created in the 18th century at the time of the development of the garden for Cole Green House and

129

Francis, 5ᵗʰ Earl Cowper and Emily Lamb who married him in 1806. Both paintings are by Sir Thomas Lawrence.

this can still be seen from the road, which runs from Poplars Green to the A414. Near the walled garden an ice house was constructed, built into a bank with the entrance facing north. It was apparently still in use, certainly until the time of Lord and Lady Desborough, in the early part of the 20ᵗʰ century. It is now, thanks to the *Herts & Middlesex Bat Group*, a Bat Hibernaculum so that the bats in the area are able to benefit from a secure home.

It is said that the building of Panshanger House did not commence until the 5ᵗʰ Earl married Emily Lamb in 1806. She was the daughter of Peniston Lamb and the sister of William Lamb, later Lord Melbourne of Brocket Hall, Lemsford, who became Queen Victoria's favourite Prime Minister. It was his wife, Lady Caroline Lamb, who became infatuated with the poet, Lord Byron, and had a mental breakdown on his death.

Emily was very beautiful, a charming hostess and she and the Earl welcomed Queen Victoria to Panshanger House. Like many other visitors, the Queen admired the wonderful collection of art and treasures. These included a large painting by Rembrandt of *'Marshall Turenne mounted on his horse'*. (This was sold to the National Gallery in 1959). Another was of the Nassau family, Dutch forebears of the Earl of Grantham, father-in-law of the 2ⁿᵈ Earl Cowper, painted by Van Dyck. Perhaps one of the most charming paintings was of *'The Children of the 1ˢᵗ Viscount Melbourne'* by Joshua

Reynolds. This shows the 2ⁿᵈ Lord Melbourne, his sister Emily, and a brother and is now on display at Firle Place, Sussex. It was purchased for the collection by the 5ᵗʰ Earl Cowper. The Panshanger collection also included a charming painting by Sir Thomas Lawrence of Emily Lamb at the age of 16. This can now be seen at Broadlands, Hampshire.

Panshanger, during the time of the 5ᵗʰ Earl, was famous as a centre of culture and lavish entertaining. It was described as *'full to the brim of vice and agreeableness, foreigners and rués'*

It was certainly a time when the Cowper family had considerable wealth and the 5ᵗʰ Earl maintained the estate very efficiently and added considerably to its size. Besides the Panshanger estate, he had land and properties over much of Hertingfordbury and Hertford, particularly in the Parish of St Andrews, and also in Bramfield, Hatfield, Welwyn and Digswell, as well as other parts of Hertfordshire, Kent and London.

After his death in 1837, the title went to his son, George, who was married to Lady Anne Florence de Grey (formerly Robinson). Two years later Emily, the widow of the 5ᵗʰ Earl Cowper, married Lord Palmerston, who twice served as Prime Minister. She lived at his home Broadlands, and also at Brocket Hall, which had been left to her by her brother, the 2ⁿᵈ Viscount Melbourne. On Emily's death Brocket Hall passed to the ownership of the Cowper family where it remained until it was sold in 1922.

Top: **Entrance to the Picture Gallery at Panshanger House where the picture** below left **of Barbara La Fiorentina by Domenico Puligo can be seen adjacent to the left hand pillar and near the centre of the photograph of the paintings,** below right. **The Rembrandt painting of Marshall Turenne on his horse on the extreme left of this general view of the gallery was sold to the National Gallery in 1959.**

Francis Thomas de Grey, the 7th Earl Cowper and his wife Lady Katrine. Taken in 1880.

Above: **One of the terraced Cowper cottages on Lower Green, showing the C of the Cowper crest and the yellow brickwork.**
Left: **A later KC crest of Katrine Cowper on one of the Churchfield Cottages.**

In 1855 there was a serious fire at Panshanger House causing considerable damage. This was later repaired. However, whether as a result of the shock of this disaster or not, George, the 6th Earl Cowper, died a year later in 1856.

In 1870 Francis Thomas de Grey, 7th Earl Cowper, married Lady Katrine Cecilia Maclean Compton, daughter of Admiral William Compton, the 4th Marquess of Northampton. In addition to the other family titles, Francis Thomas de Grey became 10th Baron Dingwall in the peerage of Scotland, and 8th Baron Butler of Moore Park in the peerage of Ireland as heir-general of Thomas, Earl of Ossory, son of the 1st Duke of Ormond. On the death of his mother, he also inherited the barony of Lucas of Cradwell. From 1880 - 1882 he was Lord Lieutenant of Ireland. He owned at this time 10,000 acres of land in Hertfordshire and considerably more in other parts of the country, approximately 38,000 acres making him one of the largest landowners in Great Britain.

In 1865 Earl Cowper was sent by Royal Command to Denmark to act as envoy extraordinary for the investiture of King Christian IX with his Order of the Garter. The Danish King was the father of Alexandra who had married the eldest son of Queen Victoria later to become Edward VII.

It was the 7th and last Earl Cowper who had the greatest influence over Tewin and the people who lived there. It appears that he had concerns about the welfare of his employees and, as a result, built many houses in Tewin and the surrounding villages. The houses were usually built in terraces or were semi-detached. They were nearly all in the same style, built of the same cream brick, possibly made on the Panshanger estate, or imported. All the groups of houses carry a crest - a coronet and a 'C' with the date. Two farms were built. Crown Farm in Back Lane was built in 1878 (see page 32) and Walnut Tree Farm in Upper Green Road, of very similar

Illustrated London News 1889. Engraving of formal gardens on the south side of Panshanger House.

design, was built in 1884. Both were constructed of red brick. In various villages, Earl Cowper, like many Victorians, *'generously'* refurbished churches. At St Peter's Church, Tewin, new pews, an organ, pulpit and panelling were given. The East window was designed by Harry Ellis Wooldridge, an assistant of Edward Burne-Jones, the great pre-Raphaelite painter (see page 58).

Panshanger House remained of great interest and in 1874 the Prince and Princess of Wales, later King Edward VII, and Queen Alexandra, visited Lord and Lady Cowper.

Beatrix Potter was another visitor, on August 29th 1882. At the age of 17 she was taken to see Earl Cowper's paintings while staying at Camfield Place, near Hatfield. She writes in her diary of the art gallery, the library and a drawing room and her thrill at seeing a painting by Raphael, of the *'Virgin and Child'*.

Besides entertaining, the Cowpers employed many people on the land and in the house and it was not until the death of this philanthropic Earl in 1905 without a direct heir, that changes began to take place.

Lady Katrine Cowper continued to live at Panshanger and tried to continue her husband's work. More cottages were built, this time in Churchfield Road. They are red brick and the letter

'K' and the date, 1909, can be seen on one of the houses. Following this, in 1910, Braziers Dairy at Archers Green was built.

On the death of her husband the Earldom had become extinct as there were no male heirs, and Lady Katrine herself died at Panshanger in 1913.

The heir to the 7th Earl was his sister, Adine. In 1866 she had married Julian Fane, a diplomat and poet, but she died in 1868 leaving a son and a daughter. Julian Fane died in 1870 and their only son in 1876. This left their daughter, Ethel Priscilla, to inherit the Cowper Estates from her uncle on the death of his wife Katrine.

Ethel, who was always known as Ettie, was regarded as one of the outstanding beauties of her day. She had been orphaned at the age of three and brought up by a nanny and various family members of both her parents. She spent a good deal of her young life at Panshanger with her uncle and aunt and also at Brocket Hall at Lemsford with her uncle Henry Cowper. Ettie was a beautiful accomplished and charming young woman and after her marriage to William Grenfell on 18th February 1887 was renowned for her entertaining at Taplow, Buckinghamshire, the Grenfell home and in later years, at Panshanger. Many celebrities, politicians and members of the aristocracy frequented the weekend house parties.

133

Left: **William Meads senior and junior, Estate workers at Panshanger c1910. William senior was a gamekeeper and lived at Keeper's Cottage in Tewin Wood. His son William later worked for Sir Otto Beit at Tewin Water and lived at Meads Cottage, Orchard Road. He later lived at Churchfield Cottages. William junior died in 1973.**

Below: **Panshanger House and Estate Fire brigade 1906.**

Ettie Grenfell (Lady Desborough) 1867-1952.

It was quite early in her marriage when Ettie became a member of the 'Souls', this was a group of young men and women known for their *'brilliance and beauty'* who had very definite and reforming ideas. Evidently it was Lord Charles Beresford who gave this name to the group at a dinner party in 1888 when he said *'You all sit and talk about each other's souls so that is what you will be called'*. Other members of the group included Arthur Balfour, George Curzon and Winston Churchill.

In 1905, William Grenfell was created 1st Baron Desborough of Taplow.

The son of Charles W Grenfell and Georgina Sebright Lascelles, William was educated at Harrow School and Balliol College Oxford. He rowed twice for Oxford and was President of the Oxford University Boat Club and the University Athletic Club. He was a member of the rowing crew which achieved a dead-heat race with Cambridge in 1877. His other rowing achievements outside Oxford included being stroke for an eight which crossed the English Channel. He was a great all round sportsman and his activities included mountaineering in the Alps, climbing the Matterhorn by three different routes and shooting in the Rockies. William also

swam twice across Niagara, crossing the pool just below the Falls. As well as these interests, point-to-point played a considerable part in his life and at Taplow he kept his own harriers, which had formerly belonged to King Edward VII. In 1908 he became President of the British Olympic Committee.

William Grenfell's career followed various paths. In 1880 he entered the House of Commons becoming Liberal MP for Salisbury and in 1892 for Hereford. In 1900 he won the seat of High Wycombe for the Conservative Party. He was appointed a Knight Commander of the Royal Victorian Order and in 1928 was admitted as a Knight of the Order of the Garter. He headed several commissions, was a Justice of the Peace and was a keen farmer and renowned conservationist. From 1924 to 1929 he was Captain of the Yeoman of the Guard. It seems that from a young man he was known and respected by many for his strong literary and artistic sense. William Grenfell was a man *'who was able to get things done'* which is perhaps why he led such a full life and had a long list of impressive achievements.

When his wife Ettie inherited Panshanger House and estate in 1913 they lived both there and at their home in Buckinghamshire, Taplow Court. From 1939 Lord and Lady Desborough lived at Panshanger throughout the year. In World War I Taplow Court was turned into a rest home for nurses, and in World War II, Panshanger House became a home for young mothers, and their babies from London.

William and Ettie had three sons, Julian, Gerald (known as Billy) and Ivo, and two daughters, Monica and Imogen. Like many, their lives were irrevocably changed when their two eldest sons were killed in the

The Desborough entwined initials on the cottages of Holly Bushes on the B1000.

135

Back row left to right: **Monica, Lord Desborough and Ivo.** Seated front, left to right: **Billy, Lady Desborough with Imogen on her lap, and Julian.** The picture was taken in 1910. Julian and Billy were killed in World War I and Ivo died in a motor accident in 1926. Monica later became Lady Salmond and Imogen married Viscount Gage of Firle Place, Sussex.

Above: **Julian Grenfell and right Billy Grenfell when they were both pupils at Summer Fields School.**

Lord and Lady Desborough with some of the young mothers and their babies who lived at Panshanger during the Second World War.

First World War. Julian Grenfell had been a distinguished First World War poet and wrote the poem *'Into Battle'*, (see page 144). Ivo was killed in 1926 in a motoring accident.

Monica married Sir John Salmond, Marshall of the Royal Air Force, and Imogen married Lord Gage of Firle Place, near Lewes, Sussex.

Although Ettie inherited Panshanger House and Estate, it is apparent that her husband took on much of the responsibility of the estate, and certainly from then on his name appears on documents, on a Deed of Sale and on purchases and sales connected with Panshanger.

The Desboroughs built one more estate house for staff at Panshanger. This was at Hollybushes on the B1000. The cream bricks are now painted over but the crest with facing 'D's on it can be seen quite clearly.

In the early 1920s a member of staff recalls the youngest daughter Imogen. '*Miss Imogen, the second daughter was lovely and we all adored her, all of us; she would have been about twenty-one, I suppose. She was very beautiful with fair, naturally curly hair. She used to ride a lot, riding side saddle, and was*

137

A Happy Christmas To dear Elizabeth from Ethel Desborough

This writing paper is almost a hundred years old — 1851.

Letter sent by Lady Desborough to Elizabeth Bishop in 1946.

very popular as a bridesmaid; every time she showed herself off in her dress to the staff.'

In 1922, Lord Desborough gave the land for the Tewin Memorial Hall, which was built by Sir Otto Beit of Tewin Water in memory of those people from Tewin who had died in the 1914/18 War. Gradually the estate and various properties were sold and the biggest sale of land by Lord Desborough was to Ebenezer Howard and the consortium who planned to build the new Welwyn Garden City. This sale of 1,458 acres took place in 1919. Lord Desborough died at Panshanger in 1945.

Lady Desborough had a great fondness for children and enjoyed the influx of babies, toddlers and young mothers who were at Panshanger during the War years. She also had her grandchildren, George (Sammy), Nicolas, now 8th Viscount Gage and Camilla, Imogen Gage's family, to stay at Panshanger. Their home at Firle Place, near Lewes, Sussex, could have been vulnerable to a possible German invasion. In the absence of the Gage family, that house was used to accommodate Canadian troops for some of the War years.

Panshanger House was at this time still full of treasures and wonderful paintings, not only in the art gallery, but along the corridors and in the living rooms. There were still visitors - often children who were friends of her grandchildren. Lady Desborough would join in their games, and a privilege for a visitor was to sit at the beautifully set tea table with its fine china and silverware with Lady Desborough presiding and pouring tea from the silver tea pot. The War seemed far away! Once a year, at Christmas, she welcomed the children from Tewin Cowper Endowed School, who would walk to Panshanger House for tea. There would be a Christmas tree of course. It is said that the first Christmas tree to be seen in England was at Panshanger House and not at the instigation of Prince Albert at Buckingham Palace. We will never know.

As Lady Desborough became more frail, she had one most welcome guest, Queen Mary, widow of George V. Ettie had been an Extra Lady of the Bedchamber to the Queen and the friendship always remained.

Sadly, after Lady Desborough fell and broke her hip, she finally died peacefully at Panshanger House in 1952. She was loved and respected by all her family and friends, and her many staff, to whom she was so kind and caring. The house was left to her eldest grandson, the Hon. Julian Salmond, and the estate was subsequently sold. Many of the treasures were removed and stored away, some at Hatfield House, but everything else was sold and in 1954 the house subsequently demolished - all except the Orangery and the stables and lodges. The land, as now, was used for gravel extraction - a very sad ending to a beautiful house and estate, which had been such an important part of our local history and the history of the County of Hertfordshire.

Panshanger Gates
These were purchased by Peterhouse College, Cambridge University, in 1954 and can now be seen in the grounds of the College.

Sale of Panshanger House and Estate
The sale of the Estate began on 15 July 1953. A copy of the Sale Catalogue can be seen at the Hertfordshire Archives County Hall Hertford. Also available are the extensive Panshanger Archives.

Freda at Longleat before her employment with Lord and Lady Desborough, 1935.

Memories of Panshanger by Freda Owen
Freda Owen - born 1915 and died in 2009.
Worked as a cook to Lord and Lady Desborough from 1937 - 1941.

Staff at Panshanger 1937 - 41
Housekeeper: Mrs Bruce, later promoted to housekeeper at Windsor Castle; *Butler:* Mr Barret; *Parlour maids:* Minnie and Kate; *Kitchen maid*: Mary Mason; *Still-room maids*; Betty who had previously worked at Longleat with Freda and Rhona, (transferred to the kitchen during the war); *Laundry maids:* Emily, Yvonne; *Odd job man*: Mr Taylor; *Ladies maid*: Miss Leah; *Groundsmen; Chauffeur.*

Management of the household
Lord Desborough's home was Taplow Court, near Maidenhead. The household moved there from February to October. At the beginning of October they came to Panshanger until February.

Taplow Court had its own dairy and supplied the kitchen with cream, butter and cheese. There was also a large vegetable garden.

When the household was at Panshanger dairy produce and fresh vegetables were sent from Taplow twice a week in a hamper.

This arrangement continued until the outbreak of war when the family moved to Panshanger - produce was still sent to them. Fish and meat was sent up from Hertford.

Traders in Hertford used by Panshanger
Groceries	Bates
Meat	Frost
Fish	Brewsters

Catering arrangements
The still-room maids made all the cakes and did teas, coffees and lunch cakes. The kitchen only made

A french oven (this one is at Longleat) but a similar one was at Panshanger. Only used in addition to the range when they were very busy for a houseparty.

desserts. Freda had one girl to help her in the kitchen but extra help was brought in for parties.

The Desboroughs were an elderly couple living on their own and liked to live simply. They could not manage beef because of their teeth and preferred lamb and chicken. No onions were allowed. Breakfast would be cereal, toast and marmalade and Bemax. Lunch consisted of two courses, meat and

139

dessert. No afternoon tea. Dinner at 8pm with three courses, soup, meat and dessert.

House parties

Every fortnight a house party of about twelve would be invited from Saturday morning to Monday morning. Guests would bring their own chauffeurs, valets, ladies' maids, and, if the children were present, nanny and nursery maids.

Freda would make a hot meal for all the staff on the Saturday and then there would be a cold table laid out for them at other times. She would always take the menu for the day to Lady Desborough at the breakfast table for approval, whether it was just for her and her husband or for a house party.

Breakfast

The guests could order what they wanted to be served in their rooms or could choose from a variety of dishes laid out in the dining room e.g. eggs, bacon. kidneys, haddock, kippers.

Lunch

Three courses e.g. An egg dish, saddle of lamb (Lady D's favourite) and dessert.

Ice cream was a popular dessert. Freda made it in an ice bucket. There were no refrigerators. The ice cream was put in a container with a tight lid and suspended across a strong wooden bucket with metal bands. All around the edge layers of chopped ice and freezing salt were packed in. A handle was turned until it started to freeze. Sometimes a bombe mould was sunk into the freezer salt.

Dinner

A typical dinner might be:- soup, clear or thick; fish, salmon or sole; meat, poussins with watercress and trimmings; dessert, ice cream and savoury, sardines or scotch woodcock (scrambled egg with anchovies).

Guests included Sir Winston Churchill and Violet Bonham Carter.

Cooking arrangements

It was an old kitchen to work in. There was no gas or electricity but a coal range. An extra set of French Ovens like the ones Freda had used at Longleat were used when it was particularly busy.

There were larders and leaded ice boxes with lids for perishables. Ice was bought from the fish monger half a hundred weight at a time. The vegetables were served on silver dishes which would be brought to

the kitchen by the pantry staff. A bell rang in the dining room. That was Freda's cue to serve up the soup or whatever was next so that by the time the parlour maids arrived at the hatch it was ready.

Lady Desborough always had a swan for Christmas. There was a staff dance at this time. All the saucepans were copper and very heavy. Jelly moulds were also copper and both were cleaned with sand and soft soap on the inside and sand, vinegar and flour on the outside.

The copper stock pot was particularly heavy. In it would be placed 10lb shin of beef and a boiling fowl. It would be simmered for hours and strained off. Some stock pots had a tap on the side. The first stock would be for consommé soup. Then it would be refilled and the second stock used for gravies and sauces.

The day's work

Morning - preparing lunch and as much towards dinner as possible. A break in the afternoon. Back again at 6pm. Dinner at 8pm.

The pantry staff washed up the dining room crockery, cutlery and silver in the butler's pantry. Freda and her helper just washed up the kitchen utensils.

In the summer Lady Desborough had groups to tea e.g. the village school and the Women's Institute. All the staff went in to help with the teas.

Many of the staff were on board wages. They provided their own meat and fish. The kitchen gave them vegetables and a pint of milk each day. The kitchen staff was small because of the existence of the still-room for cake making.

The War years

Life changed at Panshanger. The family stayed there all the year. There were no still-room staff any more and Freda and her assistant moved to the still-room where there were two big larders.

Part of the house was let and the kitchen was let with it. When Freda was there it was a home for unmarried mothers.

The big house parties were ended and visitors came in smaller numbers for one or two nights. It was decided that everyone should sleep in the cellars. Freda hated this and became ill with the heat of the pipes. She had a holiday and when she returned said she wanted to return to a bedroom which she did. Lord and Lady Desborough slept in the cellars for the entire War. Life was difficult for Freda. It was hard to cope on rations because the same standards were expected. Every time the siren went she had to leave the kitchen and go down to the cellars. She would return to find the range had gone out and the food was spoiled. In 1941 Freda decided to leave Panshanger. Lord Desborough died in 1945. Freda visited Lady Desborough in 1947 with her baby daughter, Valerie, and had tea with her on the lawn. Lady Desborough died in 1952.

Social life at this time
The Village Hall was run by stewards and was open every lunch time and evening. There was a yearly subscription to the club. Staff from all the big houses, Marden, Panshanger, Tewin Water, together with village people used to attend.

Facilities included: a radiogram for dancing, a billiard table and a dart board.

The end of Panshanger
When Lady Desborough died she left the house to her grandson, Julian Salmond. He did not want to live in it and put it on the market. A demolition contractor bought it. It was pulled down brick by brick and there were auctions held every month to sell off the materials e.g. fireplaces, bricks, stone and even the wallpaper was sold. It was taken off with a razor.

People were responsible for removing their purchases. Freda's son-in-law lived in a house in Potters Bar whose extension was built with bricks from Panshanger - sold to a local builder.

Childhood Memories - 1920s & 1930s
The school children from Tewin Cowper Endowed School were invited to Panshanger for a Punch & Judy Show. They walked there in a crocodile and sat cross legged on the floor in a big room. They were given a bag of sweets and an orange.

Memories of a young member of staff 1925-26
Lady Desborough was very tall, gracious and slim, a regal lady. She used to always keep St. Thomas' Day, which I think was a custom from Lord Cowpers' time. We had warm ale, bread and cheese, which of course the still-room prepared, and all the various house and ground staff came.

Once when the staff were going back to Taplow, she told me I must stay behind and she and I would wash all the china. So we did.

Above: **Bookplate of Francis Thomas de Grey, 7th Earl Cowper taken from a volume formerly in the library at Panshanger.**
Below: **The Orangery, (in 1995), and the stables, (page 129), were the only parts of the Panshanger House main buildings left standing following the demolition from 1953 to 1954.**

A member of staff at Panshanger recalled that Lady Desborough had told them:
The family name of Cowper was always pronounced as it was spelt not 'Cooper' (as is sometimes used today).

She added:
Lady Desborough always called the staff by their christian names.

Top left to right: **North Lodge on the B1000, South Lodge at Cole Green.**
Middle left to right: **West Lodge at Poplars Green, East Lodge at Old Thieves Lane.**
Below: **Map showing the location of Panshanger House and Lodges.**

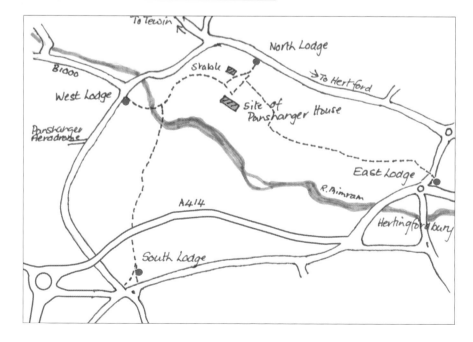

Captain, The Honourable Julian Henry Francis Grenfell D.S.O.

Julian Grenfell

1st Battalion Royal Dragoons.
Born: 30th March 1888, London. Died of wounds on 26th May 1915 aged 27 years.
Parents: William & Ethel Grenfell (later Lord & Lady Desborough of Panshanger).
Educated at Eton College and Balliol College, Oxford.

In 1905 his father was created Lord Desborough. In 1910 Julian joined the Royal Dragoons and was posted to India and then South Africa. In October 1914 the regiment was sent to Ypres and were involved in the First Battle of Ypres. In February 1915 his battalion went to the trenches at Kleine Zillebeke, and on 14th April after two days in Paris the second Battle of Ypres started. It was at this time that Julian wrote his most famous poem *'Into Battle'*.
On the 12th May 1915 a shell landed a few yards from Julian - he was wounded and had a splinter of shell in his head. His condition soon deteriorated and Lord and Lady Desborough with their daughter Monica arrived at the hospital in Boulogne.
'Between the 15th and 23rd Grenfell underwent two operations but on the afternoon of the 26th May he died.'
Julian was buried on 28th May 1915 in the cemetery above Boulogne's Eastern Cemetery, looking across the battle fields. His parents, his sister Monica and a few friends were there but none wore mourning. His mother wrote : -
'His grave was lined and filled with the wild flowers from the forest and the green oak leaves which had just come out.....it was a very windy day, he had always loved the wind'.
On the same day, the announcement of his death and his poem *'Into Battle'* were published in The Times.

Into Battle

The naked earth is warm with spring,
　And with green grass and bursting trees,
　Leans to the sun's gaze glorying,
　　And quivers in the sunny breeze;
And life is colour and warmth and light,
　And a striving evermore for these;
And he is dead who will not fight,
　And who dies fighting his increase.

The fighting man shall from the sun
Take warmth, and life from the glowing earth;
　Speed with the light-foot winds to run,
　　And with the trees to newer birth;
And find, when fighting shall be done,
　Great rest, and a fullness after dearth.

All the bright company of Heaven
　Hold him in their high comradeship,
The Dog-star and the Sisters Seven,
　　Orion's Belt and sworded hip.
The woodland trees that stand together,
　They stand to him each one a friend;
They gently speak in the wintry weather;
　They guide to valley and ridge's end.

The kestrel hovering by day,
　And the little owls that call by night,
Bid him be swift and keen as they,
　As keen of ear, as swift of sight.

The blackbird sings to him, 'Brother, brother,
　If this be the last song that you shall sing,
Sing well, for you may not sing another;
　　Brother, sing'.

In dreary, doubtful, waking hours,
　Before the brazen frenzy starts,
The horses show him nobler powers;
　O patient eyes, courageous hearts!

And when the burning moment breaks,
　And all things else are out of mind,
And only joy of battle takes
Him by the throat, and makes him blind,

Through joy and blindness he shall know,
　Not caring much to know, that still
Nor lead not steel shall reach him, so
　That it be not the Destined Will.

The thundering line of battle stands,
　And in the air death moans and sings;
But Day shall clasp him with strong hands,
　And Night shall fold him in soft wings.
　　　　　　　　Julian Grenfell.

Julian Grenfell in France 1915.

Chapter 10
Occupations & Shops

The location of the present Tewin Stores, at the end of the fencing, on the Hertford Road c1920.

Tewin, along with many other small villages, has over the years had many shops and businesses, until the present day (2009), when there is only one 'village' shop. These would all have been well supported because of the number of people living locally. In the 16th, 17th and 18th centuries there were five large mansion houses, each with its own extensive gardens, as well as substantial farmhouses and cottages. The mansion houses and farms employed large numbers of servants and labourers who would have needed a variety of shops and businesses for everyday life.

Some of these shops were around both the Upper and Lower Greens, but there is little or no trace of them now.

The 1759 militia list has a John Walby, butcher and churchwarden, followed in 1768 by a Simon Walby, butcher, possibly a relative. It is interesting to note that the Walby butchers also appear in Codicote as late as the mid 20th century.

According to Carrington there were at least two bakers in Tewin in 1808, Thomas Grigory on the Upper Green and Rowley on the Lower Green. Bearing in mind that Hertford Road was then part of

Lower Green it is reasonable to assume that Rowley was baking in what is now Tewin Stores. They both apparently sold their bread in three local shops, Deard's, Smart's and Allen's.

Henry Gullet, the son of a mason working on the construction of the Digswell viaduct, tells us in his memoirs, that when his family came to Tewin in 1849 they took lodgings at Lower Green. At that time there was a pond in the middle of the green and a variety of tradesmen living in the same row of cottages that they lodged in, a blacksmith, a baker, a shoemaker and a brewer. However he omits to tell us where these artisans carried out their trades, so it is probable that they were employees and not tradesmen on their own account, although a brewer and beer retailer, Lucy Maria Cannon, was working here in 1855. Henry Gullet was later to become the editor and part owner of the Sydney Telegraph.

By 1851 there was only one baker, a family called Goldsmith, baking in what is now our last remaining shop. In the same year the Upper Green had its own grocer, Thomas Wish. The Goldsmiths were still baking here in the early part of the 20th century and were using a horse-drawn cart for deliveries. The

145

The first post office seen on Lower Green in the left-hand cottage in the foreground. These cottages were later demolished leaving the Cowper Cottages in the background overlooking the Green.

horse was kept in a field at Lousehole (a relatively recent bastardisation of 'Household') Bottom. The gateway for the property can still be seen in the southern hedge of Lousehole Bottom. In the 18th century it was also known as Flexleys Gate, Flexleys Wood being that part of Marden. Similarly, Dead Lane, leading from Upper Green to Margery Lane, was originally Dead Mans Lane, having been used to carry coffins from Upper Green to the Church. The incline towards Hertford was known as Goldsmiths Rise. The Goldsmith family graves are in the southeast corner of the churchyard.

The shop in Hertford Road then went to the Wenham's, (a relative of the Goldsmiths) the last bakers in the village, who had a delivery round using a small motor van. With the advent of the motor vehicle came the travelling baker, firstly Grays of Kimpton followed by Coulsons of Welwyn, Rayments of Hertingfordbury, Wrens of Hertford and O. Kimpton of Woolmer Green, and this saw the demise of many local bakeries. It wasn't long before the Wenhams moved on, the bread round taken by Wrens and the shop by the Misses Preston. It was then taken on by the Mouldens who ran it as a shop and tearooms as a stopping off point for cycling clubs coming out from London.

Over the next 50 years or so the shop has had a great many owners, Mrs Neale, Miss Farrow, Jim Forsyth, Peter Howells, Dick Gale, John Boreham, Roger Temple, Peter Cole and, in 2006, John Pilbeam.

The post office has had a variety of homes; the earliest being in a row of cottages in front of what is now 13 to 19 Lower Green. First built as almshouses in 1717 they were later known as workhouse yard when the original workhouse opposite the pond on Upper Green was closed in about 1800. In 1859 the office was being run by a sub-postmistress, Jane Ballentine, who was there until at least 1869. By 1882 the sub-postmaster was Charles Briant and later his wife Ellen. When the cottages were demolished it was moved into a cottage at 9 Lower Green. It was later moved into a custom-built corrugated-iron building, where number 8 Lower Green now stands where it was run by Mr Richard Ravenshear. When he retired it was taken over by his nephew Harold Briant. In the 1960s Mr Briant felt that he could no longer cope with the post office and it went to its present home at Tewin Stores. The shop in the iron hut was bought by the Mawer family who ran it for a number of years until the land was sold to build numbers 5 to 8 Lower Green.

From at least the early 20th century the village had its own greengrocer on what was known locally as the garden field. In fact it was the village allotments and the Chalkley family, (see pp 156 and 209), ran it on ground rented from Walter Hale who farmed at Tewin Hill. The shop was in a wooden shed selling local produce grown on the allotments. Sadly this came to an end in the 1970s when the land was sold to build Harwood Close and Godfries Close.

Another business, that of haberdasher, was run by Miss Haines from number 14 Hertford Road (Cheyne Cottage, previously Rose Cottage) so named, not as according to local folklore because of the chains at the front but because a previous tenant had moved there from Cheyne Walk in Chelsea. Although, it was not a shop as such, just a waggon, parked on the grass verge on what is now the front garden of number 12 Hertford Road.

Other businesses have included tailors; three between 1773 and 1798, shoemakers [cordwainers], eight between 1735 and 1801, weavers, and of course all those trades we associate with a rural economy.

In fact as recently as the middle of the last century a Richard Taylor was still working here as a cobbler. Known locally as Dick snob [snob; a colloquial term for cobbler] he pursued his trade at what is now 21 Upper Green Road. He is first mentioned in 1912.

From 1773 until at least 1798 there were three tailors working in the parish although one of these, James Ambrus (sic) Ambrose was at Grubbs Barn, now called Attimore Hall, this was of course when the parish was much larger.

Hertfordshire in the 17th and 18th century was famous for its wheat and barley. The bulk of London Porter Malt was produced in the county. Arable farms were labour-intensive and employed many workers and tradesmen so there was a plethora of trades associated with agriculture; hurdle makers (which means that there were probably a great many sheep), wheelwrights, and blacksmiths. The first available figures show that in 1885 Hertfordshire was home to at least 160,000 sheep which reduced to less than 50,000 by 1962.

Of course we still have blacksmiths today but their role has altered considerably. Where once they were the rural engineers of their time they are now almost solely farriers and their engineering skills have been taken over by others. In the village context we now have garages and in the case of Tewin in 1908 there was a motor garage at *The Rose and Crown*, then owned by the Herts Public House Trust. William (Bill) Gamble started the garage on its present site in the 1920s. Later taken by George Ambrose who, assisted by John (Winnie) Churchill, kept the local vehicles going for many years. David Knight of *Wellspray*, Welwyn Garden City then took it on and, with a slightly larger workforce, managed it until it closed in 2007, (see pages 156-157).

Between 1758 and 1801 there were at least five blacksmiths who worked in the parish and between 1768 and 1798 three at one time. The last forge, that

The former forge on Lower Green, in poor condition on right side of the photograph, prior to its collapse in a gale in the 1950s, with the Old School House (see The Yarborough School, pages 81-85) on the left, and Cowper cottages behind.

147

on Lower Green, was demolished by a gale in the 1950s. The forge actually faced the small grass triangle in front of the Old School House, known as Herons Green. This made way for numbers 26 and 27 Lower Green.

The last blacksmith to work the forge was Arthur Digby who lived next door at number 28 Lower Green and whose ancestors had been blacksmiths here since the 1880s. He then went on to work in a factory in Welwyn Garden City. The blacksmith's wife had been a wardress in Holloway prison and in 1923 had been companion to Edith Thompson while in the condemned cell. The manner of Thompson's execution is said to have contributed to Mrs Digby's later suicide in a water butt at the forge.

The hurdle makers William and James Ray (1783 - 1792) also described themselves as lath(e) renders, i.e., making the laths that went into building the cottages in the village or into basket making. Examples of coppiced Ash and pollarded Hornbeams can be seen in Lambdell Wood and Flexleys Wood.

Whilst these were all thriving businesses in their time they were not shops as such but workshops or workrooms where the owner or tenant plied their trade.

With the abundance of straw available, straw plaiting was a common cottage industry, certainly at least until the middle of the 19th century. The plaiters would sell their product to the hat makers in and around Luton.

Straw was also used for thatching, and at one time Tewin had its own thatcher, Harry (Joe) Brand who in the late 19th and early 20th century lived at Nancybury Cottages near Queen Hoo Hall. Nancybury cottages were originally built as ten back-to-back, one-up, one-down militia barracks. They were later converted into five two-up, two-down cottages. Joe's principle job was rick (i.e. hay and straw stack) thatching but he also worked on cottages as well e.g. Rats Castle in Burnham Green Road.

Hertfordshire straw plaiter

In particular straw plaiting was carried out by women and children in the counties of Hertfordshire and Bedfordshire.

Straw plaiting work is recorded as taking place in Tewin in 1851 although it is likely to have been carried out earlier. It is no longer mentioned in the 1901 census.

In 1851 the population of Tewin was 522 with 253 being female. Of the 52 women employed, nine are recorded as being straw plaiters. That is 17.3% of those in employment.

In addition to those recorded, children as young as five were involved. Whilst girls continued working into their teens, boys would go off to work as agricultural labourers when they were about ten to twelve years old. They would return to plaiting in the winter when the weather was poor.

Straw plaiting provided a substantial supplement to the family budget and, with the hat trade, was of considerable importance to the economies of Hertfordshire and Bedfordshire in the 19th century. It produced good wages from the late 18th century until the end of the third quarter of the 19th century.

An embargo on imported straw during the Napoleonic wars (1803 to 1815) resulted in huge wage increases for plaiters. For example, a woman plaiter in Hatfield is recorded as having earned 22 shillings a week whereas a male agricultural labourer at that time was earning from 10 to 12 shillings a week.

In 1831 in Hatfield the wage was about 8 to 10 shillings a week with 3 to 5 shillings for children.

During the slump, from 1832 to 1834, straw plaiting was recorded as being vital in providing winter work in Welwyn. Unlike other counties, who did not have the opportunity to work in straw, those in parts of rural Hertfordshire were thus able to increase the family income substantially.

Despite mechanisation in the middle of the nineteenth century, straw plaiting continued to expand until 1871 with 45,000 workers altogether, 93% of whom were women.

Cheap imports of straw plait from China and Japan in the 1870s resulted in a fall in numbers of one third in one decade. They halved again in the 1880s. Part of this decline may have been due to the introduction of compulsory schooling. By 1910 rewards were derisory and there were very few left in the industry.

In the early 20th century milk could be purchased from the Briant family at Vine Cottage (30 Lower Green), which was then part of Crown Farm. After they left, the house was taken over by the Shadbolt family who ran a coal round and farmed a few acres

Barton's milk cart

including Cannons Meadow and the adjoining fields.

Milk delivery was first started in the village by two firms in Burnham Green, C. Burgess who had a farm at the top of White Horse Lane and Mr and Mrs Andrews who ran their business from a bungalow in Orchard Road. They soon had to compete with Barton's Dairy at the Marden Dairy, situated at Archers Green.

Two more milk rounds began just after the war. George Clark in School Lane and George Tebbutt at Burnham Green.

Built in 1910 by the Cowper Estate, in its day the dairy at Archers Green was what we would call *'state of the art'*, with standings for sixty milking cows, loose boxes for calves of various ages and a miniature railway track to carry trucks when mucking out. Barton's first began deliveries in Welwyn Garden City in 1927 under the slogan *'Barton's Health Tonic'*.

Petrol rationing during the war years meant that all dairies had to deliver in designated areas and it was not until the 1950s that this practice was scrapped, so it was only then that Barton's was able to start a milk round in Tewin.

By this time both the Burgess and Andrews Dairies had been swallowed up by the A1 Dairies, (later to become part of Express Dairies). Barton's was later sold to Braziers of Watford who still use the Marden Dairy buildings as a dry dairy.

Running alongside the river Maran (Mimram), from Kings Bridge to Archers Green, were the watercress beds, producing in their hey-day, large quantities of top quality cress. Fed primarily by three bore-holes each 110 feet deep, and one or two springs lower down the system, the water reached the surface at a constant 12 degrees centigrade, making ideal conditions for growing. The cress beds were rented

from the Panshanger Estate in the 19th century by John Hatton who had a small holding on the Upper Green and then in the 20th century by Basil Welch and his son Howard. They employed a small force of local labour, including Alfred Welch, a brother, and Frank and Harry Shadbolt. Much of the produce was sent to Covent Garden, Spitalfields and Southend, while a little was supplied to the greengrocers of Hertford. Later tenants have been a Mr Moule of Stanstead Abbots and a Mr Ginger who also had beds at Widford and in Norfolk.

When it closed on the death of Mr Ginger it was sold and became a trout farm, rearing trout from fry to fish of over 1lb. As in the case of the watercress beds, the water quality was conducive to such an enterprise.

Later it was used purely as a retail outlet for the sale of imported koi carp and other exotic fish, until it was finally closed in 2006.

The Mimram was also able to run a mill, known at least since 1086 and mentioned in the Domesday Book, (see chapter 2).

The first recorded Police Constable was George Clarke in 1886, followed in 1906 by Charles Gooch and PC Reeves, (see below).

Since then Boston Compton, George Leeds, (his wife Molly was the cub mistress for a number of years), Stanley Darton, Vince Micaleff and Brian Luker have all held office.

David Bond was the last village policeman before Tewin fell under the jurisdiction of Hertford and Welwyn Garden City. Although, from 1758 to 1798, for the purposes of militia duty John Ward and Theophilus Thurrowgood were listed as PCs.

Other Tewin village police taken from the list compiled at the 2000 History of Tewin exhibition included James Hart 1881, Frank Turner, Tony Moir, Janet Smith and Graham McCrone.

In the 1940s PC Reeves was Tewin's village policeman. He was previously with the London Metropolitan Police Force, and received a medal for bravery for saving a woman's life in a fire.

149

1881 Census Occupations

Agriculture

Agricultural workers during the late 19ᵗʰ century.

At the time of the 1881 census the majority of the working population living in Tewin, were agricultural labourers, a total of 88 being registered. The youngest ones aged nine and eleven years old, were the grandsons of a family named Fordham who lived in Upper Green.

One of the two twelve-year-olds employed as agricultural labourers was Robert Ephgrave, a family name that continues in the village to this day. Other familiar names in this group are Brand, Tyler, Shadbolt and Chalkley.

Whilst their sons worked as labourers, George Brand, was a bailiff. James Ephgrave was a woodman; in one family of Shadbolts, Arthur Shadbolt was a gardener and in a family of Tylers, William Tyler worked as a cowman.

Tewin had nine farmers in total and their land ranged from 583 acres at Tewin Bury Farm to the 34 acres farmed by the miller.

Two of the nine farmers were female. One was a 63-year-old widow who farmed at Queen Hoo Hall and the other, aged 79, farmed Hunts Farm.

Three farmers were born locally with the rest being incomers from as far away as Scotland and Leeds.

Other jobs on the land were that of gamekeeper (2) woodman (2) cowman (5) shepherd (5) and a watercress grower.

Service

Thirty-three people were registered as being in domestic work with twenty-seven of them being born outside the area, from Scotland to Dorset.

The largest employer of domestic servants (11) was Richard Hoare, an East India Company Merchant who lived at Marden Hill Mansion. He employed a butler, footman, cook and coachman as well as a head nurse and governess for his children who were aged 15, 13 and 5 years old. In addition there was a lady's maid, a kitchen and a scullery maid, a nursery maid and an under house-maid.

Shopkeepers

Several shopkeepers are registered as living in Tewin at the time of the census. They include a butcher. a baker, a blacksmith, a brewer, a draper, a grocer and a greengrocer. It is not known if these shops were all in Tewin itself.

There were two public houses *The Rose & Crown* and *The Plume of Feathers.*

Professional and Skilled occupations

Living in the village was a policeman. a rector and curate, 2 teachers and 2 wheelwrights. There was also a dressmaker, a carpenter, a bricklayer and a clerk.

Only 2 people are registered as unemployed. One a road surveyor, the son of the widow at Queen Hoo Hall, and the other a domestic servant.

Tewin occupations extracted from the 1901 Census

The following extract of occupations retains the wording recorded in the census and therefore a number of people who obviously carry out the same work may have their occupation described slightly differently. Occupations held by females are marked (f).

Agriculture (63)
Agricultural Labourer (10)
Cowman - Labourer on Farm
Cowman on Farm (5)
Dairyman
Dealer in Cattle
Farm Labourer (10)
Farm Labourer - Horse Keeper
Farm Manager
Farm Stockman
Farmer (6)
Farming with brother
Foreman on Farm
General Farm Labourer
Horse Keeper on Farm (5)
Horseman on Farm

House Keeper on Farm
Ordinary Agricultural Labourer
Ploughman on Farm (3)
Retired Farmer
Stockman on Farm (4)
Shepherd on Farm (2)
Waggoner on Farm
Watercress Labourer
Watercress Man (2)
Worker in fields (f)

Baking (2)
Baker
Journeyman Baker

Blacksmith (4)
Blacksmith (3)
Shoeing Smith

Bricklaying (5)
Bricklayer (2)
Bricklayer's Labourer (3)

Carpenter (2)

Corn Milling (6)
Carman for Corn Miller
Corn Miller
Corn Miller - Manager
Flour Miller (2)
Miller at Flour Mill

Clergyman of the Church of England
Companion (f)
Domestic Help/Servants (30)
Charwoman (f)
Coachman - Domestic (2)
Domestic Servant (f) (2)
Footman
General Servant - Domestic (f) (3)
Groom (4)
Houseboy
House Keeper (f) (3)
Housemaid (f) (9)
Kitchenmaid (f)
Scullerymaid (f) (2)
Washerwoman (f)

Forestry (13)
Forester of Woods
Labourer - Woodman (4)
Labourer in Woods
Woodman (6)
Woodman - Labourer

Gamekeeping (3)
Gamekeeper (2)
Rabbit & Mole Catcher

Above: **Tewin-born in 1855, gamekeeper J. Matthews was the son of the head keeper for Earl Cowper on the Panshanger estate and was given the rare accolade of being featured on the front page of** *The Gamekeeper* **in November 1900. At this time he was head keeper at Balls Park in Hertford. He was the brother of Hertford police officer Michael Robins' great-grandmother, Anna, who was also born on Lower Green, Tewin, (in 1857). Rosemary Robins discovered the cutting when researching the family history and brought it to an Apple Day at Tewin Orchard.**

Joe Baldwin continues the tradition of ferreting rabbits. This humane and efficient method of management uses a natural predator in the burrows and the rabbits are caught in nets. He is seen in 2009 at his home in School Lane.

Gardening (23)
Foreman Gardener - Fruit & Plants
Garden Boy
Gardener - Domestic (2)
Gardener - not Domestic (8)
Head Gardener & Bailiff
Journeyman Gardener (2)
Labourer in Gardens - not Domestic (6)
Retired Gardener
Working Gardener
Labouring (16)
General Labourer (11)
Labourer (2)
Labourer - Stoker in engine room for electrical lighting to Mansion
Occasional Labourer (Pensioner on Lord Cowper's Estate)
Navvy
Manufacturing (8)
Carriage Maker
Joiner & Cabinet Maker
Labourer in Beehive Factory
Mechanical & Electrical Engineer
Packer in Beehive Factory (2)
Piano Manufacturer
Secretary British Cake & Oil Mills (Male aged 48 - probably Company Secretary)
Parish Clerk
Shops/Services (14)
Deliverer of letters (f)
Dressmaker (f)
Grocer - Shopkeeper & Village Post Office (f)
Itinerant Greengrocer
Letter carrier (f)
Licensed Victualler
Linen Draper (f) (aged 81)
Needlewoman (f)
Overseer General Post Office, London
Police Constable
Publican & Farmer
Small Sweet Shop Keeper
Telegraphist in Village Post Office (f)
Trained Nurse
Teaching (4)
Infant School Mistress (f)
Organist & Teacher of Music & Asst. Overseer
School Teacher (f) (2)
Transport (6)
GNR Platelayer
Railway Gateman
Roadman (4)

Wheelwright
A total of 203 residents with occupations listed.

Boundary of the Enumeration District:
On N. by line drawn from Infant School near Burnham Green, along N. boundary of Punchetts Wood, to S. boundary of Grove Wood & Nicholsons Wood. Then direct S. by W. side of Barbers Close, W. side of Symonds Wood, along N. boundary of Park Wood & Beales Wood, along E. boundary of Bacons Green to N.W. corner of Hooks Bushes & proceeding S. across Welwyn Rd. to Poplar Grove. Then W. across Cole Green Road, by S boundary of Henry Wood to Attimore Hall, then along G N Railway to Gutteridge Grove, then full N. to Black Fan Well, across Welwyn Rd. along W. side of Tewin Water, and N. to Burnham Green Infant School.

Contents of Enumeration District:
The whole of Tewin Parish, including so much of Burnham Green as is within the same, Upper Green, Lower Green, Marden Hill, Tewin Water, Tewin Hill, Tewin Mill, Tewin Bury, Mount Pleasant, Attimore Hall, Grubb's Barn, Poplars Green, Nanceybury, Queen Hoo Hall, Tewin Rectory, Tewin Gate, High Wood, Green Wood, Black Fan and Archers Green.

Houses: 105 Inhabited, 5 Uninhabited.
Persons: 260 Males, 232 Females, Total 492.

Occupations in Tewin at the end of Twentieth Century
After the Second World War life in the village began to change. The estates were sold and the farmland bought by the tenant farmers. The skills that were dependant on the land and estates, such as the blacksmith's, were no longer required. People could go further afield to shop and obtain services such as the cobbler, the draper or the baker and these shops and services closed.

More particularly, Tewin was a convenient distance for those who worked in Hatfield or Welwyn Garden City, or commuted to London via Welwyn North Station. By the year 2000 the village had expanded to around 565 households and the occupations for those living in the village were extraordinarily varied and exciting. Few people still worked on the land but some were involved in farming, horticulture and the food industry. Although only one was a farmer, several described themselves as being gardeners, both landscape and maintenance, and tree surgeons.

The retired folk include a former gamekeeper, crop consultant and a seed merchant. There were many occupations in the food industry, a butcher, baker, fishmonger, caterer, chef, milk roundsperson, a restaurant owner, two publicans and an hotelier.

A significant number of people now work from home and are listed on the Tewin Business page of the village website. Their occupations are varied from photographer to beautician, pond design and maintenance to public relations.

Other occupations reflect local industry which is still there or which has closed in recent years. For example there are a number of retired aeronautical engineers and other jobs associated with the former De Havillands (later British Aerospace) at Hatfield. There are people who do research in the scientific or pharmaceutical industries in Welwyn Garden City. The growth of the automotive industry in the twentieth century is seen in that there was a garage proprietor, vehicle examiner and auto sales and marketing person. There were also a number of drivers including HGV, taxi, chauffeur and fork truck in the village.

Other aspects of life in the twenty-first century are listed here: Financial sector: there are people in banking, insurance, credit control, accountancy, foreign exchange dealing, equity trading, stock broking, actuarial services, payroll and book-keeping, with advisors on tax, business development, pensions and reinsurance.

STILL ROCKING: Marty Wilde in action; *inset,* a young Marty   (s)

The medical, caring and nursing professions are well represented. As well as carers, childminders and au pairs, looking after the young, old, and infirm, there are a whole range of nurses, SRN, Macmillan, and District. There are dentists, GPs, occupational therapists, a paediatrician, orthopaedic surgeon, health visitor and anaesthetist, and those supporting the Health Service, such as home care and primary care managers, a medical secretary, and a medical device specialist.

Education: The village has a nursery assistant and nursery teacher, playgroup leader, lecturers at college and university, schoolteachers, and coaches. Supporting them are school cleaners, and midday supervisors. Adult education includes English as a foreign language, yoga, music and art teachers.

Perhaps the most surprising occupations are those in the field of the arts, media, sport and entertainment businesses. Tewin has its own TV sports reporter and radio researcher. There are professionals in badminton, golf, motor racing, motor racing management and football, as well as a polo horse trainer, sports promoter and tennis coach.

A well known pop star from the 1950s, Marty Wilde, has made his home in Tewin since the 1960s. Other people in the entertainment business include musicians, a dancer, an actor, an actress, and a singer. Other artistic people include a soft furnishings advisor, a textile conservator, dressmaker, interior designer and antique restorer.

Tewin has many writers with published authors and journalists, a publisher, book binders, map historians, graphic artists and designers, photographers and illustrators and our own quiz master. There are also antique and art dealers, architects and a sculptor.

As a reflection of the changes in technology in the modern world, there are a number of people who work in information technology. They describe themselves as IT/computer analysts, consultants, engineers, managers, operators, programmers, project managers, software technicians and trainers.

Tewin often has building works in progress around its estates. It is unsurprising therefore to find amongst its residents a builder, bricklayer, carpenter, plumber, electrician, and two fencing contractors. Associated occupations include a chartered surveyor, estate agent, plus many types of engineers including building services, civil and structural.

The largest group of the listed occupations are in administrative, managerial or office work. These include local and central government officers, press,

153

public relations, marketing and sales, secretarial, human resources/personnel, company chairmen, directors and a company secretary, receptionist, recruitment and general assistants.

Other service industries are represented by a fire fighter, hairdresser, telephone engineer, postman, librarian, embalmer, cleaner, pilot, stewardess, shop owners, managers, and assistants, and Tewin's own cattery, which has been here since just after the War. Only one railway worker (a retired signalman) is listed, and a retired lighthouse engineer has chosen to live his last years in Tewin, rather a long way from the sea!

Tewin has a share of people associated with the law: policemen, a security officer, lawyers, solicitors, a patent agent and a trademark attorney, a court usher, a registrar and a probation officer have all made their homes here.

Finally there are other scientists and engineers essential to the modern world: a geologist, zoologist, chemist, physicist, microbiologist, metallurgist, petroleum engineer and oil company managers. Nor would the village be complete without its own Life Peer.

A wonderful mixture of people from all walks of life, many parts of the British Isles and elsewhere, and of all ages.

Whilst we have many retired people here, there are also young families in the village and a fair mix of people in their 40s and 50s.

Inns, Pubs and Alehouses

'Forasmuch as His Highness the Lord Protector of the Commonwealth' (Carrington wrote) *'hath taken special note of the mischief's and great disorders which are daily committed in Taverns, Inns and Alehouses...and the justices of this county of Hertford are enjoyned to take special care for the effectual suppressing of all such Alehouse Keepers as are or shall be convicted of the prohibition of the Lords Day by receiving into their houses any company or of swearing, drunkenness, suffering tippling, gaming or playing at tables...etc or any other games!!!'*

Pubs do not seem to have played a significant part in Tewin's history, but probably no less than any other village that was not on a major coaching route and later bypassed by the railway. The two pubs in the village today have both been here for centuries and are much the same size that they were when they were built perhaps five hundred years ago.

The Rose and Crown, as we know it today, is thought to have been built in about 1650 on the front of an older building that stood on the site and which now forms part of the present kitchens.

One of the first times it is mentioned is in an agreement of sale in 1730 when it was sold by one Samuel Pryor of Nast Hyde to Richard Warren of Marden for £500. This is the same Richard Warren who later was to assist John Carrington to take the tenancy of Bacons Farm and who named Carrington, as an executor of his will. In 1791 Carrington's son

The Rose and Crown pictured in the early 1900s.

Top: *The Rose and Crown* pictured recently.
Middle: **Eliza Austin and Agnes at the door of what was then called *The Feathers Inn*, c1900, (via Michael Creasey).**
Below: *The Plume of Feathers* c2002.

Jack took the tenancy of *The Rose and Crown* and was there until 1833. Carrington tells frequently of visiting *'son Jack's'* and of the many meals eaten there.

A Tewin estate bailiff gave a dinner at *The Rose & Crown* including *'a fine Turkey wt 18 pounds' and pork and greens. This was followed by 'Roley polley in the parler'* a game of skittles apparently not the pudding.

As with many local pubs *The Rose and Crown* would have run a small farm or smallholding in conjunction with its main business of selling alcohol so the food would have been very locally produced, in fact many of the subsequent landlords often described themselves as *'Publican and Farmer'*.

Below are the first two verses of a highly derogatory poem to the *'cloth'* that hung behind the bar of *The Rose and Crown* certainly at least until 1913.
'Money! Oh, money thy praises I sing.
Thou art my saviour, my God and my King,
'tis for thee that I preach and for thee that I pray
and make a collection on each Sabbath day.
I have candles and all sorts of dresses to buy,
for I wish you to know that my church is called high;
I don't mean the structure of steeple or wall, but so
high that the Lord cannot reach it at all.'

Very little is known about the origins of *The Plume of Feathers* but it is probable that it was first built in about 1500 or even earlier. However, like *The Rose and Crown* it figures quite often in Carrington's diary, and he tells us that the landlord at that time was Joseph Whittenbury, one of the Whittenburys of Queen Hoo Hall, another of whom had been involved in the killing of the footpad Walter Clibbon in 1782.

A report in the Times on 25th October 1837 told of the murder of William Bennett. His body was taken to *The Plume of Feathers* for identification. See a longer report of the incident on page 236.

Also on the Upper Green at one time was Brown's Ale House, but where it was is impossible to tell. The only reference is again from Carrington dated 14th April 1766.

Allotments in Tewin
The first allotments in Tewin, certainly being worked in the 1920s and 1930s, were situated on the present site of Harwood and Godfries Close on land known locally as Garden Field. The entrance was opposite *The Rose and Crown*. They were very large plots, keeping many families in vegetables.

155

The Chalkley family ran the allotments on land rented from Walter Hale who farmed at Tewin Hill. Charles Chalkley ran a greengrocers business at the allotments selling produce from a wooden shed on the site. He also kept pigs, chickens and rabbits and lived in a cottage on Lower Green in what was called the Alley, by the blacksmith's forge. The pigs were killed on the allotments and hung on the walnut tree in the cottage garden before being cut up and sold.

After the Second World War as people gave up their allotments Mr Chalkley took them over to keep them going. He sold the produce at Hertford, Hitchin and other local markets and also took it to London.When he became too old to continue he sold the part of the allotments, which he then owned, to Mr David Hale of Tewin Hill Farm and eventually the land was developed into Harwood and Godfries Close in 1971/2.

At the Victorian school building on Lower Green there were small plots where the boys were taught gardening and vegetables were grown and used for school lunches.

New allotments were later started in the late 1970s on land next to the new Tewin Cowper School building in Cannons Meadow. There were about

Above: Left to right. **Mr. Ambrose, Derek Compton and 'Winnie' Churchill, 1978**
Middle:**Tewin garage 2000**
Below: **Derek Compton serving a customer in the 1970s.**

forty plots. They nearly closed in the mid 1990s due to declining support but in recent years their popularity has increased and there is now a waiting list in operation. The growing interest in organic gardening is well represented and some plots are used for flowers, a wildlife pond and for rearing chickens.

Tewin Garage

Built in late 1920s the garage originally consisted of one building built for George Allen and William Gamble.

In the 1930s it was sold to George Ambrose and George Clarke. By 1939 George Ambrose had bought George Clarke's share in the garage when the latter went into the R.A.F.

A second building was added in the late 1950s using concrete beams taken from prefabricated buildings used by the R.A.F. Vehicle Reserve Unit based at Marden Hill, (adjacent to the Tewin-Hertford Road) during World War II.

David and Chris Knight purchased the garage in 1987 and in 2007 the garage closed down and was sold to Welwyn Associates.

Tewin Stores

At one time The Old Bakery, No 16 and Cheyne Cottage were a single property called The Long House. Later, when they were owned by Peter Howells, they were separated, and in the 1970s, the Old Bakery and No 16 were converted back into one house. By the late 1970s they had returned to their present state. The shop housed the bakery and was owned by the resident of the present 'Old Bakery' house.

Shop Owners 1930s / 40s
Len Moulden was the owner and, at that time, the general store was very small. Most of the space was devoted to a tea room where a cycling club met regularly on Sunday afternoons. They left their cycles in the yard to the left of the existing shop (now No. 20 Hertford Rd). A door lead from the yard into the tea room on the east wall of the shop. On his retirement Len had No. 22 Hertford Rd built. The shop passed to Mr and Mrs Neale in the late 1940s.

1950s / 70s
Miss Farrow owned the shop and continued with the tea room. She moved away in the early 1960s. It was then owned by Jim and Ethel Forsyth until the early seventies and later Peter Howells. The shop was then sold to Dick Gale and in 1978 he sold it to John Barham from Freezywater.

1981/2009
Roger Temple took over the shop in 1981. From April 2000, the owner was Peter Cole. On 21st February 2008 Tewin Stores was officially re-opened by Roger Temple as a community shop. Generous grants from the *Friends of Tewin* and Ian Toye of the Village Retail Association were acknowledged. The shop is now run by volunteers from the village.

Left: **Tewin Stores at Christmas time c2005.**
Above: **The familiar face of Roger Temple 'over the counter' in Tewin Stores.**

157

Chapter 11

Natural History

Tewin Nature Trails, Nature Reserves, Orchards and Countryside

The first *Tewin Nature Trail Guide* was produced by the Tewin Society in 1976/77, but there is such a well appointed structure of actively enjoyed footpaths and bridleways in and around the Parish that all are nature trails in their own right.

The 1987 edition of the Guide explains that new elms had been planted that year along the concrete path below Dawley Woods. Perhaps the most dramatic alteration to the appearance of the countryside, especially marked in the centre of the village, was the loss of the great elms due to 'Dutch Elm Disease'. This fungal infection which is transmitted via the elm bark beetle came in imported wood from Canada, but the scientists who identified the problem were in Holland and the title *Dutch Elm Disease* was used. The beautiful, tall trees, typical of

so many English villages, disappeared within twenty years after starting to show dead boughs in the early 1970s. Ironically, there are probably more elms in our hedgerows now than ever before as the young trees grow in profusion without the hindrance of shade, from spreading underground root systems, but they only achieve 10-20 years of maturity before succumbing to the disease.

Thanks to Green Belt protection, the nature reserves established in Tewin are linked to each other by open countryside. The valley of our river, the Mimram (see Chapter 2), is singled out especially in planning considerations as being of very high landscape and natural history value. An attractively illustrated appraisal of the lower valley, *Welwyn to Panshanger Park,* was prepared by the Tewin Society and Tewin Parish Council in an undated document from about 1992. It does not deal directly with the importance of the valley to wildlife, but gives valuable advice to

158

planners on the 'substantial scenic value and historic significance' of the area and includes reference to the mansions and park landscapes which distinguish the area.

There is also a quotation from E M Forster's 'Howards End' (1910): *'Over Tewin Water it was day. To the left fell the shadow of the embankment and its arches; to the right Leonard saw up into Tewin Woods and towards the church, with its wild legend of immortality...Over all the sun was streaming, to all the birds were singing, to all the primroses were yellow, and the speedwell blue,...'*

Although there are sites for orchids throughout the village, these rare indicators of ancient, 'unimproved' grassland habitats are most frequent in the Mimram valley, where, in the pastures near South Lodge and Tewin Mill, there have been years when over 300 Southern Marsh orchids have appeared amongst the grasses. Through management agreements with the Wildlife Trust, the pastures of Tewin Bury around the reserve and east to Archer's Green are managed by Longhorn cattle that are moved from field to field to maintain the grassland conditions needed for the continued presence of the richest diversity of flora. From this follows the invertebrate and vertebrate diversity.

Dr John Dony included Dawley Warren in Tewin in his landmark *Flora of Hertfordshire* (1967), under The Lea Valley Region (map 7) and noted that chalk

Previous page: **Bluebells in Tewin Wood in 2009** Below left: **Dawley Warren in 1968, showing the chalk outcrop where the Tewin Beaker was found and part of Dr Dony's 1967 survey of the wild flowers took place; path to Dawley Woods, showing the remnants of Margery Wood** (left) **and Workhouse Wood** (right) **which were grubbed up in the early 1960s.** Right: **The Nature Trail Guide.**

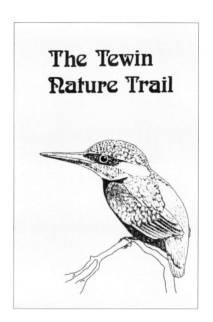

outcrops still appear as on the spoil heaps of the Welwyn tunnels and at Dawley Warren. Dawley was Habitat Study 67 *'altitude 300ft; soil Upper chalk; surveyed 20 May 1962. A large disused firing range and chalk has been brought to the surface to provide firing platforms.'* Part of the Mimram valley, it is still one of the outstanding sites in the Parish for flowers of the chalk, such as *Yellow-wort* and *Autumn Gentian,* and snails, which provided material for a workshop by Pryce Buckle for the *Hertfordshire Natural History Society* here in the 1980s.

Tewin Orchard was one of the first community orchards which combines nature reserve status (managed by *The Hertfordshire & Middlesex Wildlife Trust*) with continued fruit production by preserving the 79 year old standard fruit trees without losing their value to wildlife.

Over 1000 visitors a year enjoy the large orchard and woodland through the evening viewing at the mammal hide which overlooks the lower field between the orchard and adjoining woodland. There are bridleways and footpaths next to the reserve which link walkers to the surrounding countryside, close to Tewin Hill Farm and Upper Green.

The tall Bramley apple trees and stand of Conference pears are a feature and volunteers enjoy fruit picking in advance of the Apple Days at which fruit, juice and information is given alongside related stalls, demonstrations and entertainments for visitors. All money raised on the reserve is spent in maintaining the hide and reserve generally, as well as planting new trees and managing the old specimen types.

159

Tewin Orchard 1931: 9 acres of apples as standards or cordons; fi acre standard pears planted.			
Block A apples 20ft apart	184	Worcester Pearmain	main plant
	23	Early Victoria	pollinators
	174	Ellison's Orange	fillers
Cordon B apples 7ft apart	324	Ellison's Orange	in rows 4.8,12,16
	1944	Cox's Orange Pippin	
	243	James Grieve	pollinators in rows 2,6,10,14, 18,21,24,27,30
Block C1 apples 18ft apart	150	Laxton Superb	
	18	James Grieve	pollinators
	76	James Grieve	fillers
Block C2 apples 18ft apart	128	Bramley Seedling	
	16	Monarch	pollinators
Block D apples 18ft apart	84	Monarch	
	13	Bramley Seedling	pollinators
	1	Newton Wonder	(in front garden)
Block E apples/pears 15ft apart	144	Laxton Superb	
	24	Grenadier	
	32	Cox's Orange Pippin	
	2	Laxton Superb pears	
Block F pears/apples	71	Conference	
	19	Laxton Superb pear	
	7	Jules Guilot & Laxton Superb	pollinators
	2	Piecose de Trevant	pollinators
	1	Fertility	pollinator
	39	Ellison's Orange apple	fillers
	1	James Grieve apple	filler

Total apples and pears picked at Tewin Orchard. Bushels for apples in brackets, 1943 -1948:					
1943	**1944**	**1945**	**1946**	**1947**	**1948**
74,062 (33)	80,750 (36)	95,081 (42)	82,244 (37)	179,356 (80)	82,886 (37)
733 pears	2399 pears	4023 pears	1948 pears	1670 pears	5188 pears
Total apple trees in orchard: c5000 with 3,500 of these in the cordons. c100 pears					

Tewin Orchard has been featured in three modern books on orchards and fruit: *The Common Ground Book of Orchards* (2000); *Apples - a Field Guide* (2003) and *Orchards Through the Eyes of an Artist* (2005). The mammal hide, first constructed by the *Hertfordshire & Middlesex Badger Group* in 1989, was replaced in 2006 by a new hide paid for by the Heritage Lottery Fund - funding which the *Hertfordshire & Middlesex Wildlife Trust* secured for 12 of its most important nature reserves. Apple Days began in 1990 at Covent Garden where Tewin Orchard's natural un-sprayed fruit sold out at what was Common Ground's first ever such event. The 21 October became National Apple Day and annual events have been held here and at centres throughout Hertfordshire.

Molly Hopkyns, who ensured the orchard's survival as a

Above: **Bruce & Susan Tyler's study of Molly Hopkyns, (right), with the Tewin Orchard livestock. Annie Perry is feeding one of the horses with a visitor on the left. Planted in 1931, the Orchard had up to 16 horses stabled there.** Below right: **Oil painting of a corner of the garden by Molly, (Florence Mary), who was an accomplished landscape and portrait painter. She studied at the Slade School of Art and continued to paint after taking over the management of the Orchard from her father in 1949.**

nature reserve in her will after her death in 1982, would be pleased to know that her wishes have been carried out. Her father William Stenning Hopkyns returned to England from work as a civil servant in India and had the 5000 apple and pear trees planted out as standards and cordons in 1931.

As well as the general visitors and volunteers who attend the work days, there are school study visits and many talks have been given based on the orchard. The site has a long history in the Hopkyns' family and Stenning (as he was addressed in letters from his relatives) bought the land from an uncle.

Tewin Orchard Fruit Summary
The information on the facing page here is taken from two sheets of pencil notes kept by Molly Hopkyns. The Hopkyns family had owned land in Tewin from the Victorian era.

The remarkable increase in the crop in 1947 when the trees were well into their prime years for production, at 16 years, was probably the result of

The Millennium Orchard is next to the
footpath linking Back Lane with the farm
fields to the rear of Muspatt's Farm. The
three plantings of UK fruit that made up the
Millennium Orchards in Tewin were opened
by the then Lady Salisbury. After the event
Lady Salisbury was pictured watching
Martin Hicks demonstrating apple pressing.
One of the local varieties established at this
time was, above, the Hitchin Pippin.

Some scenes at Tewin Orchard: the long pond, 1996, one of a number of orphan deer (a Roe kid in this case) reared with the help of a Jack Russell foster mother, 'apple bobbing' by Angela Kourik and cider tasting on Apple Days, and a Great Spotted Woodpecker by Les Borg, who used to take many pictures from hides in the Orchard.

163

the very cold weather conditions of the previous months, followed by floods. This exceptional winter would have meant that many more fruit buds were set. Twice as many apples as usual were picked. (Pears seemed to benefit in the following season).

The notes in pencil are the only surviving record of crops because most of Molly's diaries and papers were destroyed following her death in 1982 on the instructions of the family beneficiaries of her will. A

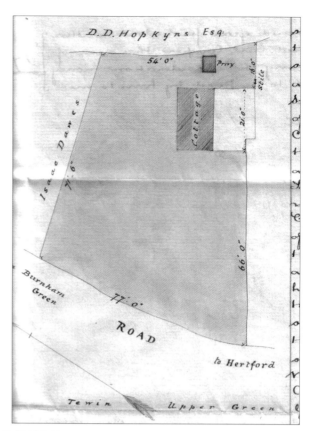

1954 log book also survives. She gave the Orchard to *The Royal Society for the Protection of Birds* and it is managed (under a 99 year lease from the RSPB) by the *Hertfordshire & Middlesex Wildlife Trust*.

Several other orchards are recorded in Tewin:

Sewells Orchard with just one old Bramley in the hedgerow of 108 Orchard Road side possibly surviving from the original trees. New plantings have been made in the Millennium Orchards scheme in Linda Adams' garden here at 106 Orchard Road.

Hunt's Farm Orchard across the road from Upper Green where there was also a very large pond (filled in long after the farm buildings were levelled to leave no trace of the barns and house).

The Coles' Orchard (see page 226) where Geoffrey de Havilland lodged at Orchard House, 51 Upper Green, close to *The Plume of Feathers,* and old trees survive well in David and Felix Green's garden.

Seven Acres where a few old trees still exist.

Crown Farm and to the field side of Churchfield Cottages where there was a poultry farm.

Orchards were associated with the farms at Tewin Hill, Warrengate and Tewin Bury, where you can still see trees, with others at Tewin Mill and Marden House. The original Tewin House is shown with an orchard - the latter's location is uncertain, but was probably to the north of the walled garden.

Patrick and Valerie Loughrey of Sevenacres, who manage their fields with Aberdeen Angus cattle, gave space for the first Millennium Orchard plantings next to Back Lane, where over 40 trees are established. Children growing up in the 1950s remember the

Above right: **The 1876 location of Piggotts' Cottage, with outdoor 'privy' marked. Below: Molly Hopkyns bequeathed her orchard to be a nature reserve after her death. She is shown with the poem quoted in the text facing this page.**

large pond known as Peacock's Pond in Hunt's Farm field for its 'big' newts, the Great Crested, and other water life and its loss was mourned, although the old one adjoining Back Lane survives. It has twice been restored by volunteers in the *Tewin Society* since the 1976 drought, when Patrick Loughrey gave help with a mechanical digger. Frogs, Toads and Smooth Newts are also present in all these sites.

The Cattery cottage (see page 227) on the road next to the entrance to Tewin Orchard appears to be the

Above : **Valerie and Patrick Loughrey provided land for the largest of the Millennium Orchards and also generously sponsored much of the habitat creation at Tewin Orchard when it became a Nature Reserve. Below: Dr John Hopkyns who gave his wood to be the first Hertfordshire & Middlesex Wildlife Trust Nature Reserve in Tewin at Hazelton Bottom, later re-named Hopkyns' Wood, in 1970, (see page 167).**

oldest building on the north end of Upper Green and originally belonged to the Hopkyns family after Dawes and Jackson ownerships described on old deeds. It appears on the early 19th Century maps and was sold in 1954 in the days when it was called Rochdale Cottage. The only surviving Orchard log book records this on 16 January. Piggotts, also adjoining the orchard land, has no link with the original cottage owned by John Carrington on this site. (His ownership is shown on the Tewin Hill Farm 1803-4 and 1785-1807 maps, with his name above

the cottage). In his diary, he describes how a Partridge and Pears were cooked for an ailing farmer in his cottage here, (probably both sources of food were from Hunt's Farm when it stood next to the cottage on the other side of the bridleway), and it is rather touching that the native Partridge and Pears can still be found here to this day. The fields across to Tewin Hill Farm also have small groups of up to 30 meadow pipits present over most winters in addition to the mixed Thrush flocks. On the east side of the village, Lapwings can visit in the winter in large groups of up to 100 and clearly find the fields towards Bacon's Farm ideal for worming. As recently as the 1950s Lapwings bred throughout the parish and it was common for people to use their eggs for food.

Proof that Carrington's cottage was demolished has come through the deeds for Piggotts, kindly lent by the present owners Warren and Tracey Stipwell: the deeds indicate that his building had been replaced by 1846 and the map for 1876 shows a cottage (and outdoor 'privy') square to the present bridleway off Upper Green. By the sale of Panshanger in 1919, the map with the deeds for the sale shows no building left on the land and the growth of the ivy on the cottage in a 1929 photograph suggest it was built between 1920 and 1925. Although the cottage was altered beyond recognition later in the 1980s, the charming front door entrance remains the same.

Molly Hopkyns had a long family association with this whole area of land round the north side of Upper Green, and described a great-great uncle, H W Hopkyns as 'a Victorian painter', who wrote a poem about Tewin in 1866 which begins:

Oh, Tewin is a lonesome place
As ever yet was seen
A few small houses built around
A little village green.

By 1876, another relative of Molly's, D D Hopkyns owned the land next to the cottage on the north side and Issac Dawes owned the property to the west. By 1919 Revd T D Hopkyns' name had replaced 'D D' and H Jackson had replaced Dawes. The Rights of Way Act 1932 deposit shows the land owned by J W Hopkyns and Hunt's Farm had disappeared by then. There was a dispute over the bridleway and users had to open a series of gates to travel down to reach the fields above what is now Hopkyns' Wood, but was then Hazelton Bottom. Remnants of these gates still remain including an ancient oak post next to the Wild Garlic pit. After an acrimonious correspondence

Above: **Ramsons (or 'Wild Garlic') in Hopkyns' Wood.**
Below: **Piggotts Cottage, which replaced the original building after 1919. The porch and Cottage survives in the centre of the present building.**

between Hopkyns and the Parish Council, the right of way was finally restored without obstacles.

It seems likely that Thomas Piggott's name survived at the side of the bridleway on all cottages built on the site of Piggott's Cottage ever since his death in 1610. He was aged 70 and this is recorded with a beautiful brass memorial in St Peter's Church (see page 56). He lived in Tewin Water House, but was known to have owned other properties in the village.

Although the deeds for the land around Tewin Orchard may seem detached from the natural history of the area, the signature of Lord Desborough  reminds us of how events leading up to 1919 changed not only the social life of the countryside, but its management and treatment of wildlife. Julian Grenfell's letters (edited by Kate Thompson, 2004) and Nicholas Mosley's account of

his life and times, (1976) describe the aristocratic life at Panshanger (see pages 125-143) and how the management of the estate must have affected the wildlife of the day. Pine Martens, Polecats and several species of predatory bird became extinct in the county due to the pressure of gamekeeping on this and the other estates which almost joined up with each other across the county - always popular for its proximity to London, yet still largely rural.

Julian's *Into Battle* (see page 144) must be published in nearly every anthology of WWI poetry and he loved to hunt with dogs and horses. However, he disliked the large social shooting parties at Panshanger which were obsessed with enormous game bags and where competitive nobles sought to outdo each other by the numbers of birds felled as they fired almost continuously with two loaders either side of them passing a freshly charged gun repeatedly as the birds were driven overhead.

The feeding of game birds does, however, benefit the song birds considerably and modern management of shoots is now much more sympathetic to other species - some of the first Buzzard chicks in the modern revival of the species bred inside the Panshanger estate, next to the pheasant release pens, and now Red Kites also fly unmolested here. Birds of prey suffered from certain chemical sprays (since banned) in the 1950s and 1960s, as did Otters when water-ways were contaminated, but all have recovered well and are now present in the county again. Protection of various species is generally respected, but lapses are given considerable publicity to at least shame those involved.

The colossal changes to society and the countryside caused by WWI culminated in many alterations to the land ownership in Tewin and the sale of Piggotts was just one small part of the events of 1919 as much of Panshanger's land was disposed of. There are no known images of the orchard at Panshanger, but it is referred to in the *Country Life* articles of the day. Large areas of sand and gravel have been excavated from this old estate, with restoration planned for a number of years ahead. The British Geological Survey's map for Tewin Orchard is typical for much of the Parish and shows the underlying geology to be boulder clay over chalk, giving rise to neutral soils, whilst the wood stands on glacial sand and gravels overlying upper chalk. There is pure clay to a depth of 2m in parts of the pear orchard, for example. The soils in Hopkyns' Wood (and most of the parish woods) are typically of woodland humus. (Flints, many found fashioned as simple scraper hand-tools, are regularly seen on the surface and badgers bring large flints from the chalk rock below ground to the open air in their spoil heaps: see page 8).

It is now described in Common Ground books as *'the first orchard nature reserve in the UK'*, but when the site was being managed as a typical village 'community' orchard, the grassland around the trees was regularly grazed by up to 16 horses, geese, ducks and chickens so that windfalls would probably have been gathered up. This kept the site quite open apart from the rows of trees. After early paid-picking, harvests of the fruit gradually became replaced in the 1950s by an early form of 'pick-your-own' where a tree was 'bought' for the year, and a 'community' orchard developed where villagers paid for, cared for, and picked the fruit from their own trees, and the orchard became open for all to enjoy, with the chance to picnic and explore. The cessation of management, however, led to scrub encroachment and the neglect of the fruit trees over much of the site, although some regular customers pruned their own trees.

Historically, Hopkyns' Wood was a part of Tewin Wood, much of which has been built on in recent decades. It was gifted to the *Wildlife Trust* by Dr John Hopkyns, (Molly's cousin in Canada), to be maintained as a nature reserve from 1972. The name changed from Hazelton Bottom to Hopkyns' Wood and perpetuates the family name here. The wood has a history of management as coppice-with-standards, now long ceased. There are photographs from the 1930s which show the hornbeams being 'singled' - turned into single stem trees from the clustered coppice stools. The old pits are the legacy of sand, gravel, flint and chalk digging. (The bridleway appears to have once been a major route to Datchworth and is reinforced to considerable depth by large flints, almost certainly taken from the pits in the woods either side at the point where the track reaches its lowest level, and it probably flooded frequently here).

Although essentially a farmed habitat, ancient orchards are today recognised as very important for wildlife, similar to wood pasture, due to the mature trees with their associated invertebrates and lower plants. Great Crested newt, Song Thrush, White-letter Hairstreak butterfly, Hazel Dormice, Water Shrews, Bats and Orchids are some of the varieties of plant and animal present or recently recorded of high conservation concern that have Species Action Plans at the local or national level.

Above: **White Letter Hairstreak butterfly and Long-eared bat, both photographed at Tewin Orchard.**

Over the 40 years since the present voluntary wardens moved to the orchard the most striking changes in the bird life have been the arrival of Collared Doves (1970s), Green Sandpiper (1980s) and both Buzzards and Red Kites (1990s). Only single records of Grasshopper Warbler (1969) and Wryneck (1969) have been made; there have been irregular winter records of Woodcock including, in the spring, their roding (courtship flights); three Goshawk sightings have been made and both Sparrow-hawk and Hobby have become familiar.

167

Declines have been most marked in, initially, Tree Sparrows and later House Sparrows (as stabling and feeding of horses ceased), Turtle Doves, Willow Warblers, Swallows (which bred in the barn up to 2000) and the seed eaters. Bullfinches have recently revived, with 2 breeding pairs regularly seen now, and Goldfinch flocks have increased considerably with groups of 26 seen and nests in the orchard gardens, too. Yellow-hammer flocks (of up to 30 in the 1990s) have declined to small numbers, and they are sometimes absent now. Reed Buntings and Bramblings are occasionally present. Lesser-spotted Woodpeckers were present in the 1970s, but recorded only once in recent years (2007); Nuthatch and Tree-creeper are always present, but there have been recent dips in sightings during the 1990s, up to 2005. Blackcaps have been the first Warblers to over-winter in the orchard.

During the winter months large flocks of Fieldfares, Redwings and Blackbirds are attracted to the reserve to feed on the fallen fruit. In summer, several Warblers breed in the overgrown cordons including Willow Warbler, (absent in 2009), Whitethroat, Lesser Whitethroat, Garden Warbler and Blackcap.

The orchard management is aimed at combining nature conservation with natural fruit production. No sprays have been used on the fruit since the 1950s and plantings have been aimed at maintaining as many varieties as possible, including all Hertfordshire cultivars and others important to the region and history of fruit. The stand of Conference and Fertility pears, for example, represent Thomas Rivers' most successful types which originated from the Rivers Nursery at Sawbridgeworth. One particular Hertfordshire early dessert apple, the Hitchin Pippin, was feared lost until a broadcast from the orchard at 6.00am on a farming programme produced a contact in Kent with the last named tree (which has since died). Grafts were made and propagated in Tewin before this happened and it is now being distributed through two nurseries.

As well as the fruit trees, the orchard borders and Hopkyns' Wood are fairly typical of the woods throughout the parish: the predominant trees are Pedunculate Oak standards and Hornbeam in the form of outgrown coppice. Also present is Ash, Wild Cherry, Hazel, Field Maple, and Silver Birch. There is a very sparse shrub layer composed mainly of Blackthorn, Elder, Holly and Hawthorn. Over 33 species of vascular plants have been recorded including some indicators of ancient woodland:

Bluebell and Dog's-Mercury are well established, and Ramsons spread out from the damp pits.

Ancient trees and hedges

Very old pollarded Hornbeams at Marden Hill.

Much has been written about hedgerows over recent years, triggered no doubt by the fact that we have been through a period where we have witnessed their removal over large areas of the countryside. The reason for this was the revolution and mechanisation of farming methods that began in the early 1950s. As is often the case, when a familiar landmark is threatened, we learn to cherish it. This phase now appears to be at an end and indeed there are some positive signs that the trend may be going into reverse; this is certainly the case in our Parish.

Although our local hedgerows are very familiar to those who walk the footpaths around Tewin, we tend to take them for granted without pausing to wonder for example who planted them? How old are they? What tree species are they made up of? What wildlife do they provide a home for?

Alan Guilford carried out a survey of one of the local hedgerows and one of his favourites is the hedge that borders Dead Lane, starting in the corner of Upper Green near the pond and ending at the large Oak tree at the junction with Margery Lane. This clearly has the general appearance of an old hedgerow and comprises a rich variety of species, particularly on the southern side of the lane. The trunks of the shrubs are gnarled and twisted and at sometime in the distant past you can see that the hedge was laid - this is more visible in the winter months. The hedge is about 200 yards long and has 10 main tree species growing in it: Blackthorn, Hornbeam, Holly, Oak, Hazel, Ash, Hawthorn, Field

Maple, Elder and Wych Elm. Other 'woody climbers' are present: Wild Rose, Black Bryony, Blackberry, Honeysuckle, Hop and Ivy, but for the purpose of dating, these have to be ignored (with the exception of the Wild Rose). A typical 30m stretch was found to have 7 species in it. The results of 6 other samples taken randomly along the hedge gave consistent results; 5 samples gave the same result, ie. 7 species, with 1 sample giving 6 species.

Using a published formula, the age of the hedge can be calculated as approximately 800 years. This does seem to be a remarkable result. Even if an allowance of 200 years is made for the 'uncertainty' factor in this method, as recommended by the authority Dr. Hooper, the age could still be 600 years. However, it is possible to establish that it is at least 200 years old by reference to Yolande and Donald Hodson's wonderful collection of old maps of the Tewin area. Dead Lane is shown on a Dury and Andrews map of the county of Hertfordshire, dated 1782, (part of which is shown below). Not only is Dead Lane itself shown, but the hedgerow on the south side is also illustrated by the row of little tree symbols.

It takes a while to work out the layout of the village from the map, as Lower Green appears not to have existed at this time. However, Hertford Road and Tewin Hill are shown and these provide good landmarks. Back Lane can be seen from its junction with Lower Green, leading north-westerly to the 'cross-roads' junction with Dead Lane on Upper Green. Dead Lane, (right in the centre of the map above the lettering 'Tewin House'), leads away in a westerly direction, turning southerly into Margery Lane. It is interesting to note that the footpath (now F12) to Harmer Green might not have existed then.

Tewin House was obviously a significant dwelling in the village, set at right angles to a complex of buildings which included the rectory. The map shows the south-westerly end of Churchfield Road, but there was no river crossing here in 1782. However, the river crossings at Tewin Bury, Kings Bridge, Archers Green and Marden are visible.

It is also interesting to note that the map shows that all the surrounding fields are similarly hedged; the inference is that by 1782 Tewin had been 'Enclosed'.

Tewin's species-rich network of hedgerows has arisen in three different ways. Some, like the recently laid blackthorn hedge marking the northern boundary of St. Peter's churchyard, have been planted. Others are the result of natural colonisation along neglected

Hedgerow on Tewin Hill Farm with intermittent saplings left to grow as vital singing-posts for birds when nesting.

features such as fence-lines, ditches, banks and trackways. The third group are historic remnants of ancient (pre-medieval) semi-natural woodlands left to mark the boundaries of fields formed when the woods were grubbed out. The herb layer associated with this latter group often includes plants collectively indicative of ancient woodland such as Wood Melick, Wood Anemone, Bluebell and Dog's Mercury.

In general the more species present in a hedgerow the greater its ecological value and wildlife interest, but managed monocultures, such as the Blackthorn hedge in the churchyard, may also have a high wildlife interest. For example, many early spring insects are dependant on the Blackthorn blossom and Yellowhammers, a species of high conservation concern, are among the birds that nest in its thick cover. Hedgerows are also important for small

169

mammals. Tom Gladwin was both surprised and delighted to see a rare Hazel Dormouse in the churchyard's south hedgerow on 5 March 2003.

Hedges were managed to provide stock-proof

boundaries between pasture and crops. For this purpose they would have been trimmed once or even twice a year. Eventually, however, the trimming results in gaps appearing in the bottom and centre of a hedge. Hedge-laying, which it is thought, may have been practised as early as 57BC, not only restores the purpose of the hedge, but also revitalises it.

Spotted Orchids growing near the ancient hedgerows around Upper Green, Tewin

New growth quickly arises from the stools, and from buds along the 'pleachers', (the term for the woven branches of a layered hedge). Birds, such as the Yellowhammers already referred to, prefer this type of hedge, and soon return to continuing pleading for 'a-little-bit-of-bread-and-no-cheese'.

An inventory of Tewin's hedges which details their origin, species composition and age would surely be of immense historical and conservation value.

Birds of the Parish of Tewin
Autumn 2007 to Summer 2008

The aim of the British Trust for Ornithology's Bird Atlas 2007-11 project, which started in November 2007, is to map the distribution and abundance of birds throughout Britain. Whilst surveying the birds around Digswell as part of this project Tom and Janet Gladwin thought it would be useful to extend their walks to transect the Parish of Tewin and produce a list of birds found there at the time of the production of *The History of Tewin*.

Habitats of particular ornithological importance in Tewin are its semi-natural ancient woodlands and other deciduous areas, orchards, diverse dry and wet grasslands, and the wonderful wildlife rich mosaic of river, lake, marshland and wet grassland along the Mimram valley. Intensive agriculture has greatly reduced the wildlife value of arable land and, particularly in winter, many birds and other animals forage in gardens where they are often supplied at bird tables and other feeding stations. Thus these and other green habitats within the village boundary are of great conservation value.

The list that follows, compiled in June 2009, is intended to provide a reference against which future changes might be determined and evaluated.

Other species may occur as rare migrants or vagrants. It is amalgamated with the list compiled of the birds recorded at Tewin Orchard.

Mute Swan	Resident. Two breeding pairs along the Mimram.
Greater Canada Goose	Resident. Several breeding pairs along the Mimram.
Gadwall	Occasionally seen in winter on Tewin Water Lake.
Common Teal	Occasional winter visitor to the Tewin Bury Reserve.
Mallard	Resident but declining. Pairs breed in most wet habitats.
Common Pochard	Occasionally seen in winter on Tewin Water Lake.
Tufted Duck	Small numbers winter at Tewin Water and the Tewin Bury Reserve. Two to three pairs breed.
Red-legged Partridge	Greatly declined resident population. A few breeding pairs only.
Grey Partridge	A once common species now rarely seen.
Pheasant	Common. Reared locally for shooting.
Little Grebe	Resident. Three breeding pairs along the Mimram in 2008.
Little Egret	One of the most recent species to colonise and breed in Britain. One to five regularly seen feeding by the Mimram in winter.
Grey Heron	Small numbers feed along the Mimram, and occasionally at garden ponds, throughout the year. Has bred in the Panshanger area.
Red Kite	Increasingly observed over Tewin. A pair, presumably from the successful releases in the Chilterns, bred in 2008 and 2009.
Eurasian Sparrow-hawk	Resident. A small number of pairs breed. Regularly appears hunting in gardens especially where there are feeding stations.
Goshawk	Seen displaying in recent summers. Probably breeds.

Common Buzzard	In recent years this species has expanded its national range eastwards and now breeds in the county. A pair bred just outside the parish boundary in 2007 and 2008. Now regularly observed over Tewin. A pair attempted to breed within the parish in 2008 and succeeded in 2009.
Common Kestrel	Observed in all months. One, possibly two, pairs breed.
Eurasian Hobby	Occasionally seen in most summers. Breeding in Tewin 2009.
Water Rail	A skulking winter visitor in small numbers more often seen at Tewin Water and in the Tewin Bury Reserve, but also recorded at Tewin Orchard.
Common Moorhen	Common resident. Breeds on ponds and along the Mimram.
Common Coot	Resident. Four breeding pairs along the Mimram in 2008.
Northern Lapwing	Winter visitor and passage migrant feeding on farmland. Numbers usually small, but some flocks of 60+ birds on Tewin Hill Farm.
Eurasian Woodcock	Occasionally seen in wet woodland sites. No longer breeds here.
Common Snipe	Winter visitor in small numbers in the Mimram valley.
[Green Sandpiper	Formerly a winter visitor along the Mimram. Not seen in recent years.]
Black-headed Gull	Common, sometimes abundant, winter visitor and passage migrant feeding and loafing on arable.
Mew Gull (or Common Gull)	Common winter visitor and abundant spring migrant.
Lesser Black-backed Gull	Small numbers seen in all months. Often observed passing overhead, especially during passage periods when it is most numerous, or feeding and loafing on arable.
Herring Gull	Winter visitor and passage migrant in varying and decreasing numbers.
Great Black-backed Gull	Occasionally seen passing overhead or loafing on arable.
Feral Dove	Resident in small numbers.
Stock Pigeon (or Stock Dove)	Common resident.
Common Wood Pigeon	Abundant resident.
Eurasian Collared Dove	Common resident.
[European Turtle Dove	Once common summer visitor now rarely seen in Tewin]
Common Cuckoo	Summer visitor in small and much reduced numbers.
Barn Owl	One, possibly two, pairs present in the parish.
Little Owl	Resident. More than four breeding pairs.
Tawny Owl	Resident. Over five breeding pairs in 2009.
Common Swift	Summer visitor frequently seen overhead. Breeding status uncertain.
Common Kingfisher	Resident. At least two breeding pairs.
Green Woodpecker	A common resident often seen feeding on lawns.
Great Spotted Woodpecker	A common resident frequently observed at garden feeders.
Lesser Spotted Woodpecker	Former breeding species now rarely seen.
Sky Lark	Small numbers present in winter. A few, perhaps five, pairs bred in 2008.

Above, left to right: **Barn Owl, (now showing signs of recovery in Tewin), Tawny Owls and a Little Owl.**

Sand Martin	Seen annually during both passage periods. Former breeding sites deserted 30 years ago.
Barn Swallow	Summer visitor breeding in small numbers. Much less common than hitherto.
House Martin	Once common summer visitor now reduced to a few breeding pairs.
[Tree Pipit	Once common summer visitor. Not recorded in recent years.]
Meadow Pipit	Winter visitor (in flocks of up to 50 birds on Tewin Hill Farm), in grassland.
Grey Wagtail	Resident and winter visitor. At least two breeding pairs along the Mimram.
Pied Wagtail	Common breeding species and winter visitor.
Winter Wren	Abundant resident.
Hedge Accentor (Dunnock)	Common resident. Population decreasing in some localities.
European Robin	Abundant resident and winter visitor.
[Common Nightingale	Summer visitor that formerly bred.]
Northern Wheatear	Occasionally seen on passage especially on stony fields.
Common Blackbird	Abundant resident and winter visitor.
Fieldfare	Common, sometimes abundant, winter visitor and passage migrant.
Song Thrush	Common resident and winter visitor. Numbers recovering after a period of scarcity.
Redwing	Common, sometimes abundant, winter visitor and passage migrant.
Mistle Thrush	Fairly common resident. Population decreasing.
Sedge Warbler	Summer visitor. Small breeding population in the Tewinbury Reserve.
Eurasian Reed Warbler	Summer visitor. Small breeding population in the Tewinbury Reserve.
Blackcap	Common summer visitor and scarce winter visitor. Birds seen in winter, often in gardens, are probably from Scandinavia.
Garden Warbler	Fairly common summer visitor.
Lesser Whitethroat	Fairly common summer visitor. Less numerous than the Common Whitethroat.
Common Whitethroat	Common summer visitor.
Chiffchaff	Common summer visitor and occasional but scarce winter visitor.
Willow Warbler	Once common now scarce summer visitor. Absent in 2009.
Goldcrest	Small breeding population in coniferous plantations. and mature garden conifers.
Firecrest	Rare winter visitor.
[Spotted Flycatcher	Much declined summer visitor. Just two pairs known in 2007.]
Long-tailed Tit	Common resident.
Blue Tit	Abundant resident.
Great Tit	Abundant resident.
Coal Tit	Common resident.
[Willow Tit	Once common, now absent.]
[Marsh Tit	Once common, now absent.]
Wood Nuthatch	Resident estimated at 15+ pairs.
Eurasian Treecreeper	Resident. Present in all woods.
Eurasian Jay	Common resident.
Black-billed Magpie	Common resident.
Eurasian Jackdaw	Abundant resident and winter visitor. (Large mixed crow roost, Tewin Wood).
Rook	Common resident. One rookery.
Carrion Crow	Common resident.
Raven	Occasional sightings in 2007/08.
Common Starling	Fairly common resident. Populations increasing after a period of rapid decline.

Tewin was a village of many great elms, but most of the mature trees were lost by the late 1970s due to a fungal disease spread by bark beetles.

House Sparrow	Resident. Population much reduced and declining.
Chaffinch	A very abundant resident and winter visitor.
Brambling	Winter visitor in fluctuating numbers. High numbers occur in years of poor crops of mast in the northern beech woods.
European Greenfinch	An abundant resident.
European Goldfinch	Present all year. Common visitor to garden bird feeders.
Eurasian Siskin	Winter visitor feeding on alder seeds but often appearing at garden feeders in late winter and early spring. Numbers subject to large year to year variations. High numbers occur in years of poor spruce and pine cone crops.
Common Linnet	Present all year in very small and declining numbers.
Lesser Redpoll	An abundant breeding species 40 years ago. Now a winter visitor in usually small numbers. Has recently started appearing at garden feeding stations.
Common Bullfinch	A thinly distributed resident. Possibly increasing.
[Hawfinch	Former breeding species more often seen in Hornbeam woodland.]
Yellowhammer	Resident. Population greatly decreased. Breeding population now probably reduced to twenty or less pairs.
Reed Bunting	Winter visitor to Tewin Orchard. A few pairs breed in the Tewin Bury Reserve.
[Corn Bunting	A common breeding species 40 years ago. Probably no longer present in the parish.]

[Indicates species not seen in recent years]

Right: **Revd. Tom Gladwin and Janet Gladwin lead a moth survey under the old apple trees at Tewin Orchard.**
Below: **Autumn scene of windfall apples left for the birds under the rows of Bramleys in Tewin Orchard.**

Opposite: **The Panshanger Oak dwarfs Trevor James** (on right) **during a** *Hertfordshire Natural History Society* **field visit in 1995. In 1855 it was described as '72 feet high' and in 1893 as 'having been recently struck at the top by lightning'. A dendrologist estimated its age to be over 500 years in 1995, planted about 1477. He considered it to be the best intact oak of its age and size in England. It was never pollarded, which made it exceptional on a national level and the 18**th **century naturalist, the Revd Gilbert White, was said to have travelled to see it from his home at Selborne in Kent.**

Top left: **A tinted engraving made by T. Medland in 1814 when he felt the tree 'was at its greatest state of beauty'.**

Below left: **Postcard of the Oak sent in the post in 1928.**

Below right: **There are older oaks than the Panshanger Oak within the estate, (all originally pollarded), and the oldest, coming into leaf in May 2009, was estimated by the dendrologist to now represent nearly a thousand years of living local history.**

Chapter 12

Tewin House and Marden Hill House

Tewin House with the Sabine family.

Tewin House

The site of Tewin House lies north east of St. Peter's Church, in the field east of the church drive. Traces of the foundations remain and part of a garden wall borders the east side of the churchyard. Nearby is a large Cedar of Lebanon, once a magnificent feature of the famous garden surrounding Tewin House. Across the road are the remains of the kitchen garden walls, adjacent to Muspatt's Farm. These few remains are all that is left of the *'spacious mansion'* described in the sales particulars of 1803.

The house had an interesting history and colourful occupants. It is thought that the first house built on the site was possibly built by John Wrothe c1540. In 1571 Dr. Thomas Montford became Rector of the church, buying the patronage of the living from John Wrothe in about 1620. He also bought a capital messuage in the Warren called Tewin House from which the right of appointing clergymen to St. Peter's Church descended (the advowson).

Thomas died in 1632 and the second Tewin House *'a fine fair house by the church'* was built by his son Dr. John Montford, c1632. He is buried in the Sanctuary and is described by the Revd. A.C.Vidler as patron of the benefice. This was a turbulent time for the church. James Montford *'parson of Tewinge'* was ejected from his living in 1643. On the memorial stone of Dr. John Montford are the words *'Anno Restaurationis 1651'*. This was the year when he was restored to his right as patron of the benefice after the time of Cromwell. Clergymen were allowed to return to their benefices and use the Prayer Book on condition that they obeyed the existing government.

Dr. John Montford died in 1651 and the house then passed through a succession of owners. It was left to Richard Rainsworth, the husband of John's daughter, Mary. The house and advowson were then sold to Sir George Boteler who died childless in 1657. His cousin, Sir Francis Boteler inherited in 1663. Members of the Boteler family had held

The remains of the original walled kitchen garden can be seen at the edge of the road in School Lane. The old wall was set back from the road edge here in the early 1950s.

Standing left to right: **Parry, Bird, James Ross, John Barrow Jnr., Sabine, Baillie Hamilton, Richardson.** Seated: **Beaufort, Beechey.** All were involved with sea explorations.

distinguished positions in the court of Charles I. When Sir Francis died, his daughter Isabella inherited and sold the house to William Gore who made *'a fair addition'* to the house before his death in 1709. His nephew, Henry Gore sold it to Joseph Sabine in 1715.

It was the new owner, the Hon. Joseph Sabine who rebuilt the house in 1716 - 1718, producing one of the most elegant homes in the county.

It was said to have cost £40,000 to build and furnish. There were two storeys above a beautifully decorated and furnished ground floor. A French traveller, César de Saussure visiting in 1725 wrote *'Nothing has been spared to make this house beautiful. It possesses two rooms in particular which are really works of art. One of these is composed of the finest marbles brought expressly from Italy and Greece, and the ceiling is painted in fresco by a clever Roman painter. The second is still more beautiful being a hall or grand staircase composed of rare or precious woods in a wonderfully clever manner with tints and colours, and has succeeded in shaping them into lovely flowers, figures and landscapes, in perfect imitation of nature. When the building and furnishing of this fine house, or rather palace was finished, many persons came out of curiosity to see it. King George I under pretext of hunting visited it twice.'* Scenes from battles of the Duke of Marlborough's campaigns were painted on the walls of a third room.

The house had a hundred foot front with *'8 chambers and 2 dressing rooms on the attic storey, 4 chambers and three dressing rooms on the principal storey, a spacious hall and staircase, 2 dressing rooms, eating room and print tea room on the ground floor, and vaults and cellaring under the house. Servants' offices adjoined the house to the north and* *around the courtyard were the brewhouse, washhouse, bakery and laundry.'*

(1788 Sales particulars)

Joseph Sabine *'laid out magnificent gardens'* (Clutterbuck). There were *'garden terraces on the south side of the mansion overlooking the lovely valley of the Mimram.'* (Cussans). Sabine closed the main road from the village to the river when he created his garden. In 1717 a writ was granted to him by the Court of Chancery in London allowing him to enclose *'a highway leading from Lower Green and which went through between his little wood and gardens to the waterside for enlarging his gardens'.* As well as turning the road he also gave land to make the wide drive down to the church which was intended as compensation to the villagers for the loss of their direct route to the river.

Across the road from the house was the walled kitchen garden which is described in the sales particulars of 1788 as *'a large kitchen garden, enclosed with lofty walls, fully cloathed and planted; excellent hot house and melon pits, beautiful lawns, plantations, woods and paddock.'* In the 1803 sales particulars more details of the *'excellent kitchen garden'* are listed including the *'grapery'*, *'hot-house'* and *'numerous fruit trees'.* The east and south wall of the old garden still remain on the corner turning into School Lane.

The Sabine family were distinguished in many ways. The Hon. Joseph Sabine who built the house is commemorated by a large marble memorial erected by his widow and now situated in the south porch of St. Peter's Church. He was M.P. for Berwick and a famous soldier serving under the Duke of Marlborough which explains his choice of battle scenes from the Duke's campaigns to decorate one of

177

his rooms at Tewin House. In 1708 Sabine led the attack at the battle of Oudenarde where his brigade of Welsh fusiliers fought and defeated seven French battalions. He was rapidly promoted and by 1713 when the war ended he had attained the rank of Major General. Two years later he bought Tewin House. In 1730 he was made Governor of Gibraltar where he died in 1739. His body was brought back to Tewin for burial and his widow Margaret left money in her will for *'repairing supporting and beautifying'* the monument erected to the memory of her husband. Any surplus was to be used for *'the purchase of yellow serge or woollen stuff therewith to clothe as many poor Tewin boys as they approve...'*

The Hon. Joseph Sabine's brother, Colonel William Sabine was the second husband of Lady Cathcart of Tewin Water whose colourful story is related in chapter seven, Tewin Water House. During their marriage they lived at Tewin House.

On the death of Joseph Sabine the estate was inherited by his son, John, in 1739. He divided his time between Tewin and the family estates in Ireland. He was a colonel in the Guards, and when the Hertfordshire militia was formed in 1757 he became its colonel. He died in 1771 and was buried at Tewin. John Sabine and his family appear in a mid eighteenth century painting with Tewin House and church in the background.

When Colonel John Sabine died in 1771 his son Joseph inherited the estate. He found that the estate was so encumbered with debt that he was eventually forced to sell it. He had nine children. Two of them were famous in their fields. His youngest child, Edward (1788-1883) spent much of his childhood in Tewin and became an arctic explorer and naturalist. He was a pioneer in the observations of the earth's magnetic fields for navigation and shipping, making magnetic maps, catalogues and tables. Whilst inside the Arctic Circle on John Ross's expedition in 1818 he noticed some small Tern like dark headed gulls with forked tails and yellow tipped black bills. Several of the birds were shot and sent to his elder brother, Joseph (1770-1837), by south bound whaler. They proved to be a previously unknown and unrecorded species which, according to the custom of the time Joseph named after his brother Edward, Sabine's Gull (*Larus sabini*). The Californian Gray Pine (*Pinus sabineana*) is also named after him.

Edward was knighted in 1869, becoming a Knight Commander of the Order of the Bath. He retired from the army on full pay in 1877, by which time he had

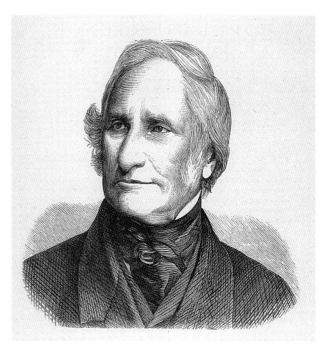

Sir Edward Sabine

achieved the rank of General.

In 1879 Sabine's wife, Elizabeth Leeves, died. An accomplished woman in her own right, she had assisted her husband in his scientific endeavours for more than half a century. Her four-volume translation of Alexander von Humboldt's monumental textbook of geophysics *Kosmos*, was published 1849-1858.

Edward was President of the Royal Society, being awarded its gold medal. Sir Edward Sabine died at East Sheen, Surrey, on 26th June 1883. He was 94 and is buried in the family vault at St. Peter's church.

His older brother, another Joseph, was also a noted naturalist. He was an original Fellow of the Linnean Society, founded in 1788 to which Edward reported twenty-four species of bird observed in Greenland. Joseph was honorary secretary of the Royal Horticultural Society and Vice Chairman of the Zoological Society. When Clutterbuck published his *'History of Hertfordshire'* in 1815 Joseph Sabine

Sabine's Gull (*Larus sabini*)

provided him with a list of eighty-eight rare flowering plants and four rare lichens for inclusion. He was awarded a gold medal by the Royal Horticultural Society.

Their father, Joseph, sold the estate to Robert Mackay who in turn sold it to a Dutchman, Charles Schreiber. On his death in 1800 it passed to his son William Schreiber. John Carrington describes the

Sabine's Puffback (*Dryoscopus sabinii*)

departure of Charles Schreiber's funeral procession from Tewin House and comments on the alterations made by his son William:

April 1800

'Saturday night the 12th died Charles Schreiber Esqr of Tewin House, aged about 80ty. Was Buired the Monday following the 21st in a Vault in Endfield Church Middlesex. Was taken away about 7 Clock in the Morning from Tewin House in Herce and Six, 3 Mourning Coaches in four, and his own Coach behind Emty, he had not Lived at Tewin above 12 years as about that Time he pirchesed the Estate of Esqr Macky for 22000 pounds......Old Esqr Schreiber was a Dutch man and he Left the Estate to his Eldest son William Schreiber, who Came to Tewin to Live their from Suffolk & made Great alterations in the offices of the House, for the Worse, & Distroyed the fine Engin which used to Serve the House and offices with water and then Sunk a well, a great Simpleton'

In 1804 William Schreiber sold the estate to Peter 5th Earl Cowper who lived nearby at Panshanger House. Tewin House is described in the sales particulars at this time as *'an excellent residence delightfully situate three miles from Welwyn, four from Hatfield and Hertford, ten from St. Albans and twenty four from London.'* It had *'numerous offices, four coach houses, stabling for eleven horses, plantations, pleasure grounds & excellent kitchen garden and several farms contiguous, containing*

together eight hundred & sixty six acres'. Detail is given of *'A noble Hall, lined and paved with Marble'*

The price of the entire estate was £35,000 but, despite its beauty and value, in June 1807 Earl Cowper commenced the demolition of Tewin House, sweeping the house and all its facilities away. Detailed records exist of the material recovered from the demolition and used by the Earl in the construction of his Panshanger mansion:
14.5 tons of lead, 909,100 bricks, 35,000 tiles, 11,187 paving tiles.
Labourers were paid £207.14s 10d for taking down Tewin House and its offices.

John Carrington describes the *'pulling down'* of *'Tewin Great House by the Church'* in June 1807.

'This month Begun pulling Down Tewin Great House by the Church the offices all down the last 2 months past, kitchen, Brewhouse, Landrey &c. Stables Coach Hous &c &c, the Mantion House 3 Story High besides the offices &c below the whole Bredth of the House, with fine Lofty rooms, & the Grandest Stair Case allowd to be in England, 27 windows East front 27 in West front & 9 in Each End, fine Large Sashes, all Brick with Large Corner Stones, flat roof with Ernes Standing all Round the top, Built by Generl Savine (Sabine) & finished in the year 1718, now Pulld Down by Ld Cowper'

So ends the story of the *'fine fair house near the church'*. It disappeared to become part of another grand house in Panshanger Park which, in turn, was demolished in the 1950s, its materials sold to many local builders and scattered throughout Hertfordshire and beyond. Now all that marks the site of Tewin House is the cedar tree above an old brick wall.

Above: **The remaining old wall at the east end of Tewin Churchyard.**

Marden Hill House

East front of Marden Hill House in 1760 before the John Soane additions.

Bicentenary 1789-1989
The following account was written
by Tom B Adams in 1989

The manor of **Marden** (Muridene, Meryden, Merden) was probably identical with the land at *'Cyrictiwa'* or Tewin, which was held about 1050 by Tova, widow of Wihtric. Tova at that time made an agreement with Leofstan, Abbot of St. Albans, by which she and her son Godwin were to hold the land for their lives, paying yearly to the Abbot at the feast of St. Peter ad Vincula (1st August) one sextar, thirty-

Terry Brand's watercolour of Marden Hill House in 2000.

two ounces of honey, and that after the death of both the monastery of St. Albans was to take possession *'without contradiction'*.

It remained with St. Albans until 1529, when it came to the Crown by the conviction of Thomas Wolsey, Cardinal of York, then Abbot of St. Albans, under the statute of Praemunire. He was, however, pardoned in 1530 and his possessions restored. The abbey was surrendered in 1539, and in 1540 the manor of Marden was granted to William Cavendish and Margaret his wife. Later it came into the possession of Edward North, Master of harriers to Edward VI, whose son Edward, Sergeant-at-Arms to Charles I, succeeded his father in 1606. Edward the younger died in 1653. His son Hugh, who built a house at Marden Hill, left two daughters, Mary, who married Arthur Sparke, and Sarah, who married Marmaduke Rawdon. These sisters, who were holding the manor in 1672, are said to have sold it to Edmund Field, MP for Hertford 1671-76, after which it was acquired by Revd. Edward Warren, who was holding it in 1700, and whose son Richard succeeded him in 1728. The latter died in 1768 and was succeeded by his son Arthur, who is said to have sold

Marden in 1785 to Robert Macky of Tewin House.

In 1789 Robert Macky demolished the Jacobean manor house (with which Hugh North, grandson of Edward, had replaced the earlier Elizabethan building) except for the still existing north wing which he incorporated into *'a handsome modern mansion'* (Clutterbuck).

IT IS THE BICENTENARY OF THIS GEORGIAN HOUSE, DESIGNED POSSIBLY BY THOMAS LEVERTON OR MORE PROBABLY BY HIS YOUNG ASSISTANT, AND LATER ENHANCED BY SIR JOHN SOANE, THAT WE ARE NOW CELEBRATING.

In 1810 Robert Macky sold Marden Hill to Richard Flower, a brewer, banker and noted agriculturist of his day. For eight years Richard Flower and his

Sir John Soane

brother Benjamin, radical editor of *The Cambridge Intelligencer* attracted to Marden Hill a large group of politically-minded friends. The house became a centre where there gathered men of dissenting views, radical politics and reforming zeal including, on occasion, William Cobbett. Anti-slavery, the iniquities of tax-gatherers and poor rate assessors, the hardships of brewers and farmers, the way the world was going to the dogs, the attractions of republicanism and the enticing thoughts of emigration to other, fresher lands, must all have been the subjects mulled over by guests and family.

With the temporary cessation of the war against Napoleon in 1814, George Flower, in the company of Morris Birkbeck, paid a three month visit to France to learn about French agricultural practices and to assess France as a possible target for emigration from England. Among the many people of rank and influence whom the travellers met was the famous Marquis de Lafayette.

On their return, Birkbeck published his *Notes on a Journey through France* which concluded that French agriculture might well benefit from the adoption of English crop rotation but, however attractive financially emigration might be, it was not a practical proposition. This not merely on grounds

of differing cultures and traditions but because *'the number and influence of the military and clergy were to persons of our republican tendencies decisive against a residence in France as civilians'*, a revealing comment in more ways than one.

Having ruled out France, the two prospective emigrants, in George Flower's own words, concluded that *'to persons of fastidious political tastes, the United States of North America seemed to be the only country left for emigration'*. And so, having turned it over in their minds and doubtless discussed it at length with family and friends, the decision to follow their *'fastidious political tastes'* was taken.

In April 1816, aboard the *Robert Burns* George Flower left Liverpool for New York as advance agent to scout the land and light upon a likely place to settle. Among the many farewells to him was a party at Marden Hill attended, on his own testimony, by seventy-three Fordham uncles and cousins.

Armed with letters of introduction from William Cobbett to various people on the eastern seaboard of the United States and, more importantly perhaps, from Lafayette to Thomas Jefferson, George landed in New York in late May or early June. His first six weeks were spent in and around Philadelphia, learning what he could of the western lands where settlement might prove attractive. While there he wrote to Jefferson, who invited him to visit him at his home, Monticello.

Returning to England in the early autumn of 1817, George found that his father had just sold Marden Hill for £23,000 and with family and servants was ready to emigrate. The winter passed in a flurry of activity preparing the family for its transfer and running an emigration office in London. By the beginning of March, a party of some eighty-eight would-be settlers was ready to sail from Bristol. In April, the Flower party with stores, cattle and sheep accompanied by some sixty or seventy others sailed from Liverpool for New York. Eventually the Flowers founded the famous and controversial settlement at Albion, Illinois.

Marden Hill was bought from the Flowers in 1817 by Claude George Thornton, who came from a Yorkshire banking family, and in 1818 he asked Sir John Soane to design a new vestibule and staircase hall. The projecting, two-storey porch does not appear on the first plans and was apparently an afterthought. A reference in Soane's journal shows that its Ionic columns had, in fact, originally been

John Soane remodelled the staircase at Marden Hill in 1818.

intended for New Bank Buildings in Princess Street. For some reason they were not used there, and came instead to Marden Hill, where they support a stone balustrade in front of the first floor windows of the projection.

The vestibule has a pedimented doorcase on either side, and pairs of Corinthian columns flanking the approach to the inner hall, where the staircase rises in a single first stage and then divides. It is constructed of wood (unusual in Soane's works, as he preferred stone for reasons of safety in case of fire), and has iron balustrading identical with that in No. 13 Lincoln's Inn Fields. The centre door of the landing leads into the famous Soane room. This has the typical vaulted ceiling with tall ornament similar to the dining room of 12 Lincoln's Inn Fields. A double flight of stone steps originally at the front entrance to the house was transferred to the garden side, and set before the drawing-room windows.

Claude George Thornton died in 1866 and his son George Smith Thornton in 1867. Eventually Marden Hill came to Godfrey Henry Thornton, son of the last-named who was holding it in 1877.

In 1903 the property was sold by the Thorntons to the late Earl Cowper, as Marden adjoins Panshanger, and its five hundred acres were in the middle of his shoot. At the time, the house was let to Mr. Hoare, a Director of the Bank of England. On the authority of his son, the late Mr. Douro Hoare, it is said that Lord Cowper told Mr. Hoare that he was going to bid for Marden and that if he, Mr. Hoare, would undertake not to bid against him, he, Lord Cowper, would give him a lease of it rent free for the rest of his life. This suited Mr. Hoare very well, as he had no intention of buying the property! Unfortunately, the old gentleman broke his neck within six months while hacking in Panshanger Park. A subsequent tenant was Lady Margaret Graham.

Between 1923 and sometime during the Second World War, Marden Hill was owned by Major and Mrs. Banbury, during which time it was the subject of an article in Country Life (August 22nd, 1941). During the war it was occupied by St. Josephs College, a small Catholic boarding school evacuated from Beulah Hill, Norwood, in London, and eventually sold at the death of the then owner Mr. E. F. Lyne in 1957 to Alluvial and General Industries (London) Ltd. (later St. Albans Sand and Gravel Ltd.), together with four cottages and about one hundred and thirty acres.

Major Banbury in 1930, when he owned Marden Hill.

Unable to demolish the listed building, but still hoping to win the gravel, the company sought a leasehold tenant for the house, one of the cottages and the gardens. Peter Adams and Colin Huntley, two young architects looking to escape with their families

Tom Adams in his studio at Marden Hill. (See page 241 for two examples of his wide range of highly acclaimed work). His text in this section is reproduced by kind permission.

from small flats in London, came to Marden Hill and, although it was several times larger than the house they had planned to find and sub-divide, the two couples decided they wished to live nowhere else.

After gathering together five more like-minded young families, Peter signed a twenty-one year lease with the gravel company in 1958 and thus the present Marden Hill community was formed. Twenty-two years later, with five of the original seven families still in residence, a co-ownership company was formed and the freehold of Marden Hill was acquired. The community was enlarged to nine households in 1987, with the building of two new cottages to replace the derelict coach houses.

Since Tom Adams wrote the above account for the bicentenary little at Marden has changed except

perhaps the people who live there. Most of the long-standing residents have moved on, to be replaced by some younger families, though Colin Huntley has now lived at Marden for fifty years.

There is a Residents' Association because the land is held in common, and there are always issues to discuss, such as the exterior maintenance of the property. Living together in such a community requires that people be extra respectful of their neighbours. There are, for example, certain unwritten customs about where families sit outside to enjoy the gardens. Each family can use part of the enormous walled garden for vegetables or keeping chickens and so on.

Descendants of the Flower party who founded Albion, Illinois, have visited Marden in the last few years. So far not one has been descended from George Flower himself, but from his servants. In 1993 Albion celebrated the 175th anniversary of its founding. Marden residents compiled and sent a book about the history of Marden and some typically British recipes.

The very peacefulness of Marden has only been disturbed in recent years by first, the threat of further gravel extraction close by, and secondly, by the sale of land located within the Mimram valley, to unsuspecting foreigners, who have been sold agricultural land, now divided into plots for later development, waiting planning permission, which hopefully will never be given (see page 254).

Marden Hill House taken in 2000.

Chapter 13

Outdoor pursuits and leisure activities

Tewin has a good story to tell of outdoor pursuits, both amateur and professional, in the village and wider. For example in the 21ˢᵗ century we have had Tom Stallard winning a silver medal in Beijing 2008 in the team GB VIII, Jo Goode winning an Olympic bronze in 2000 for badminton; National, Regional and County representation by Bruce and Susan Tyler in Clays shooting, Patrick Holden and his dogs in Obedience and Working Trials, and County bowls and bridge players. In addition we have had National (Bahrain) and Championship football management and coaching by Keith Burkinshaw whose clubs included Tottenham Hotspur, Newcastle United, Aberdeen and West Bromwich Albion.

In 2006 Lewis Hamilton was selected for the McLaren Formula One Team. Since then he has gone on to immense success in his rookie year and in 2008 became the youngest-ever Formula One World Champion.

Whilst, as elsewhere, sports clubs wax and wane, we are pleased to report that the majority of the activities covered still flourish.

Lewis Hamilton MBE

Lewis Hamilton's impact on motorsport has been astonishing and has attracted intense media coverage since he became a Formula 1 driver in 2007 and achieved the best debut season in F1 history.

It is now well documented that his racing career started at an early age when his father, Anthony, (centre, above, in the group photograph), introduced him to Karting. Very soon afterwards, at only 10 years old, Lewis won the British Karting Championship, with more championship wins to follow.

His racing career progressed further when he won the British Formula Renault, Formula Three Euroseries and GP2 Championships. Lewis' talent was soon spotted and he was signed to the McClaren and Mercedes Benz Young Driver Support Programme in 2007 and achieved the best debut season in the history of Formula I drivers with the most consecutive podium positions (9), the most consecutive podiums for a British driver (9), the most wins (4) and most pole positions (6).

184

Left: **The Hamilton family Christmas card 2008, sent from their home in Tewin and signed by the whole family in the year Lewis became Formula One World Champion.**
Above: **The local papers have followed Lewis' career in great detail. This is an example from the *Hertfordshire Mercury*, and the *Welwyn & Hatfield Times* has been equally supportive, with full-page spreads on the races.**

These were history-making achievements which lead to Lewis being runner-up in the World Drivers Championship, but more was to follow when, in the following year, he became the youngest driver ever at 23 years, 8 months, 26 days, to win the Formula 1 World Drivers Championship. He took 1st place in Australia, Monaco, Great Britain, Germany and China, 2nd place in Turkey and European, 3rd place in Spain, Belgium and Singapore. This left him needing to achieve 5th place or higher in the final race in Brazil. Millions of people throughout the world tuned their television sets to see a thrilling race, culminating in Lewis overtaking the Toyota in the final lap to take 5th place and win the title.

Lewis' development has been managed by his father, and Anthony has also become a familiar figure in the racing world and to the thousands of people who have followed Lewis' progress. Lewis has not only given excitement and pleasure to established motor racing enthusiasts, but also to thousands of others who have been drawn to the sport through his wonderful achievements and people in Tewin feel particular pride in one of their local champions, none more so than when Her Majesty The Queen awarded him an MBE in the 2009 New Year Honours.

So far the new season has proved difficult for the team, with new regulations over car design, but these are early days in Lewis' outstanding career.

Tom Stallard

Olympic year 2008 was a special year for Tewin rower, Tom Stallard. As a member of the Great Britain Men's Eight crew, he was watched by millions of people as his boat crossed the line in second place to take the coveted Silver medal in Beijing. This was the culmination of a winning year for Tom as he and his crew had already won Gold, Silver and Bronze medals in the World Cup Series.

Tom started rowing at the age of 13, coached by his father, Matthew, a distinguished Orthopaedic Surgeon, and a former University rower himself. It was soon apparent that Tom had inherited his father's talent and in 1996 he took part in the Junior World Rowing Championships as a member of the Men's Four which came fifth. He won his first medal in 1999 with a Bronze in the World Junior Championships, and in the following year he again took Bronze in the U23 World Rowing Championships, whilst finishing fourth in 2000.

A Cambridge Blue, Tom rowed in four University Boat Races from 1999 - 2002, winning on two occasions, and in 2002 he became Cambridge President. He gained his first senior GB vest in 2002 when he won Gold in the Men's Coxed Four in the World Championships in Seville, followed by Silver in Milan in 2003. This led to his being chosen to row in the Men's Eight at the 2004 Olympic Games in Athens, where the team finished in 9th place. In the next three years, Tom enjoyed further success in the World Championships and won a Bronze in the Amsterdam World Cup in 2007, which was followed in 2008 by his wonderful achievement in the Olympic Games.

Since then Tom has taken a Masters degree in motorsport engineering at Brunel University and has joined the McLaren F1 team where, no doubt, his

Tom Stallard (with medal) and family

185

understanding of competitive sport will be of great value, but it is as a rowing champion that Tom is now proudly regarded in Tewin.

Joanne Goode MBE

Joanne Goode and her Badminton partner, Simon Archer, won the Bronze Medal in the Mixed Doubles at the Sydney Olympic Games in 2000, which was the first time Great Britain had won a medal for Badminton.

Jo Goode MBE

Joanne had already enjoyed a successful career in her sport, first winning with Simon Archer a Mixed Doubles Silver Medal in 1996 in the European Championships. Then in the 1998 European Championships she won a Bronze Medal in the Women's Doubles with her partner, Donna Kellogg, as well as another in the Mixed Doubles. The same year she won two Gold Medals in the Commonwealth Games in Kuala Lumpur, one for the Women's Doubles, the second for the Mixed Doubles. Her medal tally grew in 1999 when she and her partner added a Silver Medal in the Mixed Doubles at the World Championships in Copenhagen, as well as Gold Medals in the Open Championships - firstly for the Mixed Doubles in the All England Open, and another for the Mixed Doubles in the Swiss Open.

Her Olympic Games success in Sydney followed in 2000, and the same year she competed in the Open Championship in Indonesia, winning a Gold Medal in the Women's Doubles and a Gold Medal in the

Mixed Doubles. She again had a successful European Championships in Glasgow, winning a Gold Medal in the Women's Doubles. The Commonwealth Games in Manchester was the next venue to witness her winning ways when she achieved a Gold Medal in the Mixed Doubles and a Bronze Medal in the Women's Doubles.

Joanne's husband, Andy Goode, has also enjoyed success in his Badminton career. Included among his achievements was a Championship win in the Mixed Doubles at the British National Championships in 1991 and again at the Portugal Open in 1992. Following this success, he was appointed Manager of the British Olympic Badminton team in 1992.

Following her successful career, Joanne has devoted a lot of time in recent years to helping up-and-coming young players and, in October 2004, she was awarded an MBE for her services to the sport.

Shooting

Shooting has had a long history, replacing archery when gunpowder was discovered. Early guns were made by separate craftsmen: the barrel by the blacksmith, the stock by the carpenter/joiner and the trigger mechanism by a locksmith. This gave rise to the expression 'Lock, Stock and Barrel'. Carrington often mentions shooting, including, for example, a match in 1801 *'at pidgons'* when birds were released from under a top hat to be shot at with muzzle-loaders: The nearest fallen bird to the centre of the circle was the winner. Carrington records he bet on the wrong side! The County Militia and Yeomanry during the Napoleonic wars used flintlock muskets and had some *'rifellmen'*.

More recently in the 19th and 20th centuries during the Boer and two World Wars we have had Volunteers rifle shooting on the range north of Dawley, now defunct, (see page 124).

Also in the late 19th and early 20th centuries Panshanger House was famous for its shooting parties. Earl Cowper's guests included Edward VII and George V. Earl de Gray, a famous shot, was praised by Lady Randolph Churchill (Winston's mother) for winning a bet by shooting 52 out of 53 pheasants one-handed.

We still have game shooting with the Gun Club which has syndicate members breeding birds in Dawley Wood and clay shooting with the Clay Club based in Home Wood. Bruce and Susan Tyler's awards include being British Open husband and wife champions in 1999.

Riding

Horses have always played an important part in the life of Tewin, and were extensively used in agriculture. Carrington mentions ploughing matches, naturally betting on the result. Following the advent of the internal combustion engine, the use of heavy horses has sadly declined. Until recently we saw Fred Cox's Shires grazing in Tewin and being used to pull a dray in a local brewer's livery.

Other memories of Shire horses include those of Ronald Brand, whose uncle was a drayman in the 1950s in London. When he delivered beer to *The Plume of Feathers* he would visit the Brand family then living in what were wooden houses at that time, on Upper Green, parking his dray outside. Barton's milk carts were pulled by horses, (see p. 149).

Horses were, of course, also used for people transport. Carrington mentions his little cart and his favourite pony - and that on a number of occasions he was so befuddled with drink that he paid a small boy to lead his pony home to Bacon's Farm with himself draped over it.

Other memories of horse transport include that of Susan Tyler whose grandfather ran the market garden on some of what was the Yarborough School's orchards and gardens (afterwards the market garden became allotments and are now Godfries and Harwood Closes). Elizabeth Wilson had her own pony and little cart back in the 1950s while Patrick Holden, among others, drove Molly Hopkyns' pony and trap with Treacle in the shafts in the early 1960s.

The Enfield Chace, the local Hunt, often met in Tewin and was a resplendent sight. Many of the villagers were hunt followers, both on horseback and on foot.

Whilst there have always been horses to ride in Tewin there has been a great increase in the number of horses in and around the village for recreational riding and in 'horsi-culture'. Indeed, it has recently been estimated there are now more horses in the village in the two stables and many fields around than there were at the time of the industrial revolution. There is certainly a bigger 'crop' of horses than of all other livestock combined.

Fishing

Tewin's river, the Mimram, which runs through the parish has a somewhat uncertain flow of water. Although in the past it has powered the Mill at Tewin Bury Farm and The Mill itself, which was a cornmill and an optician's grinding mill at various times, the water flow for game fish has been variable.

In addition to the usual small boys fishing for 'tiddlers' and other waterlife, there is now a thriving fly fishing club on the Mimram. This was given impetus by the introduction of a trout farm which originally grew trout to pass on to other fisheries. Inevitably a number escaped and helped increase the breeding and the trout stocks in the river south of the farm. It is here that the Mimram Fishing Club now operates.

Walking (and Jogging)

Tewin is blessed with a good network of footpaths and rights of way dating from the time when local folks needed them to ride their horses or, in most cases, simply walk to their place of work. While a number of these rights of way have been lost, particularly over the period of the Second World War, we still have a network of which we can be justifiably proud today.

Walking in the countryside has been shown by a survey conducted by Hertfordshire County Council to be the biggest participative outdoor leisure activity

Walkers on the footpath below St. Peter's Church.

bar none. It is certain that the Tewin network is extensively used not only by residents but also by other visitors. Indeed, at a recent planning appeal, 14 clubs and groups represented in person or by letter successfully supported the network, which has been described by the Chairman of the Herts & Middlesex Ramblers Association as *'the best footpath network in Hertfordshire and Middlesex'*.

The Tewin Society has been instrumental in protecting the network by ensuring that blocked paths have been opened and illegal obstructions

187

removed including a dangerous horse, an illegal sign *'Beware of the Bull'*, as well as paths wired across with barbed wire and locked gates. Indeed members of the Society were known to carry wire cutters. Now most of the landowners are supportive of the aims and objects of the Ramblers and the Country Code.

Tewin is pleased to have won a number of awards for work on the network not only countywide but also nationally. One such award was won for the production of the *'Map of Tewin and Its Rights of Way'*. This was one of the earliest village maps in Hertfordshire and the first to double up primarily as a walker's map and secondarily as a wall hanging. It has since been used as a template for several other parishes. Well over 50 people were involved in its production, making it a truly village effort. Over 3000 copies have been sold and they can be found worldwide in places as far apart as China, Japan, Australia, Papua New Guinea and USA. Indeed, for a period of time because of the problems in producing the map to avoid paying copyright fees, our map when produced was more accurate than the local Ordnance Survey itself and was used in planning applications and appeals.

Some eight paths have been added to the Definitive Map ensuring that they are available for future generations of walkers, (See p. 242-243)

Tewin is proud of the fact that all footpaths are accessible, provided that appropriate footwear is worn. The paths are now signposted, waymarked and all kissing gates and stiles are in good repair.

Dogs

In addition to walking on footpaths, many Tewin folk also exercise their dogs on them. In addition to walking dogs, dogs are trained on both Upper and Lower Greens as well as elsewhere.

Competitions for dogs have been held in Tewin: Gun Dog Field Trials in and next to Dawley Woods, Obedience Competitions on Upper Green and a

Patrick Holden's Obedience Champion Bramble TDEx , an honorary member of the Tewin Cricket Club for finding a large number of cricket balls, with his son Thorn.

Good Citizen Exhibition on Lower Green. A Tewin dog, Ob.Ch.Melnola Bramble T.D.Ex, was not only the lead dog for the winning Southern Inter-Regional Obedience Team at Crufts but also an Honorary Member of the Cricket Club for finding their balls. Other sports are alleged to have happened including otter hunting, hare coursing, lurcher competition and even badger baiting. There are lurchers still in use in the village today for their appropriate use of keeping down the rabbit population.

Tennis

Tennis was originally played behind the Village Hall until the area was resurfaced to form the current car park.

The first public meeting to discuss forming a Tennis Club in Tewin took place on Tuesday 28th September 1971 and was officially opened at the end of October with one court. The following year there were 208 members including 88 juniors, with junior coaching. ladies' afternoons and the Club tournament. Philip Arnold was treasurer, Peter Beale Chairman and Ruth Harrison Hon. Secretary with Bill Osterberg doing the coaching. The cost of membership then was just £2 for adults and £1 for juniors.

Fundraising ensued and a second court was laid in 1973. Resurfacing was done in 1984 and the pavilion and patio were constructed in 1987 with help from East Herts District Council who paid 50% of the cost.

The club has always put a strong emphasis on junior coaching with Bill Osterberg and Chris Ktori encouraging them to enter various local competitions. In 1984 the team made it to the Welwyn Garden City finals and gained their first trophy in 1985. In 1987 Bert Robinson qualified as a coach and the junior section has gone from strength to strength winning many Herts league competitions. Bert Robinson has remained with the club for over 20 years!

Despite membership being limited to the Parish of Tewin, the club has continued to put out very strong teams for both junior and senior matches. The first team came first in the senior Datchworth Summer League in 1991 and the club has four teams playing in the league. It also has teams in the Orchard Ladies League and the first ladies team has won the trophy on a number of occasions. The club has its own tournament, together with fathers and sons/mothers and daughters tournaments, and novice/newcomers tournaments. There are ABC matches on Friday evenings and other friendly league matches

Recent Tennis Club winners by the courts on Upper Green. (See also page 255).

It sounds like a variety of ninepins played within a square frame with a bowl weighing from 6-8 lbs.

There was certainly bowling in the village both between the wars and after. For example, Roger Temple and Susan Tyler remember their fathers going off to bowl on the green behind the village hall, while the ladies took tea within. That green was converted first into a tennis court and now into a car park. Tewin Bowls Club then folded.

It has been reincarnated as Shire Park Bowls Club (Tewin). This started life in the early 1990s when 17 ex

organised by various members of the Club.

The Club has prospered over the last 35 years. For the Millennium the Club had the courts resurfaced and constructed a brand new practice wall. The Tennis Club continues to thrive in the 21st century.

Bowls

Bowls and bowling have an extensive history in Tewin. It is mentioned in Carrington's diaries (c1790) although whether this was skittles or green bowling we have no record.

Carrington mentions bowling *'at the four corners'*.

members of what was the ICI Club in Welwyn Garden City bought some land at the back of the village hall. The original members built the bowling green themselves (a huge undertaking), and bowling finally commenced, with friendly weekend games and a few additional members in 1996. Initially a Portakabin was used as a changing room, the scout hut for lavatories and *The Rose & Crown* provided after match teas.

Eventually, with the help of a Lottery Grant, a clubhouse was built and opened for use in 1999. The bowling green matured under the dedicated volunteer

Shire Park (Tewin) Bowls Club has a beautiful setting on the edge of Lower Green, overlooking the fields to Dawley Woods.

189

care of first Bill Archer and now Gordon Price (both founder members), until it is now widely acknowledged to be amongst the finest in the county.

An extension to the clubhouse was opened in 2005, giving larger male and female changing facilities and lavatories, a much bigger kitchen and a large bar/lounge area. This, together with a beautiful playing surface, has allowed the club to stage major competitive matches, and the first County games (both male and female) were staged in Tewin in 2005 and it is now one of the major venues for County games. Club membership stands at 90 in 2009 and many are Tewin residents.

All standards of play are accommodated: the

Above: **Names were recorded on these two of the many Tewin Cricket Club groups photographed over the years.**
1953: Back row, **MarySmith-Palmer (sec), Laurie Sorrel, Ernie Temple, Les Eagle, Sid Owen.** Bottom row, **Glynn Davis, Bill Smith-Palmer, Bill Rhodes, Ken Mainwaring, John Booth and Derek Archer.** Lower photo: **The Club in 1987:**
Back row, **Andy Luck, Ted Kavanagh, Brian Haughton, Tim Joiner, John Gibbs, Phil Brice (Umpire) and Graham Fish.**
Bottom row, **William Edlin, Richard Sheppard, Gil McCreadie, Ted Tyler and Chris Pool.**

membership includes several County members, both male and female, and Area (South Herts) players, together with a large number of purely 'social' bowlers and there is room for new members.

The green is in constant use from April to September, and in the winter months the clubhouse hosts various activities for members, such as social events, carpet bowling, art and yoga classes.

Cricket

Tewin has an enviable history of cricket. Carrington covers matches both single and double wicket at all seasons of the year on both Upper and Lower Green. For example *'on 29 November 1805 went to Tewin to diner Rose & Crown... the dinner was plaid for at cricket and quites'*.

Popular on a smaller scale was the single wicket game; we hear of one man against three and of two against two. And there was one particularly memorable occasion: *'Memarandom, I plid after they had done, after Dinner on the Lower Green, with Chesher Church clark at Hardingfordbury for 2s 6d and I Beete Chesher 6 noctches Single Wicket & Woon of Hardingfordbury Men 15 shillings, spent at Dinner, whome 12 dined at Jacks, 5s, Leg Moton Boyled, sholder Rost, Pudings, &c &c'.*

Tewin saw many exciting contests on one or other of its two greens. Sometimes it played away matches and John followed his side with all the enthusiasm of a modern fan. We hear of matches between married men and *'batcheldors'* and between the village of Tewin and the carpenters and joiners building Lord Cowper's new mansion at Panshanger. The real popularity of cricket may be gauged by the *'great cricket match at Tewin Upper Green against the County for 11 guines, but the County beat Ware people allmost the first Innings, fine day and supposed to be 1500 people there'.*

Remember that Mr Lord founded his eponymous Lords Cricket Ground currently described as the *'Headquarters of English cricket'* only in 1804 well after cricket was being played on the two greens at Tewin (see page 109).

Unfortunately, little more is known in written form of cricket in the village for the next 100 or so years, although cricket was certainly played at the schools and on Upper Green between and after the wars.

The current Tewin Cricket Club was founded in 1953 by a group of residents after an informal chat at the bar at *The Plume of Feathers*. From the outset the team has played all its home matches on Upper

Above: **Mick Fuller (left) with captain Andrew Whawell open for Tewin Irregulars v Ex-Hong Kong Bank. Simon Barnes occasionally refers to the Irregulars in** *The Times.*

Green. Years ago the conditions were in marked contrast to the superb playing conditions enjoyed now.

In the early days of the club the team changed and took tea in *The Plume*. However, in 1956 the club acquired its first pavilion in the form of an old builder's site office. It has to be said the conditions were fairly cramped but in 1971 the club joined forces with the football club and the present pavilion, designed by local architect Ken Feakes, was constructed. This was later extended to accommodate the tennis club. From the outset the club only played friendly matches and apart from winning the Datchworth Seven-a-Side in 1971, no other competitive cricket was played. However, in 1997 after much soul-searching the club entered league cricket. This has proved to be a great success with the club finishing runners-up on two occasions.

Graham Fish's record of the birth and running of the current Tewin Cricket Club is now in the Archives. It has also been recorded elsewhere in its own book *'The Tewin Story 1953-1990, A History of Tewin Cricket Club'* by Phil Brice and *'Cricket in Hertfordshire'* by R G Simms. *The Times* Senior Sports Editor Simon Barnes established 'Tewin Irregulars' and continues to mention them from time

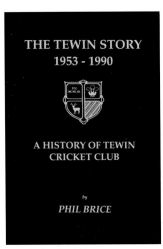

THE TEWIN STORY
1953 - 1990

A HISTORY OF TEWIN
CRICKET CLUB

by

PHIL BRICE

Phil Brice's Tewin Cricket Club book cover.

to time in his articles on sport in the national newspaper.

Cycling

There is a lot of cycling in Tewin, as would be expected in our beautiful village with its easy access to the nearby towns of Welwyn Garden City, Hatfield, Hertford and Stevenage. Moreover London's Congestion Charge and terrorist outrages on public transport have made cycling to work in the Metropolis very appealing and Tewin commuters are as active as any!

Some cycle for fun on most Sunday mornings for a relaxed 20-30 mile ride through the Hertfordshire countryside. The *Tour de France* it certainly is not, but enjoyable it certainly is; it has been going on for ten years now in (nearly) all weathers. There are also events organised by the Tennis Club and others and even long distance holidays (eg Lands End to John O'Groats).

Several long distance races come through the village, although not many villagers themselves are racers.

'Cycling is fun to do, good for you, and exceptionally effective exercise - the BMA rates it the best form of exercise for most people, more so even than swimming or walking', writes Mike Horsman, *'Tewin offers great opportunities for all who are interested in such benefits'*.

Football

Tewin FC was formed in 1914 and it competed in the Hertford & District League thereafter. They were Division 1 champions in 1914, 1918 and 1923. In those days they played on Grass Warren (since the eponymous housing estate). In more recent years they won Division 3 in 1977/78 and in the same season they were finalists of Division 3 cup and were promoted to Division 1 in 1978/79 under the chairmanship of Dickie Dunn. They were finalists in the Welwyn Hospital Cup in the 1980/81 season at which Bruce Tyler was the Manager and indeed there were no fewer than three other Tylers in the squad.

Football has been played in the village over the

centuries. Post-war it has been played on Upper Green and improved from humble beginnings to a properly marked-out pitch with goal posts and corner flags. Later in the 1950s the Football Club shared the pavilion which they used in the winter months whereas the cricket club used it in the summer months.

Although football is still played in the School (whose team reached the Home Cup final in 2006) the Tewin Football Club itself is currently moribund in Tewin itself. We must hope that like other sporting clubs and societies (tennis, cricket, bowls, horticulture), it will be brought back into life in the village in the near future. Meanwhile Tewin Athletic FC play at King George V playing fields in Welwyn Garden City and Datchworth FC are playing on the pitch at Upper Green.

Keith Burkinshaw

Keith Burkinshaw is a legendary name in football history. Not only did he manage the Tottenham Hotspur team which won the FA Cup twice, as well as the UEFA Cup, but his name passed into football folklore when he achieved one of the game's greatest transfer coups. In 1978 he travelled to Argentina and brought back to England and Tottenham the World Cup winning partnership of Ossie Ardiles and Ricky Villa. Such transfers were unheard of at the time and this became a significant moment in the history of the game.

Before this Keith had enjoyed a long career in the game as a player and a manager. During his playing career he had a brief spell at Wolverhampton Wanderers before joining Liverpool FC from 1953 to 1957. Player/Manager roles at Workington AFC and Scunthorpe United followed, and from 1968 to 1975 he was appointed Assistant Coach and Coach, at Newcastle United FC. There followed the most successful period of his career when he joined Tottenham Hotspur FC in 1975, during which time they won a number of tournaments, the most notable being the FA Cup in 1981 and again in 1982, the FA Charity Shield in 1982, and the UEFA Cup in 1984.

After leaving Tottenham in 1984, Keith coached the Bahrain National side for a while before becoming Manager of Sporting Lisbon in Portugal for four years. Managerial and coaching roles at Gillingham, Swindon and West Bromwich Albion football clubs followed and then in 1997 he was made a director of Aberdeen FC. He returned to the game in 2005, when he was appointed Assistant Coach at Watford FC.

Above: **Presentation to Tewin Football Club Members 1982/83.** Left to right: **Jimmy Johnson, Bruce Tyler, Philip Tebbutt, Sue Tyler, Alan Brazil (ex Scottish International footballer who, during his professional career, played for Tottenham Hotspur, Ipswich Town, Manchester United and Coventry City)** Sitting: **Gary Marshall, Alan Thomason.**
Below right: **Keith Burkinshaw and his wife, Joyce, with the UEFA Cup in 1984 after his team, Tottenham Hotspur, beat RSC Anderlecht in the final.**

The following year they were promoted to the Premier League, but Keith resigned in 2007.

In May 2004 Keith was honoured by Tottenham Hotspur FC when he was inducted into their 'Football Hall of Fame' at a special occasion attended by many famous footballing personalities, including many of his legendary players who had achieved so much under his leadership.

Alf D'Arcy

Alf D'Arcy was voted Amateur Footballer of the Year in 1958-59, during which season he played for Barnet FC, who won the Athenian League and were Runners-up in the FA Amateur Cup.

Alf won his first international cap against Northern Ireland and subsequently went on to play for England more than 30 times, captaining the side on many occasions. In 1960 he was appointed Captain of the British Olympic team at the Rome games – the last time a British team qualified. He was also a member of the 1964 Olympic team.

Tewin Football Team 1913-14 on Upper Green (note the well and *The Plume of Feathers* in the background).

Alf D'Arcy, captain of the winning Enfield team, after receiving the FA Amateur Cup at Wembley in 1967.

Alf played at the old Wembley Stadium on five occasions, and apart from the achievements mentioned, he also represented Great Britain and England, and also played for the Football Association, the London FA and Hertfordshire. A good indication of his status in the game was summed up in the Press, which commented - '*In every international game he has been the outstanding player in his country's side.*'

When he retired from football, Alf set up a successful sports promotion company which has taken top football league clubs, and international teams, on tournaments around the world. Alf has now retired and his sons have taken over the company.

Horticulture and other activities

Gardening for profit and pleasure has been a feature of the village throughout its life, with allotments on what is now the site of Godfries and Harwood Closes. The current site by the School is fully utilised. Towards the end of World War II Upper Green was ploughed up for crops including wheat. Digging matches were held, for example, in 1954, when one event had 70 competitors countywide and was covered by the BBC. Prizewinners from Tewin had such well-known village names as Ephgrave, Shadbolt, Izzard and Whyman (see Chapter 14).

There was the Village Produce Association which metamorphosed into the Horticulture Society. This wound up in the 1980s, but has risen phoenix-like with arts added as **THACS** (Tewin Horticultural, Arts & Crafts Society) in 2001 (see page 202). There is a new tradition of 'Open Gardens'.

Other activities include **Ballooning:** Carrington

The opening in 2006 of the new National Lottery funded badger hide at Tewin Orchard by Audrey Randall, chair of the Hertfordshire and Middlesex Badger Group.

The scene on 26th November 1954 when Tewin held a digging competition, (see page 201). Left to right: **Mary Wallbutton, Joy Barker** with her son, **Geoffrey, Emily Tyler, Andrew** and **Carol Sinclair, Mrs Lily Collet** with her twin grandsons, **David** and **Antony Wallbutton.**

mentions Lunardi's balloon in 1784 and still in the 21st century we have an individual with a balloon taking off at times from Upper Green, **Car mountain trials** take place at Tewin Water. Classic car events are currently held annually on Upper Green. **Ferrets:** a number of which are in the village both working, (see page 151), and as pets. There are also ferret races at the annual Fête. The village has Clubs, Societies and other associations promoting outdoor activity including **The Tewin Society, The Countryside Alliance** and **Tewin Allsorts** (a ladies' club following the defunct W.I., described on page 196,) who have outdoor as well as indoor activities.

Wildlife Watching

Tewin has a wide diversity of wildlife. This is covered elsewhere, but a walker may encounter birds such as Kingfisher, Green and Great Spotted Woodpeckers, Grey Wagtail and Green Sandpiper while the fauna include Muntjac deer, Badgers, Foxes, Grey Squirrels and even a Polecat has been seen. Tewin has two nature reserves and a SSSI (Site of Special Scientific Interest) protecting species such as the rare Great Crested Newt, the Marsh Warbler and Reed Buntings.

Our protected habitats not only provide areas of wilderness, but link with other refuges such as The Commons Reserve in Welwyn Garden City to allow birds to disperse safely. The mammal hide at Tewin Orchard, described in Chapter 11, can be booked for watching at dusk between April and October through the Hertfordshire & Middlesex Wildlife Trust and Badger Group via tewinorchard.co.uk.

Scouts, Guides, Brownies, Cubs and Rainbows

Guides, Cubs, Brownies and Rainbows have all been strongly represented in Tewin. Brownies and Rainbows still remain in the village.

The beginning of Scouting in Tewin was linked with the troop in Letty Green run by David Walker.

Ken Hartfield, in his book *'Scouting in Hertford District'* describes these early days:

'The connection arose after one of the Letty Green Scouting families moved there from Birch Green and were dismayed to find no facilities for young boys in the village. There was a period when 'bussing' between Tewin and Letty Green occurred at 1/- per head, organised by an enterprising parent who owned a mini bus. This did not last long and pressure began to build to provide local facilities in Tewin. At that time Tewin was in the Welwyn Garden City Scout District and their DC was unable to offer any

1st Tewin Brownies. (See also 1st Tewin Guides, page 255).

prospect of re-starting the 1ˢᵗ Tewin Troop which had closed in 1939. After discussion with WGC District, Tewin was transferred to Hertford District and some ten boys began attending the troop at Letty Green on a regular basis. Tewin parents then began agitating for a Cub Pack in the village and the 1ˢᵗ Letty Green (Tewin) Pack was formed when Mr Ben Macalmont and Mr Jack Castle volunteered to act as leaders. The first meetings were held in Tewin Memorial Hall before Mr Barton, owner of Barton's Dairies, kindly gave permission to use a former cookhouse at Bericot Green as their HQ, being shared with Warrengate Farm Social Club. This was officially opened by CC Mr Melville Balsillie in May 1970. Carole Body and Dennis Carlton received their Leader permits and Jack Castle received his Leader's Warrant.'

In those days Jack Castle was Pack Leader, (Akela), assisted by Sheila Hampson as Baloo. Pauline Brown and Sheila Hampson ran the pack in the early eighties and Sheila retired in 1988 after sixteen years service. She remembers the week at camp every year whether it took place in Minchinhampton in Gloucestershire, Haversage in Derbyshire or Witham in Essex. Weekend camps were also arranged. Gerry Murphy took over when Sheila left until the pack finally closed in 1995 due to a lack of leaders.

Brownies was started on 14ᵗʰ February 1966. The pack met in Tewin Memorial Hall with Kathleen Arnold as Brown Owl and Marilyn Mead as Tawny Owl. A Jumble Sale was held every year to cover rental of the hall until, after more fund-raising, a purpose built hut was erected next to the Memorial Hall. It was formally opened by the Mayor of Hertford on 30ᵗʰ September 1978 and was used by the Cubs and Brownies and also Guides. When Kathleen gave up the Brownies, Marilyn Mead took over helped by Anne Sullivan. Anne became Brown Owl in 1984 joined by Ann Kevis as Tawny Owl in 1986. Due to demand a second pack was started in 1989. Anne retired in 2004 after twenty-eight years running the Brownies in Tewin. Mandy Clark took over for two years and at present Ann Kevis is keeping things running until the new Brown Owl, Claire Curley, is warranted.

Rainbows was started by Anne Sullivan as Rabbit and Ann Kevis as Hedgehog in the 1990s and is still active. The unit helpers are Fiona Hay as Squirrel and Gillian Walker as Dormouse.

This group is for the five to seven year olds and there is a full pack. They work on a similar basis to Brownies. Many of the activities are to do with helping others and learning about their country. They have their own distinctive uniform - a bright red and blue track suit.

Before the new hut was opened in 1978 the Guides met in Tewin Memorial Hall and were run by Jean Kirkham and Mrs Blamire - Brown. Wyn Carlton and Ann Kevis re-opened the Guides in September 1979 after a break and a new flag was dedicated at St. Peter's the following April, (see page 255). The company which had started with twelve members had now risen to twenty six. Money had been raised for the new flag by the Guides themselves. Wyn left Guides when she moved to Welwyn and Ann kept it going until Andrea Ford took over in 1986. The company was finally closed in the late eighties, but Brownies and Rainbows still continue to thrive.

Half a century of Tewin Players

During the 1950s a group of residents in Tewin Wood formed an amateur dramatic society named 'Tewin Wood Players'.

Originally only residents in the Wood could be members and each new member had to be proposed to the Committee, who then voted on the application.

Performances, usually comedies, were staged twice a year in Tewin Memorial Hall, where members designed and made a stage extension and scenery. The Front of House Manager, a local Bank Manager, always wore a dinner suit at performances.

Royal Academician, John Haggis, designed the motif *'TWP'* for the lavish blue velvet curtains.

Auditions for parts were conducted very seriously and acting standards were good enough for successful entries in both the Welwyn and Hertford Drama Festivals.

Gradually, with changes of residents, a wider membership was admitted and eventually the name was changed to 'Tewin Players'.

The village, plus a wider loyal audience, continued to be entertained by usually two performances each year until it became impossible to find enough men to act and build the sets, with members able and willing to direct, manage and stage plays.

The last production was *'My Friend Miss Flint'*, performed on 5ᵗʰ, 6ᵗʰ and 7ᵗʰ April 2001.

Tewin Women's Institute 1920-1986

The monthly evening meeting of the ladies of Tewin was a highlight of their lives when husbands looked after the children, allowing an hour or two of

A performance of *The Mikado* by the Tewin W.I. in the 1930s. Winifred Lyles 3rd from right in back chorus line.

friendship and fun and opportunities to develop domestic skills as well as acting, singing and a fair selection of crafts.

In 1952 when rationing was still around, and money seemed a lot scarcer than it is today, the mode of 'make-do-and-mend', a philosophy from the war still existed.

There were many talented and skilled teachers like Dorothy Wenborn who was a fierce but excellent needlework exponent and very fussy about fitness! Ever tactful though, she never implied you were fat, but just said *'you're a bonny girl.'* Peggy Morton was an 'ace' at presentation and designed so many displays at the district and county shows. She also taught the group how to make silk-covered lampshades.

Other crafts learnt were glove-making and millinery. One year a hat was made for the then President, Muriel Kindell, to wear at the Albert Hall for the A.G.M!

There was always a drama festival and this was another feature of W.I. involvement as there were several quite talented actresses and producers who led on to a Gold Star or two! The Gold Star was the acme of achievement as the standards were high and they were not given lightly.

Then there was always the cooking. Mrs. Izzard was an expert at cake icing and members learnt a great deal from each other during the lessons.

Concerts to raise money were organised which were always enormous fun.

For many years the W.I. entertained visitors from East London, from the Fern Street Mission. The larger groupings of district and county and ultimately, national institutes brought home to us wider issues of great interest and concern to women. Someone always came to enlarge on the resolutions which had been selected for the Albert Hall. One year there was a plea to widen the turnstile entrances to ladies public loos! Dear Kaye Petrie, of blessed memory, who was of ample proportions, wished it to be known that she had not put that particular one forward! Much hilarity ensued.

By 1986 it was farewell to the happy days of The Women's Institute that had included dancing, singing and acting. Many hours had been spent stitching and in cheerful, friendly rivalry.

Thanks are due to those whose efforts have left so many fond memories and useful skills learnt over the years.

Above: **Annie Perry second from right.** Right: **The Women's Institute Victory bell '***Cast with metal from aircraft shot down over Britain'***. The bell depicts Churchill, Stalin and Roosevelt and the inscription '***1939-1945 R.A.F. Benevolent Fund'***.**

Above: **Possibly '***Merry England'***, a production by the Tewin W.I in Tewin Memorial Hall. The Revd. Stebbings front row, among the group are Gerry Edwards' grandmother, Lillian Lyles, on the extreme right at back. Winifred Lyles second from right at back also with moustache and Mrs Digby in black bodice next to her.**

Left to right: **Margaret Tebbutt, Mavis Haggar, Hilary Tipping, Peggy Wilson, Rita Robbins, (at back), Alison Burleigh, Sylvia Brown, Menna Searle, Caroline Berkley, Linda Crawford, Julia Tizard and Anna Clark** at Julia's house during the Allsorts New Year's party 2005.

Allsorts (founded 1987)

After 66 years of the Women's Institute in Tewin, the third evening of the month felt oddly empty.

Many ex-members had become personal friends, of course, yet a handful (of perhaps the noisier or nosier variety) also missed the monthly lively interchange of conflicting opinions, the different talents, the experiences of new activities which had been part of the W.I.

Over a casual 'cuppa' one day, the idea grew that the essence of the old Institute could be upheld as long as the inherent pitfalls were avoided. They planned to meet up on the third Wednesday of each month, but with no formality, no committee, no hierarchical structure, no membership (keeping to a small group who would find a chair to sit on in the most modest of homes), above all no fees.

Several members would now claim to be the one who thought of the name (they are 'that sort of person'), one which suits the definition, *'that we are all sorts of ladies, doing all sorts of things, in all sorts of places'*. The group 'transforms',- people go, people appear. In 2007 the group celebrated 20 years of life with Allsorts, and in planning the next year's programme each September, ideas still freely flow.

Activities enjoyed? Too many to list but, for example: art, music, crafts, countryside pursuits, theatre, eating, walking, a guest speaker (with costs divided by the number of folk present on that night), talking, often being just ridiculous, and laughing.... just like the original W.I.

Tewin and Tewin Wood Village Produce Association 1942-1961

On February 18th 1942 Miss Talbot, from the Ministry of Agriculture, gave a talk to the Womens Institute on 'Rabbit, pig and potato clubs'. The members expressed a wish that a Village Produce Association be started in Tewin. Following a public meeting the Tewin and Tewin Wood Produce Association (TPA) was formed on the 6th March 1942 under the chairmanship of Mr C. Duvall Bishop of Sevenacres.

Mrs Spratt was elected secretary and remained so for 17 years until May 1959 when she retired on health grounds. A farewell supper was held to thank her for all her work. She moved away from Tewin and was greatly missed.

The first committee meeting, held on the 9th March 1942, followed the 'Model Rules for Produce

199

Associations' and Lady Beit was invited to become president. Two Auzani hand tractors from the Hertfordshire Agriculture Committee would be available. No one wanted to join a bee section and although a pig section was set up, nowhere could be found to house pigs. The minutes of March 30th 1942 record that Mr Hale could not grant the use of the pig-sties at Walnut Tree Cottage. The Government had taken over the use of his farm buildings and the pig-sties were being used for storage purposes. An attempt to start again, in 1946, failed as no one was found to take on the recording duties.

A secretary volunteered for a poultry section, but little was reported, although it was recorded that permits for wire netting were required and in April 1947, warnings about fowl pest were recorded. It closed in 1952.

Home Guard duties prevented some people from attending meetings and the secretary and chairman were interviewed several times for the radio over the years.

Potato Section

In the first year, Mr Neale offered the use of 2 acres of land at a rent of £1 per acre which was accepted. By May, the ground had been fertilised and the potatoes planted. Mr Neale arranged for ridging to be done during the week as it was cheaper than at weekends. The Saturday rate being-time-and-a-half and Sunday double-time. The Auzine plough was to be used to 'earth up' the potatoes but this task was in fact undertaken by Mr Chalkley with a horse and plough.

The plots were then pegged out and sprayed. Some were not taken up so Mr Duvall Bishop and Major Osman agreed to take these over and a draw for plots was made. Unfortunately, by August, due to pressure of work, Mr Neale could no longer run the potato section. Members were advised to retain half a hundred weight (cwt) of the seed potatoes, per plot, for the next year's sowing and Lady Beit would be asked if they could be stored at Tewin Water Farm.

As members had had difficulty in finding labour to lift the potatoes, and no one could be found to supervise the plots, it was decided to cultivate only one acre for potatoes next season. Members would work co-operatively and carry out the weeding. Mr Bishop agreed to rent the other acre for kale. Members could buy the potatoes at cost price and the remainder would be sold at market price.

In September 1943, the lifting of potatoes was again discussed with various estimates for the work.

Mr Bennett had given a price of £4 for the lifting and 30 shillings (£1.50) for the carting. It was agreed to ask Mr Neale to interview Bennett and ask him to do this work, first obtaining a written contract and price. It was also agreed to ask boys to pick up the potatoes. Plot holders would be allowed not more than 3 cwts of potatoes per plot with any surplus being sold for the benefit of the funds.

Unfortunately the crop was not cost effective and it was decided to ask Mr Dunnett to take over the land, (minutes of October 4th 1943).

Rabbit Section

Stud fees for the Rabbit Section were agreed at the first meeting in March 1942. Mr Clarke agreed to be Records Secretary with one shilling (5p) being the section joining fee.

The names of 18 members were needed so that the quarterly application for bran rations could take place. When received in August, members were asked to leave a labelled sack at Mr Clarke's house for their rations. Wire netting was limited, but some was obtained by July. There was supposed to be a demonstration, but '*Mr Reeves was unfortunately unable to kill and skin the first rabbit for any member so that they might see it done correctly*'.

Mr Clarke resigned in September 1942 and Mrs Read took over as Records Secretary, followed by Miss Dunn in April 1946.

This section appears to have continued successfully over the years with very little in the way of recorded comments until April 1951, when, due to the increased price of bran, membership had declined '*a little*'. In June 1952, bran was still being distributed, but Miss Dunn had become very ill and could only continue as Administrative Secretary. She was re-elected at the AGM in July 1952, but no further mention is made of the section.

Winter Greens allotments

Tewin Wood residents asked for communal allotments on which to grow winter green vegetables. Lady Beit offered some land at Mr Mead's cottage for winter greens and one acre was accepted. Some paperwork had to be completed to enable them to get a government grant for the section. The land was subsequently found to be rather acid, but worth cultivating if lime was added. A second acre which was rather better had been offered by Mr Gage and this was also accepted.

In May 1942, due to the drought, only the first acre had been ploughed and limed. It was agreed to split this land into 25 plots in the proportion 2 parts Brussels sprouts, 1 part kale and 1 part broccoli. The second acre would be sown with swedes. Members would be able to buy the crop at cost price with the remainder being sold at the controlled price.

Strict rules of ownership of the plants were implemented: '*plants on a boundary line should be deemed to belong to the owner whose plot was nearest to Mr Meads cottage*'... Plots were again drawn for.

However, in June 1943, two thirds of the plants had died due to bad planting by Mr Clarke's two young assistants. Members had to step in and replant under supervision and the subs had to be raised to 15 shillings, (75p).

In May 1944 it was agreed that the greens should be planted co-operatively and subs must be received before plots were allocated. A request for the Association to hold a produce show in aid of the Agricultural Red Cross was turned down, but a donation of £5 was sent.

The swedes failed due to fly, and it was decided not to replant them. Instead, members could rent for half a crown (25p), a 10 foot strip to plant turnips, carrots or leeks. The field was sodden by September.

In 1945, lime was still being used on the fields and a permit had to be acquired for fertiliser.

At the annual meeting in St Albans of the county association, (reported in June 1945), the speaker had stressed the need for every effort to be made to increase the production of food for the coming winter.

In January 1947, there was a new owner of the land and he served a notice to quit by 27 April 1948.

In July 1949, it was decided to keep the Produce Association to benefit members. Bulk buying of lime, bran, fertiliser and seed potatoes continued.

At this AGM a request to hold a flower show (which had, apparently, been very popular years ago) was made and a sub-committee set up to arrange this. A ladies sub-committee to organise the teas was also agreed. Honorariums were allocated and payment made for storage of bulk buys.

Also in 1949, a Tewin quiz competition was held to decide which members would be chosen for the county competition.

In 1950 there was a garden competition open to those not employing paid labour, but very few entries were received. Produce could be entered providing no more than 3 days labour was employed.

The first profit from the Produce Show was in 1951, which included cakes; this profit was invested in the Post Office. An annual show was held in September.

A 'shindig' in aid of the Memorial Hall was held with TPA providing a produce stall.

In 1953, for the Coronation, shrubs were planted on Lower Green which members looked after. There was also a *'most colourful garden'* competition. A much admired Ronson cigarette lighter was presented to Mr Shoal.

A digging match on a field owned by Messrs Burgess was held in 1954, (see page 195), in the age groups: over 65 years, under 65, ladies, and children under 14. Eighty competitors took part and it was filmed for the television newsreel, and Countryside in November. The 1954/55 winter was very harsh.

In 1955 a compost competition was held with Messrs Ephgrave, Clarke, Tyler, Whyman and Izzard mentioned.

Mrs Izzard started the wine guild in 1956, and the first Harvest supper was held in November 1956 when '*100 people sat down to a supper of hot soup, various cold meats and salads, tarts, pies and cheese savouries and, of course, home-made wines. Walter Savage entertained with his inimitable songs and games and dancing concluded a most enjoyable evening.*'

There was also a digging match in 1956. A daffodil and narcissus competition was held on March 3rd 1958. In 1961 it was decided that the Tewin Produce Association no longer described the core activities and it was terminated. The Tewin Horticultural Society was set up in its place.

In 1964 a request was made to the BBC for *Gardeners Question Time* to come to Tewin. This duly took place 20 years later on September 12th 1984!

Joint speaker meetings were sometimes held with the Tewin Society and two Horticultural shows were held each year. An evening meeting proved to be very popular. The Harvest supper continued and a bench was bought for Upper Green. It was varnished by the long-standing secretary Richard Nodder. Bryan Hammond was treasurer for many years.

Unfortunately, due to lack of support from members and no volunteers for the committee, the society was wound up by Alex Graham in January 1988.

It was re-started in 2001 as **THACS** from a committee organised by Anna Clark to include the arts as well as horticulture.

Above left: ***THACS*** Spring show exhibits. Above right: ***THACS*** Autumn show exhibits. Below left: **Mick Lloyd arriving with his pumpkin entry.** Below right: **Elisabeth Buchanan leads a *THACS* pottery workshop. Open Gardens, guest speakers on gardening topics and the arts, visits to exhibitions, craft shows and many other actiivties are organised by the committee. Frequent updates appear on the village website, with regular newsletters and pictures.**

THACS
TEWIN HORTICULTURAL ARTS & CRAFTS SOCIETY

Due to the enthusiasm of gardeners and artists of all kinds in Tewin, and the momentum following the Millennium Fund activities (which included plant sales and a trip to the RHS gardens at Wisley), a new committee chaired by Anna Clark developed some ideas and the society known as ***THACS*** was formed. It was hoped that by including the arts it would encourage a much wider membership and result in a more varied programme of activities.

The society has since attracted over a hundred and eighty members, both Tewin residents and postal members, and many successful events have taken

place. ***THACS*** holds Spring and Autumn shows covering horticulture, arts and crafts, photography, culinary and children's classes. There are talks and demonstrations; pottery, flower arranging and creative writing and gardening workshops; painting and photography days in and around the village; visits to gardens, churches and galleries; open gardens, featuring members' gardens; sales of plants and exhibitions of artists' work.

In 2004, to mark the RHS 'Year of Gardening' which celebrated their bicentenary, ***THACS*** arranged a special *Year of Gardening Weekend* with many gardens open to view, a sale of plants and an exhibition in the Memorial Hall. Proceeds from this weekend went to five charities, including the RHS, who at this time were asking for donations to build a massive new glasshouse at Wisley. The **THACS** contribution was recognised by the Society's name being engraved on one of the glass panels outside the new glasshouse, naming all the significant sponsors. Open Gardens are now held bi-annually with 15 or more gardens open to view.

The Society has also run projects with the local school children and encourages the Under 5s, the Rainbow and the Brownie groups in the village to enter the children's classes at the annual shows.

The Children's Playground, Upper Green

In the late 1950s a children's playground was provided on Tewin Upper Green, but with very basic equipment which was little used. With the arrival of the 'compensation culture', where someone must be to blame for any accident, it was decided to remove the equipment.

Some years passed before renewal for such a facility was voiced. A poll of residents showed that over 80% were in favour of having a playground and a similar poll with the schoolchildren put the desire for the playground at the top of their wish list.

Many attempts were made by the Tewin Parish Council to find a suitable location and a public meeting was held. All suggestions were ruled out for reasons such as traffic danger, noise affecting neighbouring properties and lack of sufficient space.

The provision of a playground became a constant and leading requirement for Tewin and a small area of the Upper Green near the tennis courts was decided as the most suitable location; being close to the other sporting activities of tennis, cricket and football pitches.

Residents were asked for their views and a clear majority were in favour of the site. There were objections from owners of nearby houses upon grounds of traffic danger, noise, vandalism, devaluation of properties, Bee Orchids, Great Crested Newts, access from the footpath and danger from cricket balls.

All these objections were sympathetically addressed. Bee Orchids were given greater protection and steps taken to discourage newts hibernating. Some re-siting of the equipment and the clearance of obstructions in the footpath access took place. Residents were shown the plans and kept informed of the proposals. High safety nets prevented cricket balls falling into the playground, child-friendly

fencing and ample litter bins were provided.

Financial support was sought and the *Friends of Tewin* led a successful application to the Hertfordshire Community Foundation's Local Network Fund for their maximum grant of £7,000. A further grant of £10,000 came from the National Lottery to enable the plans to proceed.

Upon receiving Planning Consent, members of the Tewin Parish Council and representatives of the Friends of Tewin visited manufacturers to view the equipment and eventually the Egham, Surrey, based company of SMP Playgrounds was contracted to provide and install the equipment.

To coincide with the opening on Sunday 15th July 2007, crowds attended a Tewin Family Day on Upper Green. Events included a classic car display, bouncy castle, play bus, face painting, hand-turned organs, pottery demonstration, a fire engine, a police 4 x 4, the Red Cross, bowls, tennis and cricket coaching, a pig roast, Punch and Judy show, bands and refreshments.

At 2 o'clock Lord Laming of Tewin, (who wrote the introduction to this book), officially opened the playground, accompanied by a boy and a girl representing the School, who presented a bouquet to Lady Laming. The playground, with all the necessary safety features, is limited to children up to eight years of age. It is carefully monitored and maintained and, particularly at school holiday times, is well used and also provides a pleasant picnic spot for the parents.

Chapter 14

Some Tewin Families

The Archer Family

Harry Archer was born on the 21ˢᵗ June 1897 which was the day before Queen Victoria's Diamond Jubilee.

He lived in Nancybury Cottages which were just north of Queen Hoo Hall, where he was brought up by his grandmother. She was friendly with Kit Nash, (see page 238). On a Sunday Harry used to go to Kit Nash's for tea with his grandmother. They had smoked herring cooked over the fire and bread and butter. After leaving Tewin Cowper School he worked on local farms and saved enough money to buy a secondhand motorcycle.

After the outbreak of the First World War he rode to Aylesbury in Buckinghamshire and signed on with the Oxford and Bucks Light Infantry. He was sent to France and Belgium and fought in the Battle of the Somme. He was shot, and the bullet passed through his arm, splintering the bone. They wanted to amputate his arm, but he refused. He was then sent to a convalescent home at Talgarth in the Brecon Beacons, Wales.

Harry was sent to a farm in Peterborough to work. On Armistice day the farmer came into the field to tell him the War was over. Harry then packed all of his belongings and caught a train to Knebworth and went to live with his aunt. Eventually he bought himself a secondhand lorry and started as a coal merchant at Knebworth station delivering to local villages including Datchworth and Bramfield. In 1927 he met his wife Eileen who was from Belfast. They were married at the Catholic church in St. Albans in 1928. They had a daughter Eileen and a son Terry, who has written these reminiscences.

During World War II the family lived at Mardley Hill and Harry who was very fond of horses bought a horse and trap and could often be seen trotting around the local villages.

The Baldwin Family

Arthur Baldwin and his wife moved from London to live in Tewin between the wars when Arthur came to work for Mr Hale at Tewin Hill Farm. Later they lived at 26 Upper Green Road.

Their son John and his wife Amelia stayed with his parents and later moved to 7 Tewin Hill. They had four children, Daphne, Joe, Gerald and David.

Another branch of the Baldwin family, cousins, lived at 2 Tewin Hill. Nellie and Jonto Baldwin had seven children Olive, Joyce, Hazel, Barbara, Maurice, Malcolm and Peter. Jonto worked at Tewin Hill Farm (see chapter 3).

Daphne who later married Roy Ketteridge in 1950 left school at 14 and went to work in Panshanger Aerodrome Canteen. She followed this with various jobs including working for Smith Kline & French, Allen & Hanburys, a post as nursing assistant at the QEII and working for Zena & Bert Booth when they were the publicans at *The Plume of Feathers.*

Memories of Tewin 1939 (World War II)
by Daphne Ketteridge 1995

Roy and Daphne (née Baldwin) Ketteridge on their wedding day at St. Peter's Church, 1950.

Walking from church with friends, we were told war had been declared. I was ten years old. For a year or so Tewin was still very peaceful. My father was working at Tewin Hill Farm for Mr W Hale. It was fun to go and get the milk after school from the dairy and spend an hour at the farm milking by hand the large herd of cows. We also used to watch the fresh milk being taken to the cooling system - it was so clean and something I will always remember - the cow sheds were spotless.

It wasn't very long before my mother was nursing and my father was transferred to the private police at Panshanger Aerodrome. We soon became very aware of the bombing of London, which changed the way of village life. People in the village became very involved and busy.

Evacuees arrived, chief test pilots, John and Geoffrey de Havilland, became temporary residents at The Plume of Feathers, Tewin, being only a short distance from Hatfield airfield, which they used to fly from. They now have a place of honour in St Peter's churchyard, Tewin.

American airmen soon became a familiar sight, going on and off duty to the look-out and control site at the end of the Panshanger aerodrome runway. Local residents soon made them welcome to join families in Tewin for living accommodation until the end of the war. By now we were beginning to understand what war was all about.

Most air raids took place at night. I clearly remember being carried from my bed by my father to look at Firwood ablaze with incendiary bombs. We could clearly see London in the distance, with the sky ablaze. Many high explosive bombs dropped all around us. The one that fell in the garden of Upper Green Road, Tewin, did not explode. The windows of our house were boarded up but the front door blew up the stairs - my brother slept through all this noise. My parents had stored some marrows on a shelf above the bed Not one had fallen on him and he was carried downstairs still asleep. We all said our prayers and remained downstairs to sleep.

We no longer had flowers in the front garden - instead my father grew vegetables to provide for the family meals. He also kept chickens, rabbits and grew fruit trees on the allotments.

Saturday evenings my mother and myself stoked up the fire and made pastry with the fat from tinned sausage meat. It was delicious for sausage rolls. Eggs were pickled in a bucket of waterglass for winter, but the family did enjoy dried egg and potato scones. My mother, despite the rationing of food, managed to have good meals for the family.

The Air-Raid Warden's post was at the local village school. Air-raid shelters had been dug - I can remember using them in the daytime. We had a very nice family at the school, Mr F Hollis and his wife. They were both teachers but the standard of education at the school was not particularly high. A Reverend Stebbing would take scripture lessons and morning prayers each day, and the one thing I can remember and enjoyed doing with a friend, often on a Friday, was the housework for Mrs Hollis at the school. On a Sunday, sometimes three times a day because I was in the choir, I would attend St Peter's Church in the village.

The two shops in Tewin were excellent. Mr Briant and Mr Molden did a very good job and fresh vegetables, fruit and eggs were brought from the garden field shed run by Mr C. Chalkley.

We also had Tewin Orchard and after school Miss Hopkyns (she owned the orchard) allowed us to pick hogweed for the rabbits and have an apple off the trees. On a Saturday morning we would go down to the watercress beds for a bunch of watercress. It is now Tewin Fish Farm, although both have now closed.

We were very lucky to have a nurse called Miss Fountain living in the village in the cottage as you enter Cannons Meadow. Children could visit her on their way to school. The school bell would ring until 9am.

The Tewin Memorial Hall was made very good use of and we all enjoyed Girl Guides thanks to Miss Nunns. Bowls were played at the back of the hall - we used to sit on the fence and enjoy watching. In the middle of the Lower Green we had a round seat and a filled-in well with a very nice frame - that still stands today as a shelter from the rain. I remember a lion's head pump we used to get water from to drink while playing or watching cricket, rounders and football. Us girls would sit and do our knitting and embroidery - we would never get bored.

We would spend school holidays down by the River Mimram, taking some jam sandwiches for a picnic. The water was so clear and clean we could swim and catch small fish. The wild flowers and grasses were beautiful. The Tewin Bury Farm with its 19th century farmhouse is still delightful on the banks of the river. We would make our way to the farm along the River Mimram to Barton's Dairies, a very picturesque spot in the Mimram valley. Tewin Mill to us was a picture *postcard setting.*

Two familiar faces always seen in the village were Mr J. Wilsher, the road sweeper, and Mr C. Geeves, the local postman, who were resident in Tewin.

Tewin Garage was owned at that time by Mr G. Ambrose and because there were not many cars around. If anybody required transport he was always available, for a small fee, to pick people up. You could also purchase an accumulator and buy paraffin from him.

There were no battery radios in those days, so for the wireless sets, accumulators did the job!

At Sevenacres, Upper Green, we had a dentist called Mr Bishop. He came to Tewin around 1932 and worked in the Tewin practice at this house. I still have the fillings set in my teeth, being the original work done by himself.

At fourteen years of age, upon leaving school I was given my first bicycle to go out to work on. My job

was at Panshanger Aerodrome. A gentleman called Wing Commander Pike had still got a training school there and it was a very busy concern. With friends from the village we built up a very good canteen team and had some very happy days there.

King Peter of Yugoslavia and Prince Bernhard of the Netherlands would fly into there and I had my first flight from Panshanger Aerodrome during this time.

When the war was coming to an end, salvage came from warehouses to be cleaned and sorted in the barns at Crown Farm in Tewin. Myself and friends would spend many hours after school working on this project.

The Rose & Crown could now get you a Sunday lunch if booked and two of our local doctors, who were later to practise in the village, could be seen sitting in the porch with Mr Johnson, who owned Crown Farm, awaiting their lunch.

Charles Barker (1884-1957) and his wife Elizabeth (1880-1918) with their children, Charles Alfred (1913-1970), Edith (1907-1967) and Thomas (1915-2002). In 1940 Charles Alfred came to work for Mr Hale at Tewin Hill Farm. He and his wife Joy and their family lived at 7 Tewin Hill. They moved to Upper Green Road in 1969.

Cecil John Barton

Cecil Barton lived and farmed at Summers Lane, Finchley where his father had also lived. Originally the family came from Gloucestershire.

When he was 19 his father died and subsequently Cecil came to Tewin and in 1927 rented the Dairy at Archers Green and Warrengate Farm house from Lord Desborough.

During the following years he developed a harness which enabled pigs to be tethered, (see page 37).

Cecil purchased Warrengate and the Dairy from the Desborough Estate in 1960. After Cecil's death in 1974, his son John continued to farm here, and later sold Warrengate.

Alfred Barclay Bishop

In 1925, the land later to become Tewin Wood Estate was sold to Homeland Garden Estates Limited. Alfred Barclay Bishop was the resident agent who showed visitors round the plots of land for sale for the new housing development. He lived with his family at Keepers Cottage, (see page 231). He remained in Tewin Wood and took an interest in the village, at one time becoming Chairman of the Parish Council. He died in 1952, a plaque to his memory is in the bus shelter opposite *The Rose and Crown*.

Cyril Arthur Duvall Bishop

Parents: John & Edith Duvall Bishop of Cuffley
Born: February 3rd 1893
Died: January 1959
Brother: Sidney
Educated: Merchant Tailors School North London and Guys Hospital Dental School
Married: 2nd wife Mabel Morris
Family: One daughter, Elizabeth

Left: **Alfred Barclay Bishop**
Below left: **Alfred and Betty Barclay Bishop (rear) with his daughters Mollie (Ingram) (b1918-) and Barbara (Sinclair) (1920-2007) children of his first marriage to Kathleen.**

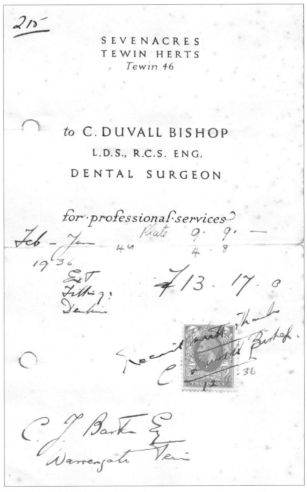

A receipted bill to Cecil Barton of Warrengate Farm for dental services, 1936.

207

Left: **Family photograph showing Cyril Duvall Bishop and his wife Mabel with their daughter Elizabeth in 1948.**
Below: **Watercolour portrait of Elizabeth by Eileen Soper (1905 - 1989). In 1948, Eileen painted a number of portraits of local children including this one. Eileen lived in 'Wildings' at Harmer Green, not far from Kit Nash (see page 238).**

Taught by her artist father George Soper, at the age of 15 Eileen became the youngest ever exhibitor at *The Royal Academy of Arts* in London. Her subjects were mainly children and wildlife, at which she excelled. It was her love of animals and her ability to draw and paint them which was quite remarkable, and is best remembered today.

One of her most important professional partnerships was with Enid Blyton, the prolific children's book author, and she illustrated many of her titles, including the *'Famous Five'* series, still in print in 2009.

After finishing his training as a dental surgeon, Cyril Bishop went into the army and served in Sierra Leone during the First World War.

He was one of the few to survive the terrible conditions in West Africa and was very ill for many years on his return to England.

Advised to take up a hobby he began to breed rabbits and Rhode Island Red chickens. He also took up conjuring and became a member of the Magic Circle. Gradually he returned to health and his career in dentistry. Finally in 1932 he purchased 7 acres of land in Upper Green Road, Tewin for £400. On the outbreak of the Second World War in 1939 Cyril gave up his dental surgery in London and moved his practice to Tewin. He also had a large pedigree poultry farm and smallholding, (see chapter 3). He wrote articles and broadcast on the radio. He was for some years a County Councillor and did a considerable amount of work for Tewin.

The Brand Family

The Brand family name first appears in Tewin as a record of a death in 1830. It is possible that the family came from North London. Since that time there are records of the family in Tewin, Bramfield and Datchworth, and surrounding villages.

Harry and Florence Brand lived at Nancybury Cottages in Queen Hoo Lane. They had four boys and three girls. One of their sons, Alfred, married Violet Daisy Bricklow and they had three children, Ronald, Daisy and Margaret. The family lived in the wooden cottages which were near *The Plume of Feathers*. Ron married and he had two children, and his son Terry is an artist, runs a village art class and also specialises in teddy bear restorations: 'Tewin's Bruins'.

Another son, Henry 'Joe' Brand, married Gladys. They had two daughters, Janet and Shirley, and a son John. Janet and her husband, William Pitman, had six children: Randolf, Alan, Linda, Eric, Colin and Jenny.

Harry and Florence Brand, Nancybury Cottages, c1940.

The Chalkley Family

The Chalkley family is mentioned in the 1881 census of Tewin with those of working age designated as agricultural labourers.

In the 1930s, Charles Chalkey, his wife Edith (née Shadbolt) and their family, (Doris, Bert, Vera, Lillian, Margaret, Willy and Johnny), moved to one of the new social houses in Upper Green Road. Regrettably, Johnny died at the age of 16.

Behind these new houses, Charles had a small-holding on land that formed part of the village allotments. He grew fruit and vegetables and kept various animals and birds including pigs, goats and chickens.

All the produce was either sold locally or taken to sell in the markets and shops of North London and to hotels and restaurants.

At Christmas time members of the family and local helpers worked tirelessly plucking the chickens and

turkeys. Sometimes 60 to 80 chickens would be prepared at a time. One of the workers reported that *'the feathers in the shed were so numerous that they came up to their shoulders!'*

In the mid 1950s when Charles died, the allotments and the land on which the smallholding was situated was sold. Later Godfries Close and Harwood Close were built on this site, (see page 222).

Robert and Gladys Cole

Bob Cole was born in Tewin, and lived as a boy in a small cottage which stood to the left of *The Plume of Feathers*. As a young man he was apprenticed as a wheelwright. Gladys was an orphan and as a young woman became a laundry maid at Tewin Water House.

They were both members of a Concert Party which performed in the village, and this is how they met. When Bob was 27 and Gladys 24 they were married. They were probably engaged for quite a while as Bob and his brother-in-law started to build the marital home, Orchard House, in 1921. It was completed for Bob and Gladys to move into after their marriage in 1924. There were two children Daphne and Marion.

During the Second World War Bob and Gladys Cole let two rooms. Land army girls lodged at Orchard House, and between 1942-1943 so did Geoffrey de Havilland.

Daphne Cole

Gladys and Bob Cole at the marriage of their daughter Marion to Dennis Walby at St. Peter's Tewin 1954. The Bridesmaids were Tina Quince, Anne and Jennifer Darton.

Daphne was married in 1942, the reception was held at *The Plume of Feathers*. Geoffrey flew a Spitfire overhead to celebrate!

Boston and Charlotte Compton

Boston Compton

Born:	1878 at Potton, Bedfordshire
Died:	March 1956
Parents:	Father was the Policeman at Pirton near Hitchin

Education:	St Mary's School, Hitchin
Married:	Great Munden Church

Boston joined the Police Force in 1899 at Royston Police Station. He was later based at Hitchin, Welwyn, Watton-at-Stone, Hertford and Tewin. He was a good athlete and entered in the 100 yards race in the police sports which he won.

While at Hertford Police Station he lived in Bengeo where he met his wife Charlotte Patmore. They were married at Great Munden Church.

There were three children of the marriage: Aubrey was born in 1915, Margaret in 1917 and David in 1924.

In 1919 Boston and his wife, Aubrey and Margaret moved to the Police House at Tewin, No 3 Lower Green, a Cowper House. Retirement came on 27th December 1924 and the family moved for a short time to South Lodge at The Mill House, while their new home, Lime Cottage, was being built. It was completed in June 1925.

On retirement Boston enjoyed his hobby of gardening and taking all the local papers to see what was happening in the criminal world in the area! He helped for a while in the garden at Marden Hill House, but his main pleasure was entering his garden for the best kept garden in the Welwyn area. He won the competition for 14 years up to the start of the Second World War.

During the 1920s and 1930s he served on the Tewin Parish Council.

Boston's cousin was the father of Denis Compton, the cricketer, who played for Middlesex and England 1930s - 1950s. Denis Charles Scott Compton CBE (1918-1997) was *'one of the greatest artists and entertainers the game of cricket has known'*. He averaged over 50 runs in Tests and scored 5,807 runs at this level. In his first class career he scored 38,942 runs, including 122 centuries, achieved 622 wickets bowling and took 415 catches.

With elder brother Leslie, he played for Arsenal FC during the winter months. He became a particularly familiar face in the media by advertising Brylcreem hair dressing.

Charlotte Compton - née Patmore

Born: 1882 at Great Munden, one of 11
             children, 8 boys and 3 girls
Died: 1963
Father: Nathan Patmore
Education: Great Munden School

Charlotte left school at 13 and went to work as a cook assistant for Mr and Mrs French of 'Frenlite Flour'. Later she moved to become head cook for Lady Longmore of Parkhill House Bengeo. It was at this time she met her future husband, Boston Compton. In Tewin, besides running her home and caring for the family, she helped to form the *Mothers Union* in the mid 1920s.

Boston Comton in 1900.

Charlotte Compton (née Patmore)

Taking a swarm of bees, possibly at the lower end of Back Lane, in 1928. Left to right: **Aubrey Compton (son of Boston Compton), Clive Shadbolt and Jack Digby.**

Richard W Dunn

Born: 12th September 1914, Wembley
Father: Richard (Dickie) Dunn
Mother: Lillian Mary
Educated: Taplow, Bucks
Married: 16th March 1940 to Joan
Children: Lesley and Richard

Dick, or Dickie as he was known, moved with his wife Joan to Tewin in 1949 from Southgate. They lived at 39 Upper Green Road.

As a young man Dickie went to work in his father's motor trade business in Euston Road, London. He had many hobbies including horse riding and cycle racing and was a keen speed-skater at Streatham Lee Rink.

In 1938, after the Munich Crisis he joined the Rangers Kings Royal Rifles, the local Territorial Regiment. In 1939 he joined the army and was based at Limber - Dickie's section was the best fed in the British Army. He used his country skills and there was always pheasant, partridge and rabbit to add to their rations.

He went with the 2nd Armoured Division to Egypt at the end of 1940. After tours of duty in Cyprus and South Africa he joined the 7th Armoured Division of the Eight Army in the Western Desert - he fought at Tobruk and Bir Hakien and was seriously wounded in the arm during the British Army's retreat to El Alamein. He was sent home and discharged from the army, and returned to the family motor trade business where he worked until he retired.

Dickie, Joan and their family continued to live at Tewin and Dickie became very involved in village life. He was a founder member of the present Tewin Cricket Club and Football Club. He enjoyed his hobbies including fishing and gardening, winning many prizes at village agricultural shows. He was particularly well known for his home brewing - many a pint was enjoyed at 39 Upper Green Road!

Dickie and Joan Dunn with Lesley and Richard, mid 1950s

He helped to run the Memorial Hall, took part in Amateur Dramatics, was a member of the Parish Council and for several years the village fête was held in the garden of his home.

Dickie is perhaps best remembered for his love of Tewin and his enthusiasm for The Best Kept Village Competition. He worked with tireless energy with one or two others, to encourage the people of Tewin to take pride in the village. Clipping grass verges, trimming hedges, picking up litter and generally tidying up the village, led to Tewin winning the competition firstly in 1967, again in 1973, 1984, 1985, 1987 and 1988.

Leonard and Lily Ephgrave

Leonard Ephgrave and his wife, Lily (née Welsh), lived at 32 Upper Green Road with their seven children, Robert, Joan, Eric, Brenda, Mick, Jean and Janet.

Leonard worked as a dairyman for Sir Otto and Lady Beit on the Tewin Water Estate. Later, he was employed by ICI at Digswell Lodge in Welwyn Garden City. Leonard died in 1981 and Lily in 1990.

Leonard was one of the seven children of Benjamin and Clara Ephgrave, who all lived at 9 School Lane. Benjamin (1882-1940) was in the First World War, where he was injured and lost an eye. After the War he worked at Tewin Hill Farm.

The earliest record of 'Ephgrave' in St Peter's Churchyard is 1905, possibly a relative of Benjamin. Since that time generations of this Hertfordshire family have lived in Tewin.

The name 'Ephgrave' is rare and unusual and is of Anglo Saxon origin, probably originating from a small village or hamlet in Hertfordshire, long since gone, called 'Ipgrave'.

The name takes a number of forms and is found mainly in London, Bedfordshire and Hertfordshire – derivations can be 'Hipgrave', 'Ipgrave', 'Ipsgrave' and 'Epgrave'. 'Ephgrave' is less common. There have been families with this name living in Hertfordshire for several centuries, particularly in or near Ayot Green.

Len and Lily Ephgrave

213

Ellen Maud Morris

William, Frank, Ellen (Nellie) and Mabel photographed in c1912.

Parents: Lt. William James Morris
               Royal Artillery
               Ellen Elizabeth (Fripp)
Born: 10th August 1904 in Halifax,
               Nova Scotia, Canada.

Ellen or Nellie as she was known was the second child in the family of two boys, William and Frank and a sister Mabel.

She was educated at various schools depending on where her father was stationed. One school was the Victoria College for Young Ladies at Westcliff-on-Sea.

Part of her schooling was in the U.S.A. where her father was based during the First World War near Pittsburgh, Pennsylvania.

She finished her education in North London after the death of her father in 1917, and she finally did a secretarial course at Pitmans.

One of her first jobs was as junior secretary to Sir John Simpson, Architect, who with his partner, Maxwell Ayerton designed the original Wembley Stadium, the opening ceremony of which Nellie attended.

For a while during the war she worked for Sir William Acland at Barnes Wood, Burnham Green. She then applied and was accepted for a post at County Hall Hertford where she was a secretary for most of the war - cycling there and back each day.

After answering an advertisement in County Hall

for a Social Worker for the mentally handicapped she was appointed to the post in the late 1940s. She had no experience but learnt about her patients, their families and all their troubles and problems. She was responsible at that time for all young people with mental handicaps in the whole of Hertfordshire. She was well known for her tireless work and her compassion for her patients - she loved her work from which she finally retired at the age of 70.

Nellie never married, but was devoted to her family and close friends. In 1932 she purchased 'The Cottage' 43 Upper Green Road from Lord Desborough for £100, where she lived firstly with her mother and later with her sister Mabel Duvall Bishop. Nellie died aged 92 in 1997.

Claude & Freda Owen

Claude

Parents:	Richie William Owen
	Millie Chapman
Born:	Letchworth Garden City April 22nd 1915
	3 brothers and 2 sisters
Married:	Freda Walton September 29th 1945
Died:	March 2008

As a child Claude and his family moved to South Wales returning when he was 10 to Letchworth where he attended Pixmore School until he was 14.

After leaving school he worked on farms at Sheppall, Kings Walden and Wheathampstead, finally coming to Tewin working for Mr Hale at Tewin Hill Farm. He also worked for Norton Abrasives (Grinding Wheel Company) in Welwyn Garden City, where except for the War years he worked until he retired.

Claude was a member of the Territorial Army and when World War II started he became a member of the Royal Engineers and was in the 334 Searchlight Company. In January 1940 he was moved to the Royal Artillery and went to France. He was injured and had many months in hospital. He came out of the Army on December 6th 1945.

Freda

Parents:	George and Annie Walton
Born:	Horden Co Durham March 18th 1915
	1 brother and 2 sisters
Educated:	Horden Girls School Higher Tops 11-14
Died:	March 2009

Freda left school and went to work for a Methodist Minister's wife 7.30am-5pm including Saturday and Sunday mornings for 5/- (25p) a week.

1930	Became a scullery maid at Stanford Hall Nottingham. There she used an electric dishwasher, potato peeler and cake mixer. She was later promoted to 2nd kitchen maid.
1935	Moved to Eastwell Park in Kent and worked for Viscount Dunsford. She remained here only six months as the family went abroad.
1935	She then worked at Longleat House home of Lord Bath the 5th Marquis. Promoted to head kitchen maid.
1938	Freda commenced work for Lord and Lady Desborough at Taplow Court near Maidenhead. Here the Desboroughs lived in the summer months, moving to

Panshanger House during the winter. When war was declared, Taplow Court was taken over by the Government, and the family moved permanently to Panshanger House, (see Chapter 9). Freda left Panshanger in 1941. It was while she was at Panshanger that she attended Tewin Memorial Hall Dances and met Claude.

On marrying Claude in 1945, they moved in with his mother in Upper Green Road and then to Cannons Meadow in 1946. They had two children Valerie, and Peter. Peter sadly died when he was 26.

Claude and Freda enjoyed village life. Freda had been closely linked with the Church, the Mothers Union and had looked after the Church linen for over 38 years. Both later joined **THACS** and Claude exhibited his wine at the first two shows, 2002-2003.

Claude and Freda Owen on their wedding day in 1945.

The Perry Family

Early in the 20th century Arthur and Emma Perry lived in the wooden cottages which stood near the front of *The Plume of Feathers*. Arthur worked as a road man round the village, sweeping the sides of the road keeping them clean and tidy. In later life they lived with their daughter Annie.

Their son Arthur worked at Norton Grinding Wheel Company in Welwyn Garden City. He was married to Edith and they lived at 24 Upper Green Road. They had four children Jimmy, Ellen, Joan and Bertha.

Ellen, like her brother and sisters, was educated at

Tewin Cowper School and when she was 12 she went to live with her aunt Annie Perry in School Lane. From the age of 14-18 Ellen worked at de Havilland Aircraft in the catering section. She cycled to and from work in Hatfield every day. It was at this time that Ellen became a member of the G.T.C. (Girls Training Corps). This was an organisation formed during the Second World War for girls to train with a view to entering the armed forces.

It was at Tewin Memorial Hall that Ellen met Don Tyler. They were married at St Peter's Tewin on March 2nd 1945 and had a family of four boys. As her children began to grow up Ellen helped her husband in his fish shop in Digswell and later became cook caterer for 26 years at Tewin Water School for children with hearing impairment.

The Quince Family

The Quince family lived in Tewin from 1913 when Edward John Quince (born 1875) and his wife, Eliza (nee Webb - born 1875) moved to the village from Bramfield with two of their children, Ivy, born in 1904, and Arthur Edward, born in 1907. Both children attended Tewin Cowper Endowed School. In 1992, at the age of 87, Ivy, who was the oldest living ex-pupil, attended the school when it celebrated its bicentenary, (see page 90).

The family lived at 1 Churchfield Cottages and Edward was a gamekeeper working for Sir Otto Beit on the Tewin Water Estate. At the start of the First World War, in 1914, he joined the Royal Engineers and his name can now be seen on the Roll of Honour in St Peter's Church.

After the War Edward returned to work at Tewin Water House. He died suddenly when out in the fields near his home in 1932.

In 1943, Ivy married Bill Hubbard, also a gamekeeper. They lived at Marden Lodge, near Hollybushes, and had one son. Ivy's brother, Arthur, married Christina Josephine Kavanagh (Josie) of The Laundry, Folly, Churchfield Road. They had two children, Edward and Tina. The family moved about a good deal, living in various houses in Tewin, among them the Stable Flats at Tewin Water and the North Lodge at Panshanger.

They finally settled in Cannons Meadow. Arthur was employed as a gardener at Tewin Water House and then he worked for Sir Knox Helm at The Old Rectory. Tina and her family now live in Welwyn Garden City.

Arthur Shadbolt & (possibly) E Hankin.

Left to right: **Mrs Atkins, Doris Strange and Mrs Taylor.**

Doris Strange

Doris Strange, who lived in Cannons Meadow, came to Tewin at the age of 16 from Gloucestershire to work as a scullery maid at Tewin Water House.

On recounting her years working for Sir Otto and Lady Beit she recalled their kindness and caring attitude to all their staff. Doris stayed with the family for many years finally becoming the cook. She remembered General de Gaulle who stayed at Tewin Water from time to time during the Second World War - *'a nice man who always remembered the names of all the staff '.*

Doris met Fred Strange at a dance in Digswell Village Hall. Fred was living in the barracks by Welwyn North Station, he was a regular soldier in the Herts & Beds Regiment. He was also a trumpet player. After the war Fred worked at Murphy Radio in Welwyn Garden City.

They married in 1942 and lived at Mr Lyles' house, 16 Upper Green Road. Later they moved to Cannons Meadow and had a son, Andrew. Doris, who died in 2002, worked at Tewin Cowper School as a cook, with Mrs Atkins and Mrs Taylor. She was there for 5 or 6 years when Mrs Grant was the head teacher.

George Ernest and Margaret Harriet Temple
George (Ernie)
Ernie was born in Hertford in 1912 at Dunkirks Farm, which at that time had the land at the top of Queens Road - now the site of Simon Balle School. Ernie was the youngest of the five children of Frank John Temple and his wife Florence Emma.

His father was reputed to have had one of the earliest milk rounds in Hertford with a cart delivering milk three times a day:- the breakfast run, the milk pudding run and the tea time run.

It was in Hertford that Ernie developed his love of the land, but at the age of 7 his father died and the family was split up and Ernie went to live with an Aunt in Eastbourne, where he stayed until he left school. It was here that he became a keen cricketer playing for his school and the Sussex Colts.

On leaving school he became apprenticed as a carpenter and joiner to his mother's family firm 'Newby Bros' in Southgate, and was part of the team who installed the first revolving stage in a London theatre, at the London Hippodrome.

In 1938 he caught polio and never really recovered the full use in his left hand. However, he completed his apprenticeship and joined his oldest brother Frank who had taken a farm at Stapleford, after helping to establish Patchendon Farm. In 1941 he was married to Peggy Day whom he had met at the Enfield branch of the Junior Imperial League. The wedding took place in the blitzed church of St. George's, Harringay, and they moved to Tewin. They had two children, Roger born in 1942 and Frances in 1947. In Tewin Ernie and Peggy initially lived at Archers Green and then moved to Vine Cottage, Lower Green. Ernie worked for C. J. Barton at Warrengate Farm for 42 years.

Ernie's great love was cricket and he was a founder member of the present Tewin Cricket Club. He helped to move the Tewin Wood Estate hut from its site on the corner of Desborough Drive to Upper Green where it became the Cricket Club's first pavilion. After retiring from playing cricket Ernie became president of the Club.

Margaret (Peggy)
Peggy Day was born in 1912 in Rawalpindi, Pakistan. She was one of nine children born to Albert and Amy Day. Her father was a Colour Sergeant Instructor in the armed forces.

Her early years were spent in Rawalpindi and it was not until her father retired in 1921 that the family returned to England. They settled in Tottenham and Peggy went with her father to White Hart Lane and became an ardent Spurs supporter.

Firstly working on the magazine *'The Gramophone'* she later became a secretary to Robert Porter of

Ernie and Peggy Temple

Robert Porter & Sons, the bottlers. She was also a part-time auxiliary nurse at the local hospital.

Besides working in the office of C. J. Barton, Peggy became involved in many village activities - the Women's Institute, The Tewin Wood Players, (later the Tewin Players), The Conservative Association, and she also became secretary of the Village Memorial Hall. She helped to test the Guides for their badges and helped with teas for the Cricket Club.

Peggy's son Roger states *'Peg was a person whose glass was always half full and never half empty'.*

Peggy died in 1974 and Ernie in 1987. The seat on

217

the piece of grass opposite Tewin Stores was given in their memory.

The Tyler Family

George William Tyler and his wife lived c1900 in the house next to *The Duck*, now Tebbutts Stores.

Behind the house was a 'sausage skin factory' (finally demolished after the Second World War) and George Tyler and his sons had the task of regularly cleaning the sewer which took the effluent from the factory.

The men were lowered down a 50ft shaft to the sewer, and on one of these occasions as he was being lowered down the shaft, George's son Ernie was overcome by the fumes and fell. His father was then lowered down to try to rescue his son, but was also overcome by the fumes and fell to his death. The two bodies were finally retrieved by another son, Albert.

Albert was subsequently awarded the Carnegie Trust Medal for bravery and his father was awarded it posthumously.

George Tyler and his wife had several children and one of their sons, Lewis, founded the Tyler Timber Fencing business.

Ellen (née Perry) and Don Tyler.

Lewis married Gwendoline May Mardell from Woolmer Green and they had six sons, and two daughters. Educated at Tewin School the children then went at 11 to school in Welwyn. One of their sons, Don, like many young men during the Second World War, enlisted and joined the Royal Navy.

He was de-mobbed in 1945. For a while he worked with his father and then opened a fish shop in Digswell. The shop closed in 1970 and finally in 1984 Don retired. For over forty years he took on the responsibility of raising the Union Jack on the village flagpole to celebrate national and village events.

Thomas and May Williams

May Williams was the daughter of Mr and Mrs Alexander Charles Hill. She was born on 1st May 1909 at Warrengate Farm and in infancy moved with her parents and sister Dorothy to The Mill House. Sadly Dorothy, who was the older of the two girls, died in childhood.

May was educated in Hertford, and in the 1920s her parents retired from farming buying 3 acres of land in Hertford Road, Tewin, building a house, 'Southleigh', where they all lived. From here May went to work during the early part of the war at Nivea, the Smith & Nephew factory in Welwyn Garden City.

She had several years earlier met Thomas (Tommy) Williams who, with his brother Billy, had come to Tewin from Carmarthen, South Wales in 1931. (see chapter 3).

In 1943 May and Tommy were married at St Peter's Church and lived at Southleigh. Ivor was born in July 1944 and Vaughan in April 1948. In 1952 the Williams family moved to Tewin Bury, (see chapter 3). In 1981 May and her son Ivor moved to No 2 Back Lane, Tewin.

May lived her life in Tewin contributing greatly in her own quiet way to the life of the village. She was a member of the Mothers Union and a wonderful cook. She entered many local cookery competitions. For a while she was a member of the Parochial Church Council, and throughout her life devoted much time working for St Peter's Church.

May died on 9th November 1992.

Thanks are due to the people that have provided information and photographs of their families and who wished them to be included in the book. Some of these items were originally presented in the Millennium Exhibition in 2000.

Howardsgate Welwyn Garden City Hertfordshire AL8 6BH

Far left: **May Williams in 1928.**
Left: **May seen on the left with her sister Dorothy and their nanny at the Mill House.**
Below: **The Williams family, left to right Vaughan, May, Tommy and Ivor in 1948.**

Above left to right: **Mrs Lily Collett, Mr Arthur Collett, Mrs Nellie Hart and Mr Brian Hart at Marden c1930**

Chapter 15

Housing Development

Lower Green showing the new Cowper Cottages behind the older, later demolished cottages with Post Office, c1905.

Tewin in the nineteenth century was described in *'The Story of my life'* by Henry Gullet (1837- 1914) and this is his view of Tewin, Lower Green.

'The house, of which we occupied a part, was pleasantly situated, facing a little triangular village green, in the centre of which stood a venerable pound, now and then briefly tenanted by an erring donkey.

Near this stood other relics of antiquity in the shape of the whipping post and stocks and close by was the well house erected over the well from which most of the neighbourhood was supplied with water.

The country round consisting mostly of the estates of the different noblemen and 'squires', the village was principally occupied by the families of some of the dependants of these gentlemen.

There were two or three gamekeepers, two stewards, a baker, a shoemaker, a blacksmith, a brewer, the schoolmaster and a number of labouring people inhabiting a row of small cottages. Such were nearly all the elements of which the population of our little village was composed.'

Lower Green

Whilst the whipping post and stocks have disappeared and many of the tradesmen are no longer about, the scene is not so very different from Henry's account above. Lower Green has a mix of houses built over the past four centuries, the oldest of which are now numbers 8 and 9. Number 8 was used as the Post Office at one time with the Post Mistress in charge of routeing telephone calls to and from the village as well as the postal services. At the rear of this pair of cottages an extension was added in the seventeen hundreds. Further extensions were made in the eighteen hundreds and about 1950. The cottages were part of the Panshanger estate until the estate was sold in 1953. The houses were timber framed made from lathe and plaster with a peg-tiled roof. Under number 8 is a vaulted cellar with brick steps leading up to both cottages. Previous owners have been Mr and Mrs Briant in number 8 and Mr and Mrs Parrot in number 9.

The houses nearest to this house are some of the newest on the Green built in the 1960s and 1970s.

The Panshanger Estate built a number of houses in

The first social housing was built in 1919 in School Lane. This was followed in the 1930s by numbers 14 - 44 in Upper Green Road.

the nineteenth century for their workers. These Cowper Cottages are familiar properties across this part of Hertfordshire, built in local yellow (cream) brick. They were built either as terraced or semi-detached housing.

The earliest record of a smithy on Lower Green was around 1550. The last forge in Tewin, adjacent to Forge Cottage, was in use until the end of World War II and then fell into disrepair. A pair of semi-detached houses was built on the site after it was demolished.

Lower Green also has The Old School House, built in the 18th century. The Old School House is one of a small group of houses on Lower Green, Tewin, which has both architectural and historical importance. Architecturally, it was built at the same time and by the same hand as *The Rose & Crown* Public House.

Across the Green from the Old School House is the Victorian School house built by the Cowpers in 1840 to educate the children of Tewin and surrounding farmworkers' families. It had a house at one end of it for the school teacher and a garden in which they grew vegetables for school lunches, (see page 86). Tewin has its own village hall, The Memorial Hall

8 and 9 Lower Green

Above: **Grass Warren** Below: **Cannons Meadow**

221

that is also a war memorial, (see pages 110-115).

Behind Lower Green new social house building took place between 1948 and 1961. Called Cannons Meadow and Grass Warren, they include a small number of bungalows for older residents. Many of the houses are now in private ownership since the Right to Buy came into existence, but some are still council-owned properties.

The Adams Huntley houses.

Further expansion of the village took place in the 1950s in Tewin Wood and the late 1960s with the construction of Harwood Close and Godfries Close on the site of the old allotments off Upper Green Road. In 1968 fifteen houses were built on the site of the Old Rectory on Lower Green. They were built by Griffiths Taylor and the architect was Adams Huntley Associates. The development won an architectural award, described in *'The Buildings of Hertfordshire'* by Nikolaus Pevsner (Second Edition 1977) as follows:-

'At the end of a pleasant elongated green, informally grouped pantile-roofed terraces with the special feature of front court yards formed by the projecting entrance halls'.

Forge Cottage

Forge Cottage, Lower Green
Probably built in mid to late 18th century. Part of the two adjacent houses with Yew Tree Cottage. A well or rainwater storage pit was found at the rear of these cottages. It is said that someone committed suicide in the well in the early 20th century. Bob Digby was the last Tewin blacksmith who worked the forge which was adjacent to the cottage.

Yew Tree Cottage, Lower Green
This was probably built in the mid to late 18th century for the Panshanger Estate. Mr Hornet was a bricklayer employed by Mabey builders and Mr and Mrs Hornet occupied the cottage when it was sold as part of the Panshanger Estate.

Water was supplied from a well at the rear of Forge Cottage.

Yew Tree Cottage, centre, with **Vine Cottage** on right.

Vine Cottage, Lower Green
Built in 1652 possibly for the Panshanger Estate. Occupants have included Mr and Mrs Shadbolt (1946-1972), Ernie and Mrs Temple (1972-1976), Mr and Mrs Smith (1976-1983), Mr and Mrs Don Southgate. (See watercolour, painted from the front gate, on page 255).

Hertford Road
The two cottages, numbers 16 and 18 Hertford Road, next to Tewin Stores, and pictured on page 145, are thought to have been constructed about 1700 as artisan dwellings. Number 16 was the bakery and had ovens in its cellar, but in 1975, when both cottages were sold, number 18 was designated 'The Old Bakery'.

Both cottages had ladders leading to the attics, which have since been replaced by staircases.

Southleigh 13 Hertford Road.

Above: **Lime Cottage 2 Hertford Road.**

Mrs Quince, wife of the gamekeeper, outside No.1
Churchfield Cottages c1920.

Southleigh, 13 Hertford Road
Built in 1926 for Mr and Mrs A. C. Hill upon retirement from farming. The land was part of the Cowper Estates at the end of the 19th and early 20th centuries.

Lime Cottage, 2 Hertford Road
The Compton family is the only family to have occupied Lime Cottage.

  Built in 1925 for Mr Boston Compton, the architect was Andrew Grey for Aubrey Ellis builders of Hitchin. Mr Boston Compton was the Police Constable in Tewin from 1919 to 1924, (see pp 210-11). The cottage was built on land purchased from Lord Desborough. It is reported that he was pleased that Mr Compton intended to build a house not a bungalow as he reputedly did not like bungalows.

Cheyne Cottage, 14 Hertford Road
The date of construction was in the early 18th century, probably built or refurbished for the Panshanger Estate. When the Panshanger Estate broke up, the property was purchased by John Barton of Warrengate Farm in 1960. It was sold again some 10 to 12 years later and is called Cheyne Cottage because the family who lived there came from Cheyne Walk in Chelsea.

Churchfield Cottages
The eight Churchfield cottages were built about 1909 to house workers from the Tewin Water estate. The date plaque between numbers 1 and 2 has the initials KC (Katrine Cowper) upon it. The cottages were built while Tewin Water still belonged to the family and leased to Otto Beit. Most of the cottages have been considerably extended, but were initially upgraded in the 1920s to provide superior accommodation, (i.e. a bathroom), for the butler and poultryman. Each garden was planted with a number of fruit trees, a few of which survive.

  Mrs Ivy Hubbard remembered that her father, Mr Quince, was the gamekeeper for Sir Otto Beit. In

223

Tewin Lodge, Churchfield Road, in the 1930s. (See also page 21).

1913 when they came to the village they lived first at number 7 or 8 and then moved to number 1. At that time the cowman lived at number 2; the ploughman (Mr Lyle) at number 3 and the estate carpenter (Mr Ambrose) at number 4. At numbers 5 and 6 were the chauffeur (Mr Atkins) and the gardener (Mr Sheath). At numbers 7 and 8 were the butler (Mr Downing) and the poultryman (Mr Key). Mrs Hubbard said Lady Beit expected the cottages to look alike and even supplied the *'spotted muslin frilled curtains'.*

Later on Cyril Geeves, for some years 'Captain of the Belltower,' lived at number 1 Churchfield Cottages. He was permitted to take a short cut across the field opposite the church and 'Geeves gate' can still just be seen in the hedge.

Folly, Farce and Sky
Built in 1908 this was originally the laundry for Tewin Water House. The water pump was housed in a brick outbuilding in the garden of number 2 Churchfield Cottages. Many Tewin people, at one time as many as thirty, worked at the laundry. The laundry was sold in the late 1950s and became private dwellings.

Tewin Lodge
Constructed c1780 as a single storey building, an upper floor was added in 1880. It was originally built as a lodge for Tewin Water House, possibly replacing an earlier lodge.

There were very thick walls with no damp-proof course in the original part of the building. The main room had a sprung floor but other rooms had mud floors. Under the path a cistern used for water extraction was found, possibly dating from before the building was erected. A Roman pot has been found in the Mimram nearby.

The ornamental lake in Tewin Lodge gardens was part of the major re-design for Tewin Water Estate by Humphry Repton.

Upper Green Road

21 Upper Green Road
Built in 1810 for the Panshanger Estate to be occupied by foresters employed by the Estate. Originally built as 2 timber-framed cottages they were later converted into one building designed by local architect Arthur Edwards.

Before 1968 E. Shadbolt, coal merchant, occupied this dwelling with Dick (surname unknown) a cobbler, at the back of the house. Pieces of his leather were found during restoration.

When preparing new foundations for refurbishment the remains of an old well or rainwater storage tank were uncovered. There is a story that many years ago, an old lady resident met her end in this well or storage tank.

21 Upper Green Road built in 1810 for foresters on the Panshanger Estate and was originally two cottages.

76 & 78 Upper Green Road

Originally constructed around 1700 it is possible that these two cottages were originally built as one house as part of a small farm called Walnut Tree Farm. In the late 19th century it was owned by Earl Cowper and the farm buildings behind the cottages were built in 1884.

76 Upper Green Road originally built around 1700.

The Cottage, 43 Upper Green Road

Originally a two-room single-storey cottage built in the mid 17th century. The upper storey was added in Victorian times.

It was purchased in 1932 by Ellen Morris from Lord Desborough for £100. Major renovations were carried out to make it habitable. It was then let for four years and it was at this time that the famous Brooklands racing driver Lord Howe visited the cottage, *'arriving in his blue Bentley dressed in a matching blue outfit'*.

The cottage was rendered in 1950 and two extensions added in 1991.

The Cottage, 43 Upper Green Road

Sevenacres, 49 Upper Green Road

The house was designed by Mr Frank Knight (who later designed Stanborough School in Welwyn Garden City), a junior partner in the firm of Sir John Simpson who, with Maxwell Ayerton, designed the original Wembley Stadium.

Sevenacres was built for Cyril Duvall Bishop on seven acres of land bought from Walter and Alfred Bishop (no relation). The cost of the land in 1932 was £400, the building itself cost £629. In 1954 the value of Sevenacres was £6000 and in 1974 it was £50,000.

The house was designed to make best use of natural light. The front of the house faced north and the kitchen, bathroom and cloakrooms were on that side of the property. Facing south were the living rooms and the bedrooms. There was limited central heating in the property. The construction was of Flemish bricks.

Sevenacres, 1952.

225

On the left a bungalow has replaced this row of four wooden cottages, (59 Upper Green). The sign of *The Plume of Feathers* can be seen. Note the elms that were felled due to 'Dutch Elm disease'.

Upper Green

Upper Green now boasts the village tennis, cricket and football pitches. But in the 19th century it was surrounded by rows of small cottages, some built on the piece of land now occupied by 'Perrytrees', others beside 'Piggotts' and some where 'Wheelwrights' now stands.

59 Upper Green

59 Upper Green is a modern bungalow, which now stands where a row of wooden cottages used to be, next door to *The Plume of Feathers* public house.

47 Upper Green was built by Mr Cole for his wife in 1921.

47 Upper Green

Bob Cole designed Orchard House and built the home for his impending marriage. It was said: *'Mrs Cole was an orphan who had never had a home so her husband had it built for her'*. Construction commenced in 1921 and was completed in 1924. They had two daughters, Daphne and Marion. Mrs Cole lived there until her death in 1992. Geoffrey de Havilland lodged with them in the early part of World War II, (p 62).

Wheelwrights

The house known as 'Wheelwrights' was originally built in 1776. This building was pulled down and rebuilt by Benjamin Read as two semi-detached cottages in 1840. Here Willie Ward, wheelwright, set up his business in the garden of one of these houses, inherited by his wife, Emma Read, daughter of Benjamin. Willie Ward, the wheelwright of Tewin, was a well-known craftsman and his yard was in an ideal position, between Burnham Green and Tewin Lower Green, to keep the wheel of this agricultural community turning. Later he was famous for his wheelbarrows, some of which lasted into the second half of the 20th century.

The two semi-detached cottages were called 'Roselle' and 'Yew Tree Cottage' until 'Roselle' was renamed 'Wheelwrights' in 1961 in memory of Willie Ward's occupation. The two houses were made into one in 1994.

'Perrytree House'

'Perrytree house' replaced a row of cottages, which fell down before the Second World War. The land was bought in the early 1950s by an architect, Arthur Edwards, (see his book on page 240), and his wife, Christine. He designed a bungalow for his family. His wife, a keen gardener, persuaded him to have the garden designer, Sylvia Crowe, draw up plans for a comprehensive vegetable and fruit garden with many varieties of trees. The house was altered after the Edwards family left and a second storey was added. The garden remains one of its beautiful features.

'Piggotts'

'Piggotts' cottage was constructed in the late 18th century by the Desborough Estates to house estate farm workers. Only one of three cottages on this site survives, and little of that remains to be seen as the house has been added to and the cottage garden and orchard have disappeared. (See also pages 164-166).

'Rochdale Cottage', 7 Upper Green

'Rochdale Cottage' 7 Upper Green, called Tewin Cattery. This house, was built about 1750 and was originally part of the Manor of Tewinbury, before becoming part of Panshanger Estates. It is believed to be the only remaining one of three identical cottages on this or nearby sites. It has underflooring of hard pitsawn oak timbers and lathes and large bricks of the 16th and 17th centuries in its structure.

The sale of the cottage is recorded in the Tewin Orchard log book kept by Molly Hopkyns shown on page 164: a cheque from Withers for £290.0s.6d, was received on 16th January 1954.

Wheelwrights, formerly known as 'Roselle' and 'Yew Tree Cottage'.

The Manor of Wimley Bury, now Sewell's Orchard
Three listed Modern Movement houses

The history of the land and how these houses came to be built.

The piece of land on which these three houses are built has had the same boundaries since at least the 14th century and probably much longer. In the 19th century the land was an orchard, hence the name Sewell's Orchard.

In the 14th century the Manor of Wimley Bury, otherwise known as Wymondley Bury, was here; the name is retained in a field at the bottom of the garden, Wimley Bury Field, see map of 1785 (p. 11).

The earliest record of Wimley Bury is in a charter, possibly of around 1250, in which Eudo de Hamle, who also held a half fee of Tewin Bury, granted a large part of his estate to the Priory of Little Wymondley (founded in 1205-7). The charter states *'Grant by Eudo de Hamle to the Prior and Canons of Wymondley of the land he holds in Tewin for one pound of pepper at Easter. For this the Prior and Canons have paid him 207 marks. Confirmed by Peter de Maunes and Jane his wife'.*

The extent of the lands is unclear but the large payment indicates that it was possibly around 200 acres. In 1326 the Prior valued the estate at fifty shillings yearly. A map of 1785 shows that Wimley Bury Manor included Hazelton field opposite (5fi acres), Wimley Bury Field (6 acres) and Punchards Wood, now part of Tewin Wood and retained in the name 'Punchetts'. It also clearly identifies the principal house or capital messuage (site of a dwelling and outbuildings), by then called Claret Hall. This house was described as being *'situated at Wymondley Green on a site of two acres by the road from Tewin Green to Burnham Green'.*

Hazelton field achieved some notoriety in the fourteenth century when it was mentioned in a royal document of Richard II. The calendar (list of prisoners for trial at the assizes) states that a pardon was *'granted to William Joyce, canon of Little*

Wymondley Priory, for the death of John Detlyng, servant of John Hurthull, rector of Tewin who was killed in a field called Haselton, as it appears that he killed him in self defence'. The reason for the dispute is not given but it could be surmised that it concerned land or tithes or maybe the rector's glebe, which was nearby.

Ownership of the Manor of Wimley Bury appears to have stayed with the Priory until the Dissolution of the Monasteries. A record of rentals in 1537, when Henry VIII suppressed the Priory, lists the following tenants: Roger Wrenne of Tewin, weaver and his wife Christiana, land and messuage, rent 13 shillings yearly; Richard Canon, farmer, certain land, rent 56 shillings and 8d yearly; John Parsonage, farmer, one messuage and land, rent 6s 8d and a tenement (Thedgalle), rent 12d; Total yearly rent, £3 17s 4d may indicate the total area leased was much the same as when the lease was first granted three centuries earlier. After the Dissolution of the Monasteries the land was bought by a James Nedham. No further records of ownership are known until James Fleet bought the estate and other properties in Tewin in the early 18th century (see chart on page 14).

Claret Hall was leased to Philip Cosgrove in 1786 for twenty-one years at a yearly rental of nine pounds. Three years earlier, we know from an extract of an obituary of Lady Cathcart, who died in 1789, that on 18th July 1783 the reversion of Lady Cathcart's Manors of Tewin and Wimley in Hertfordshire, together with other property, particularly at Bear Quay in London, was advertised to be sold in chancery. It is understood that it was then that her property was bought by the 3rd Earl Cowper. After this there are no records for why Claret Hall disappeared, but in the 19th century the land was an orchard.

In the early 1930s Ralph and Muriel Crowley bought the land after their daughter Mary qualified as an architect. The Crowleys were Quakers who lived in Digswell and were part of the Quaker community in Welwyn Garden City. Mary, with her friend Cyril Kemp, had been to Stockholm in 1930 to an exhibition at which they saw houses with monopitch roofs, and large, light, airy rooms. They persuaded their families to enable them to buy land and build similar properties. The houses were designed in 1934 and built in 1935/6.

Mary Crowley, whose parents occupied the centre

house, designed the two houses numbered 102 and 104 Orchard Road. The third house number 106, was designed by Cyril Kemp for his own personal use. Mr and Mrs Miall, who were related to the other families, lived at the third house.

The houses were designed for communal living with a front entrance leading to three garages and a communal back garden. The fronts of the houses face north east and the back, south west. They are staggered on the site so that none of them takes light from the others. The houses are built from local yellow Hertingfordbury bricks, with a plinth course of blue bricks, with Staffordshire pantile roofs. All the living space, which gets most of the sun during the day, is at the back of the house.

The houses had fitted kitchens, central heating for radiators and towel rails, and a maid's room. There was only one fireplace, in the lounge, very unusual for houses built at this time.

The furnishings were very simple and plain with large airy windows and doors letting in lots of light. There are tiled floors in hall, kitchen and downstairs cloakroom and upstairs in the bathroom and toilet. All doors were plain and a concrete staircase with original bannisters remains. Fitted cupboards with flush handles, airing cupboards, light fittings and fitted shelves still exist.

Tewin Wood
From forest to prestigious housing development

Old plans show that the original name was Tewin Big Wood, and name parts of Tewin Wood as 'Punchetts Wood' to the west and south, 'Swanhill Wood' to the south east 'Synods' to the east and 'Great Oakcroft Wood' to the north.

In the early 1800s the first residence, 'Keepers House', (now known as 'Keepers Cottage' in Desborough Drive), was built in Punchetts Wood. The 1881 Census shows the occupants as Joseph Howe, Gamekeeper, aged 25, his wife Ellen aged 27 and his two daughters Jessie, aged 1, and baby Frances of 3 months. Becoming part of the extensive estates of the 7th Earl Cowper in 1870, the wood provided timber and fuel for their Panshanger House and was a good game-hunting area, and remained in that ownership until the death of the Earl's widow in March 1913, when the property passed through marriage connections to Lady Desborough and her husband Lord Desborough.

Lord Desborough in turn, sold the approximately 150 acres of Tewin Wood for £9,300 in August 1925

to a four-man consortium. Before this time the game rights had been retained by Sir Otto Beit of Tewin Water House together with 'Keepers Cottage' until 1st February 1921. The consortium was made up of Benjamin Arthur Brown, Francis Alfred Brown, Stephen Charles Edward Brown and Edward Charles Elsmore. The Browns were timber merchants and felled and extracted much of the timber. It appears part of this family occupied 'Keepers Cottage' and had steam traction engines based there. The agent for the estate was Albert Bishop who resided at 'Holborn Cottage', Knebworth Station. The Wood does not appear to have been developed until it was sold to the Homelands Garden Estate in January 1932 with the intention of selling plots for residential use. The sales prospectus describes the Tewin Wood area of *the quiet woodlands, winding lanes, stretches of meadow, and streams that thread their course between gentle alternatives of hill, and dale, stamping Hertfordshire with inimitable grace*. It goes on, *to the artist, book-lover, musician, the city worker, who desires emancipation from the tyranny of mud, bricks, and motor, there are spots, which furnish all they desire for moderate terms*.

'Tewin Wood Estate' included all the wooded land fronting the south side of Burnham Green Road, almost reaching to Bulls Green, and both sides of Orchard Road.

Large plots of well over half an acre sold for, now quite unbelievable prices:

Tewin Road. (now Orchard Road).
0.5 acre sites   £130 - £175.
4.5 acre sites   £300 - £400.

Desborough Drive.
0.5 acre sites   £175 - £300.
1.5 acre sites   £400.

Bulls Green Road. (now Burnham Green Road).
0.5 acre sites   £200

A sale document of a three quarters of an acre site, listed as Plot 21, in the South Western corner of Tewin Wood, was sold to Mr John Alfred Haggis on the 5th November 1925 for the total price of £135. The Vendor is recorded as Edward Charles Elsmore on behalf of the Homestead Garden Estate.

On the 1st January 1932, the Browns sold their shares in the Estate to Edward Elsmore who set up the Homeland Garden Estates Limited.

Mr Brown had, in 1925, sold 'Keepers Cottage' to

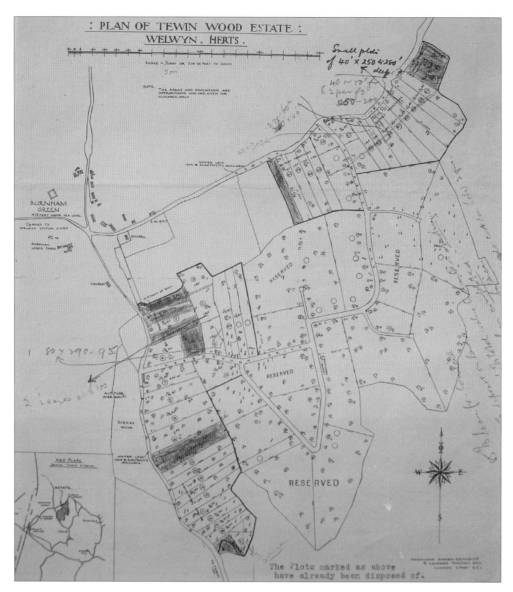

Mr Alfred Bishop. Alfred died in 1952 leaving a wife and two daughters.

On the 7th January 1932 the title to Homeland Garden Estates Limited passed on in one part to Sarah Susan Innes Bishop, the wife of James, brother of Alfred, and the other part to Mary Edith Bishop, Sarah's daughter. At that time, both ladies lived in Maida Vale, London. Sarah Susan Innes Bishop died intestate on the 20th March 1944 and her share passed to her daughter Mary who now became the sole owner.

Due to the economic depression of the 1930s and the threat of a new European War, sales of plots came to a standstill until after 1946 when a few were sold. In 1952, being unable to service the loan originally obtained to purchase the Wood, the Title of the remaining plots of a total of about 40 acres, was transferred to Barclays Bank Limited.

Miss Mary Edith Bishop, who had moved to 7 Firs Walk in about 1950 sold a few more plots, on behalf of Homeland Garden Estates Limited. In 1963, when the remaining plots were sold to the property developers, Prowtings, they rapidly built large houses on them. New roads were built and the original tracks metalled. These remain private with occupants holding one share of Tewin Wood Roads Limited per household, paying twice a year a sum for maintenance based on the rateable value of the properties.

During the Second World War, a Canadian Forestry Corps cut out the fir trees to replace lost timber imports, the stumps of which can still be clearly seen. In more recent times, due to the removal of so many splendid trees, a Tree Preservation Order was placed and strictly applied. During the Second World War, Tewin had one of the two village First Aid Posts with

230

volunteers and an ambulance driver. An air raid siren on a tall pole was at the 'T' junction of Desborough Drive and Cowpers Way. A red public telephone box also occupied this position for many years until its removal in about 1964. The only wartime 'incident' was during the night of the 15th November 1940, when a single 250kg high explosive bomb fell in the back garden of 12 Desborough Drive without causing serious damage.

Considered to be an exceptionally pleasant area to live, and with the rapid increase in house prices nationally, the values of the houses in Tewin Wood have 'rocketed' with some prices passing the £1m mark. Large plots were sub-divided and some smaller or older houses, purchased just for the building plot. These were then demolished and larger houses built.

Keepers Cottage, 7 Desborough Drive
Tewin Wood
The original cottage was constructed in c1761 for Earl Cowper's gamekeeper. In 1854, the left-hand side, (see above), was added to the building. In 1926 the centre part was rebuilt and in 1992 the right-hand side was added. The building was totally renovated by Norris of Hertford.

Part of the original cottage, including the fireplace, still exists as does a well which is now covered. When Tewin Wood was used as a hunting area for Earl Cowper, Keepers Cottage was probably the only building in the wood.

Nancybury Cottages
At one time, opposite Nancybury Gorse in Queen Hoo Lane, there was a row of five yellow brick cottages situated at a right angle to the road.

It is thought that in Elizabethan times, between 1558-1603, there were buildings on the same site, possibly used by the guards and servants of visitors to nearby Queen Hoo Hall. Queen Elizabeth I was also a likely visitor. In addition, records show that

these cottages were used by the First Hertfordshire Rifle Volunteers (founded in 1859) as living accommodation when stationed in the district. At that time the buildings were divided into 10 back-to-back cottages in one-up and one-down units.

After that period, the five cottages were restored to two rooms downstairs and two upstairs, one of which included the landing. There were no facilities and tenants of the cottages obtained water from an outside pump, although Tewin resident, Janet Pitman, née Brand, who was born in one of the cottages, recalls her mother washing her hair with water from the nearby well.

All the cottages had large gardens and each had a wooden shed with a red pantile roof, plus an outside toilet, but there was no drainage. Another member of the family, Ron Brand, recalls that his grandfather hung pheasants, rabbits and other game around the shed, and did not consider the pheasants were ready for eating until he saw the first maggot drop to the ground!

In 1944, the cottages were owned by Woodhall Estates and the last tenants were the Brand, Marshall, Izzard and South families, all of whom, over a period of time, moved into new houses in the village. One cottage was rented to one of his farm workers by Mr Hale of Tewin Hill Farm.

The cottages were pulled down in the 1950s, and the major part of the site is now occupied by large, attractive houses. When the Drews built their bungalow, Highfield, the last property facing the wood at the top of the hill, they had the now unsafe well filled in and built their garage over the site.

Nancybury Cottages no longer exist, but they are well remembered by many present-day Tewin residents and remain an interesting part of the history of the village.

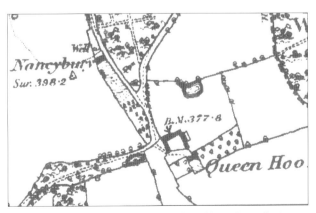
This 1884 map gives the location of the Nancybury Cottages and the well from which families originally drew their water.

Chapter 16

A Tewin Miscellany
John Carrington's Diary

A watercolour by William the thirteen year old son of Joseph Strutt (see page 79) May 30ᵗʰ 1790 of Bacon's Farm, near Bramfield, the home of John Carrington. There is no known portrait of the diarist.

John Carrington, the diarist, was born and brought up in Tewin, the son of a gardener, and is buried next to his wife, Elizabeth, in Tewin Churchyard. He was devoted to her and, when she died in 1797, he wrote this epitaph for her grave:

She was virtuous and good
And as fair as ere stood
In the Balance of Justice and Fame
She was generous and kind
With a Noble Mind
And blessed be her name.

It was after her death that Carrington began his famous diary which he continued until ten days before his own death in 1810, aged eighty four years. John Carrington was born in 1726 and started work as an under gardener with Lady Cathcart at Tewin Water House. By the 1750s he was working for Richard Warren at Marden Hill in the parish of Tewin and, in about 1760, he obtained the tenancy of Bacon's Farm, Bramfield, near the boundary of

Tewin Parish, from Richard Warren. He lived there until his death in 1810.

In 1760 he married Elizabeth Waple of Watton. They had three children, John, Mary-Ann and William. John (Jack) became the landlord of *The Rose and Crown* public house in Tewin. John Carrington was a successful farmer but, by the time he wrote his diary, his younger son William was carrying on the day to day routine of the farm whilst Mary-Ann looked after the house. In 1771 he had been appointed one of four Chief Constables in the administrative area known as the Liberty of St. Albans, supervising the constables of seven parishes. For forty years he was Tax Assessor and Collector for Bramfield and, as Overseer of the Poor and Surveyor of Highways, he was a leading member of the Bramfield Parish Vestry.

Carrington's diary was written on any scrap of paper available to him including the backs of auctioneers' bills, lists of deserters from the army or militia, licensing regulations and instructions for Tax Assessors. He used little punctuation. The text is peppered with capital letters and his spelling is bizarre. He wrote in whichever direction he felt like according to the space available on the paper, horizontally, vertically or diagonally, sometimes writing directly over original text. Every now and then, his daughter would stitch a bundle of his notes together and label it *'Memorandums for* [a particular period]'. The original diary was given to Hertfordshire County Record Office in 1943 by Miss Hilda Wickham of Hertford, one of the few surviving members of the Carrington family.

The diary provides a fascinating view of a farmer's life during the Napoleonic Wars, including much of local interest. In his various roles Carrington travelled widely in the area and he gives us many descriptions of meetings and social gatherings, often held at his son's pub *'The Rose and Crown'*. Food and drink are prominent features of the diary. Carrington lists in great detail what he ate and drank and what it cost him:

'Dinner at Son John's Rose and Crown Tewin on a Rosted Hear & a Hashed Hear & Boyled Sholder of Mutton & lonions, pudding &c Spent each 6s 6d, plenty of Punch & Good Company.' (Friday 18 March 1808).

The company of eight included Mr Rowley, a baker from Tewin, Mr Lamburne a gardener from Tewin Water, Henry Cowper and Mr Carter, plasterer at Lord Cowper's *'New house building at Panshanger.'* Carrington was obviously a very sociable character,

often entertaining friends at his farm. He also had stamina as this entry for his 80th birthday in July 1806 indicates: *'Being my Birth Day..... had a few friends at Bacon's at supper....we was merry till 2 Clock morning.'*

The farming year brought its own celebrations and, again, they continued until late.

'...Barley Slight, Gates & Wheat Good, Went to Bell's Harvest home... Good Supper & plenty of punch-Didn't Brake up till 2 Clock...' (27 August 1807).

Sometimes drink got the better of him, as when he fell off his horse or got lost in the small field by his farm after an evening out: *'Got fuddled and fell of my Poney O for Shame.'*

The diary is crowded with his friends, neighbours and acquaintances, amongst them, the Revd Bourchier of Bramfield, Mr Warren *'my good old master'*, John Pridmore, the schoolmaster, and Joseph Strutt, engraver, author and antiquary who lodged at Bacon's farm for four years. Family members visit or are visited and there are frequent mentions of being entertained by the upper servants at Marden and other great houses:

'....in Evening went to Esqr Mackeys at Marden as Being invited by Mr & Mrs Moulding, his Bayleff & Houskeeper, to spend the Evening their...... plaid at Cards & Suppt Sumptuosly, Good ale, Brandy Ginn & Water & Wine & good Cake & some Scotch ale, home 1 Clock' (Saturday 25 January).

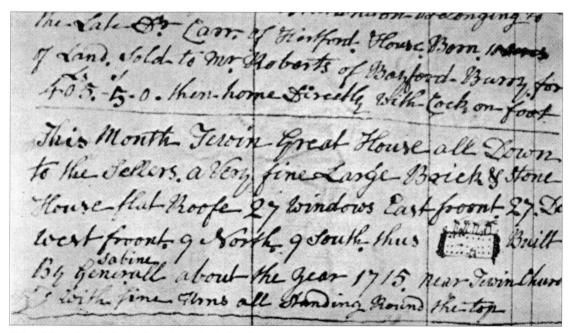

Extract from Carrington's diary, 1807, including his little sketch of Tewin House it was later demolished (to his great regret). *'The late Dr Carr'* referred to was the recent headmaster of Richard Hale School in Hertford.

Music is sometimes a feature of gatherings as when Mr Otway the schoolmaster from Welwyn brought over the '*Wellin Band of Musick*' to the Rose and Crown. '*4 Carernetts, 2 Buzzoons, 1 french horne, Tumbrean (tamboureen) & Simbolds &c &c.....Cold Round of Beef for supper, plaid Severall pieses of Musick Well, Mr Otway plaid the flute as Master.*' (14 May 1807)

Carrington describes the funerals of local gentry and of more humble funerals which nevertheless were followed or preceded by the usual feast:

'*To Mr. Frances Deans Funerl at Tewin Church, Carried on Men's Sholders from his House on Tewin Lower Green......a Good Dinner provided at Sons Rose &Crown for the Bearers & Some Neighbours and a good Dinner at his house for the 6 Pall Bearers 7 Mourners. Buired about fi past 2 oclock, then Came Back to the House had Tea, wine and Cake. Dined before went to Church on Veal & ham, Rost Beef, the Pall Bearers had Silk Sashes & hat Bands and Silk Gloves.*'

Carrington was a keen cricketer describing matches played at both Lower and Upper Green, usually for a prize of food or supper at the pub. On September 3rd 1807 there was a cricket match on Upper Green between the builders of '*the New House at Panshanger against all Tewin for a whole sheep Dresed at Son's Rose and Crown, 2 Leggs Boyled, Saddle Rost, 2 Sholders Baked.......the Tewiners Beat them shamefully*'

Occasional journeys were made to London by coach, entailing overnight stays. Every week he went to Hertford market and walked to Ware or Hertford until well into his eighties. At other times he travelled in his '*little cart*' around the locality in his various roles. In May 1807 aged eighty one he describes driving to Hertford in the cart with Mr Cock who was going on to London. He then '*walked to Ware Park to Esqr Bydes, then to Hartford again.*' At the end of the day he '*Brought the grist from the mill home 9o'clock.*' Quite a strenuous day even for a much younger person!

Carrington's generous nature is revealed in his visits to Tewin Workhouse, on Upper Green. In June 1805 he goes to '*Tewin Poorhouse to see Blind Willimson the Scotchman and to Treet the poor their in Beer, gave them 22 quits of Beer & Lofe & Cheese & Smoked a Pipe with them...*'

Every Christmas he gave a feast to the residents of the workhouses at both Bramfield and Tewin. He transported the poor from Tewin in his cart and took them back afterwards. On December 25th 1805 he '*had the poor, 4 from Bramfield and 5 from Tewin to Dinner*' and '*made them all merry.*' The following Christmas Day in 1806 '*....all the old poor came to Dinner with me in little cart and carried them back.*'

In January 1809 there was a very heavy snow fall and on Monday 23rd he describes going '*to Bramfield to give the poor families wood and some relief in this sharp frost and snow..*' W. Branch-Johnson notes that they were not forgotten in the instructions that Carrington left at his death. Loaves of bread were given to the poor in Bramfield and 30 quarts of Beer to the poor in Tewin Workhouse as well as a gift of 2/6 (12½p) each for the widows in both.

As Constable, John Carrington attended the quarter sessions and assizes, checked the weights used by shopkeepers, chiefly bakers, dealt with the renewal of ale house licences and supervised the hiring of farm and other labour. In his day there were two hundred capital offences on the statute book. In his book '*The Hertfordshire Pepys*' Branch-Johnson relates how Carrington made great efforts to save a young man with a wife and four children from the gallows. Thomas Witty had stolen a sheep worth one guinea (£1.05). John Carrington travelled to London to lobby Hertfordshire MPs, Hertfordshire peers and other influential people. A reprieve '*came down to me at Bacons about 3 ours before the hanging*'. Witty was sentenced to seven years transportation.

One Sunday evening in August 1806 Carrington was robbed himself after collecting money at the Rose and Crown '*off Insome Sackcarrier for wheat Sold yesterday*' He graphically relates the incident:

'*...was Robed on my ass as I Came home about ¹/₂ past 8 o'clock by 2 Irishmen, one on one side my ass & the other on the other side, Within 4 pole of Flexley Gate after you Come up the 2nd Hill from Tewin, they Clapt a pistel to my Head & Demanded my money & they blow my Branes out if I made a noise...*'

But Carrington was too clever for them;

'*...I told them my puss was in my wastcoat pocket which they took with my knife & some halfpence & Hankerchieff..... So off they went Down the road towards Tewin & I walked on a Little way with my ass, then got off & Runn & Hollowd Down to Marden, so I escaped with my other money, Near 20£ in Notes, in a little pocket in the Lining of my wastcoat, So my loss but small, about 4sh in my puss & knife & Hankerchieff, the 2 men was Drinking at my sons while I was there...*'

We do not hear whether the men were apprehended for the crime.

A picture of a busy and thriving rural community is built up in the diary. Carrington records the changes in corn prices for thirteen years and other prices at market are carefully noted. The effects of the weather on the farming year appear throughout the diary: '*Peas none in Generall this year, Dry wather & Green bugg, not worth threshing.*' Church attendance at both Tewin and Bramfield was a regular part of his life. He tells of charity sermons, for example, one preached in 1808 by the Revd. Joseph Hollet-Batten, a teacher at the East India College Hertford (now Haileybury). He mentions work on the '*treble bell of Tewin Church being Crackf*' and '*New Cast by John Briant of Hartford at a cost of £10*' (see page 55) and of the same John Briant being given '*5sh per year to keep the Church Clock in good order Which gose well*' Celebrations for the marriage of Lord Cowper are recorded when the eighty-seven boys and girls of Tewin Sunday School were given '*a good dinner at the schoolhouse.. and plenty of good drink*'. Changes in ownership of the great houses are noted and the demolition of '*Tewin Great House by the Church*' is described in June 1807:

'*....the offices all Down the 2 Last months past, kitchen, Brewhouse, Landrey &c Stables Coach Hous &c &c, the Mantion House 3 Story High besides the offices &c below the whole Bredth of the house, with fine Lofty Rooms & the Grandest Stair Case allowd to be in England, 27 windows East front 27 in West front & nine in each end..... flat Roof with ernes Standing all Round the top, Built by Genrl Savine (Sabine) & finished in the year 1718, now Pulld Down by Ld Cowper.*'

He gives a fascinating glimpse of the impact made on a small rural community of more momentous events of the time. For example, George the Third's Golden Jubilee is marked by the poor of Bramfield being given food and drink.

More significant is the impact of the war against Napoleon. As Chief Constable, Carrington was responsible for raising men for the Army and Navy. In 1803 he wrote: '*...we are threatened to be invaded by one Boneparte by the French & England is to be Divided among the french..... So we are Raiseing of men from 17 to 55 one Class and 15 to 60 the other class so Nothing but Soldiering three times a week...*'

In 1799 as Tax Collector he was involved in collecting the first income tax to help the war with Napoleon.

The price of wheat was affected by the war:

'*Markets dearer on Account of Said going to Warr againe and fitting our Shipps out.*' (Saturday March 6th 1802)

Carrington travels to London in 1803 to see the Review of volunteers in Hyde Park:

'*27 thousand vaulenteers in and about London & supposed to be 500000 spectators. I never saw such a sight all my days.*'

After the Battle of Trafalgar he writes on Sunday 15th December 1805 that '*a Collection Was at Tewin Church today for the widows etc in Nelson's Battle £14*'

John Carrington emerges from the pages of his diary as a warm and generous character. He was well loved and respected, a fact reflected in the description of his funeral on 30th May 1810 by his son, Jack:

'*....on Wednesday May 30th 1810 he was buried in Tewin Churchyard by the side of his wife. The Rev. Mr Bourchier of Bramfield buried him by his desire. Mr Judd and Mr Bowman and others from Hertford sung a funeral anthem and Mr Pridmore and the children of Tewin School sung the 39th psalm. To show that he died as he lived, respected by all, his funeral was attended by upwards of 1000 persons, Men, Women and Children.*'

Footnote:

Hertfordshire Archives & Local Studies

Anyone studying the Carrington material nowadays has the benefit of the considerable volume of authoritative work undertaken by W. Branch-Johnson in the twentieth century.

Carrington's original diary is available to view at HALS, County Hall, Hertford, together with the two volume transcript by Branch-Johnson which presents the diary material in legible typewriting, whilst retaining Carrington's idiosyncracies of spelling and punctuation.

William Bennett Murder Tewin 1837

On the 25th October 1837 William Bennett a 59 year old army pensioner from Burnham Green was mugged in Scrubs Wood, Tewin. His body was discovered next morning and taken to *The Plume of Feathers.*

After collecting his pension of £8 0s 3d, Bennett had gone into *The Cold Bath*, a pub in Hertford, where four local unemployed labourers, George Fletcher, William Roach, Thomas Taylor, and David Sams (whose father lived in Tewin), were seen asking Bennett if he had collected his pension. Later three of them were seen in Scrubs Wood.

Fletcher and Sams were arrested on 27th October, Roach on 9th November, but Taylor got away.

At the Hertfordshire Lent Assizes; Fletcher and Roach were found guilty of murder and sentenced to be hung on the 14th March 1838, but Sams was acquitted as he had not gone into Scrubs Woods with the others as he was afraid of being recognised by Bennett.

The popular view that Taylor was mainly responsible for the fatal blows, together with growing opposition to the death penalty, gave rise to a petition for mercy and commutation of the death sentence which was sent to the Home Office. The petition was rejected by both the Prime Minister, Lord Melbourne of Brocket Hall, Lemsford, and the Home Secretary Lord John Russell.

Fletcher and Russell were hanged in Hertford before a crowd of 4000. Taylor was caught in September 1838. He had enlisted in the army, under a false name, and been sent to Ireland. He was found guilty of murder at the Hertfordshire Lent Assizes of 1837 and executed on March 13th 1839.

Sams was transported for life for larceny in 1841.

Vincent Lunardi

On September 15th 1784, all London was agog to see the first flight in England of a balloon with a man on board. It is reported that over 100,000 people crowded into the Honourable Artillery Company grounds at Moorfields to view the take off (seen on page 237).

The architect and pilot of the project was 25 year old Vincent Lunardi, a native of Lucca in Tuscany working in London as Secretary to the Neapolitan Ambassador.

His balloon envelope was 32 feet in diameter and made with red and blue striped oiled silk. The nacelle was open, fitted with wing-like paddles and carried

Vincent Lunardi

sand as ballast. For the flight the envelope was filled with hydrogen prepared under the direction of a Dr Fordyce, lecturer in chemistry at St Thomas's.

Lunardi prepared a detailed journal of his flight. Lunardi's name, coupled with the fact that his launch site was near the location of Bedlam, prompted a response from the media which would not be amiss today. In fact, in his journal he notes that just after his launch *'I recollected the puns on my name, and was glad to find myself calm'.*

Lunardi had on board with him a pigeon (which escaped early), a cat and a dog. Provisions included cold chicken, bread and wine.

Take-off, heralded by gunfire, was at 2.05pm As the balloon climbed slowly to the north, it was seen by King George III, who was holding a Council of State at St James's Palace. He said *'Gentlemen, let us adjourn and take a last look at poor Mr Lunardi'.*

The flight was full of new experiences but uneventful. After about an hour he vented some gas and at low altitude tried to talk with people by megaphone, without success. At 3.30pm he landed briefly near Welham Green and freed the cat, which was in a very poor state.

He decided to continue his flight and having dropped the last of his ballast rose to an altitude at which ice formed. Having reached his highest altitude of flight, dropped various messages and flown near clouds, he used his remaining paddle (he lost one at take-off) to assist his descent.

At 4.20pm he landed after a flight of 2 hours 15 minutes at Standon Green End. He was famous!

Let us give the last word to John Carrington, who lived at Bacons Farm and saw the balloon over Tewin. He notes in his diary:

'...Lunerday assended in a Boolone at the artillery ground London to a great hithe over Barnat, North Hall, then went for StAlbans, then took his Course East over Codicote, Wellin, Tewin, Bengeo & Landed him self in a Little Meadow at Standon Green End, he Throwd his line out & was pulld down by a young woman in the meadow who was fritned at first and runaway, thought it the Devill, till he made her sencable and gave her 5 Guineas, it was a very fine hot day, I saw him plane as he came over Bacons, he was at a great Hight for his Boloon was 30 feet round but appeared no biger than a Boys Kite,.....

Wm Baker Esqre of Bayfordbury took him home..... & Baker had a great pibple Stone..... remooved to the place he fell & a Brass plate put theiron with the account'.

Above: **Launch at Honorable Artillery Company grounds.**
Lower left: **An artist's impression of the first balloon flight in England that passed over Tewin.**
Right: **The pudding stone at Standon Green End, near Ware.**

Old Bottles Found In Hertford Road

In Autumn 1996 a large number of old bottles were found when foundations were dug for an extension to a house near the shop in Hertford Road. They were found at the rear of the property and when the area was fully excavated to a depth of almost two metres, the remains of a brick structure were discovered which had obviously been used as a dump.

The owners researched the history of the site and found that a building had been there, possibly a farm building. Previously they had found old tiles and long nails when digging the garden. The present house was built in 1968.

Their conclusion was that their find was probably a rubbish dump for the shop/tea room and other houses in the road. Dozens of Camp coffee bottles were found, together with lemonade bottles, including a Hiram Codd's bottle with a marble in its neck, manufactured in the late nineteenth century. Also found were ink bottles, medicine bottles and stone bottles for beer and ginger beer. Other interesting finds included a very old Pond's Cream jar, several glass stoppers and a tiny ceramic pig.

The bottles found date from approximately the late nineteenth century to the 1920s and 1930s.

Kit Nash of Harmer Green

Local people said that Kit Nash was a witch. She was certainly a notorious poacher, but it seems probable that she was just a very eccentric lady.

Kit was the illegitimate daughter of Sarah Nash and they lived in a two roomed cottage on the site of what is now Kit's Corner on the road between Burnham Green and Harmer Green.

A fine looking woman, Kit's parentage was a mystery - some said she bore a resemblance to the then Lady Cowper. Certainly Lady Cowper took an interest in Kit, whom she always called Katie. In 1879, Kit married Jack Darnell, whom she always called 'Sackings'. They had three children and Kit and her husband both continued their careers as poachers! Finally, Jack was caught poaching on the Panshanger Estate, was convicted, and said to have been despatched to Australia.

Kit achieved fame in the district when she took a shot at PC Summerby when he tried to interview her at her tumble-down cottage.

She was a tall figure, who never washed, and appeared very unkempt. She wore a man's hat and had a sacking apron over her ample skirts, under which she concealed her poached pheasants and pheasant eggs. She was well known to all the local gamekeepers, police and publicans.

There is a story of how Kit was caught poaching in Earl Cowper's woods (now Tewin Wood) by his gamekeepers. They lifted up her skirts and found pheasants hanging from her waist. When she was brought before Earl Cowper, he was horrified to hear that his gamekeepers had looked under her skirts. She was released at once and told she could catch pheasants in the woods whenever she wished.

Kit died in the Hatfield Workhouse on the 9th October 1930, aged 81. There is a memorial to her in Digswell Churchyard.

It is doubtful if Kit's husband was, in fact, transported to Australia at such a late date. If he married Kit in 1879 and they had three children, the date of his conviction and punishment would be in about 1885. Transportation to Australia ceased in 1853 and to Tasmania in 1864.

'Kit' Nash (born Caroline Darnell) seen on the left with her mother and two children outside their cottage at Harmer Green. 'Kit' was a poacher and achieved notoriety when she shot at a police constable. She died in 1930 and is buried at Digswell.

Jean Havilland

In 1975 Jean was the 'Babycham girl' in a very big advertising campaign and one of her photographs from that time is currently being used on a retro-style greetings card that is on sale in WH Smith and John Lewis. Jean has appeared on numerous magazine front covers, posters, mail order catalogues, advertisements and in commercials for many clients including Lyon's Maid Ice Cream, Woman's Own, Ribena, Harp lager, Marshall Ward and L'Oréal. She also played the Devil Woman in Cliff Richard's video of this recording!

Rob Duncan, Jean Havilland and Gemma McPherson in a publicity still taken in Tewin Orchard in the 1980s.

Rob Duncan

Well known for his appearances in several successful television programmes including *'Drop The Dead Donkey'*, *'The Bill'* and *'Casualty'*, for many years Rob Duncan and Jean Havilland's home was in Tewin and they still keep in contact with local people.

Albert Richard Whitear

Albert Whitear lived in Tewin with his wife, Lena, and family from 1955 to his death in 1989. Up to his death, he worked as an illustrator and painter from their home, 'Farce', on the edge of the village.

He was born in Hornsey, North London, in April 1906. As a child, he contracted polio and broke his pelvis. He explained later that this meant he had to 'learn how to fight' - the only way for a 'cripple' to survive in his tough school.

It also meant he could not always participate in the world, but had to be still and observe. And he spent months in bed, where he occupied himself by drawing. He later turned what he saw of the world at that time into art and did this for the rest of his life.

After Hornsey Art School, he started his first job at 16 years of age with a sign painter. He then worked as a commercial artist in any style required for advertisements, restaurant murals or books.

After he married Lena in 1955, she became his agent, and persuaded him to work solely for publishers, as she found them more civilised to deal with than advertising agencies! It earned him less money, but great satisfaction in working on a vast range of children's books and book jackets. (His cover drawing for the Tewin Society Newsletter is shown here).

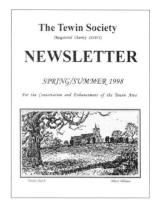

He was proud of the fact that he never had to earn a penny, except through his art. While working on his various commissions, he always created his own pictures.

These ranged from an extensive set of abstract reliefs in polystyrene, which he exhibited in Germany in the 1960s, to the strange, and disturbing 'dream' paintings he exhibited in Cork Street in the 1980s. It is a testament to their power that, as well as selling pictures in the exhibition, someone took the trouble and risk to steal one.

He left a wide body of work, now distributed to people's homes across the world. He also left vivid memories to those who knew him - perhaps particularly within Tewin, of seeing him speeding through the village in a roofless Land Rover, with the wind blowing back his white hair.

Literary Tewin: 'Writers Bloc'

Hertfordshire has been a fruitful place for authors including such heavyweight writers as Charles Dickens, H G Wells and George Bernard Shaw. More recently and close to Tewin are the popular Frederick Forsyth, Ken Follett and the late, pinkly prolific Barbara Cartland.

The village of Tewin itself, specifically the area from the edge of the Wood, Lower Green and Marden has produced no less than 19 published authors with over 100 books. There are 8 around Lower Green alone!

The subjects covered range from the arcane (e.g. statistics) to the mundane (e.g. dog training), from the cerebral (e.g. aesthetics of art) to the practical (e.g. household DIY). Novels, childrens' books, (some not only written but illustrated by local artists), archaeology, town planning, buildings and structures, autobiographies, have all flown from the pens of locals starting with two earlier books on Tewin by Miss Brettell, and the Revd. Vidler, now brought up to date with this volume.

Tewin Writers

Author	No. of Books	Description
Georgie Adams	30	Children's books
Pauline Adams	4	Patchwork Quilts
Luke Bonwick	1	Windmills
Phil Brice	1	Tewin Cricket
Miss Brettell	1	Tewin History
Michael Clark	10	Mammals
		Badgers
		Mammals, Amphibians and
		Reptiles of Hertfordshire
		The Mysterious Greatwood
		Apples: a field guide
		The Cuffley Story
		(with Patricia Klijn)
Arthur Edwards	2	Town Planning
		Aesthetics of Art
Paul Griggs	1	Diary of a Musician
Lewis Hamilton	1	Autobiography
Dr Donald Hodson	6	Maps inc. Military
Dr Yolande Hodson	1	History of 1 inch
		Ordnance Map
Patrick Holden	7	Dogs Training & Behaviour
		Local History
		Rights of Way & Map
		Limericks*
John Lee	1	Archaeology*
Malcolm Ross McDonald	13+	The World from Rough Stones
		and 12 other novels
Barty Philips	12	D.I.Y.
		Tapestry & its History
		Interior Decoration
Michael Plews	1	Statistics
Tewin Society	2	Nature Trail
		The History of Tewin
Rev. Vidler	1	Tewin History
Andrew Whawell	6	Quizzes

100+ titles

*in preparation

Paul Griggs (on extreme left) author of the book *Diary of a Musician*. Pictured with Frank Sinatra who appeared on the same show as Paul's group Guys n' Dolls.

Tewin Artists and Illustrators

Author	Description
Tom Adams	Illustrator, designer Agatha Christie covers
Terry Brand	Artist, designer
Elisabeth Buchanan	Potter, designer
Anna Clark	Portraits
Michael Clark	Illustrator, designer *Punch* - cover and cartoons *Private Eye* - cartoons
Jim Fish	Commercial artist
Molly Hopkyns	Artist
Menna Wynne Searle	Artist
Albert Whitear	Artist and Sculptor
Linda Williams	Artist

Terry Brand's watercolour of woods at Marden Hill.

Above, top: **A Tom Adams cover for Agatha Christie 1943 and an illustration from *Swift* magazine**

Michael Clark's cover for *Punch* magazine 1968

Albert Whitear's sculpture of *Comfort Cobbani*

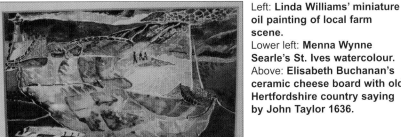

Left: **Linda Williams' miniature oil painting of local farm scene.**
Lower left: **Menna Wynne Searle's St. Ives watercolour.**
Above: **Elisabeth Buchanan's ceramic cheese board with old Hertfordshire country saying by John Taylor 1636.**

Anna Clark's watercolour portraits of the Datchworth author Diana Norman and film critic Barry Norman's grandchildren

241

The Mapping of Tewin

The village of Tewin has a fine reputation for footpaths, not only well cared for, but also well documented. *The Tewin Society's* Patrick Holden, handing over responsibility after many years, looked back on the great publishing venture that became an example to all:

It all began in 1985 when *The Tewin Society* determined to produce a survey of Tewin's rights of way to celebrate the 900th anniversary of the Domesday Book of 1086. Each of the 40 plus paths was allocated one or more 'surveyors', all members of *The Tewin Society*, who walked their paths and recorded them for each season. Having thus logged all the paths and their problems, it then made sense to clear the various blockages.

Barbed wire was cut (wire cutters were carried), gates were unlocked, paths were re-instated or marked out by boots - and later tractor wheel - after farming operations, and illegal signs were removed, as was a dangerous horse. For this work *The Tewin Society* was awarded Hertfordshire Society's Jubilee Conservation Award in 1987, including the first prize of £250.

Both walkers and landowners needed an accurate map of the footpaths. Legal rights of way are shown on the Definitive Map: those in Tewin are on two sheets of the map. Hertfordshire County Council were charging £10 for each sheet plus £1 postage, i.e. £21 for a complete copy of the map. It was decided to spend the prize on the production of a village map. No other village had produced a walkers' map before although one other village had produced an attractive village map. It was resolved that the map would be an accurate one rather than an artist's impression. It would be in four colours, 1:10,000 scale with a legend suitable for walkers and riders. It would be A2 size but foldable. It would have the Definitive Map allied statement on the back with updated notes on the routes. As a secondary consideration the *Society* agreed to add colour illustrations by local artists and details of the flora and fauna on the space available. This would then make the map not only a walkers' but also a village map.

The problems that were faced in addition to the mapping itself were those of copyright, finance and printing. The County Council map was expensive because of their need to pay copyright to HMSO on each sheet. Most of this need was bypassed by starting the map with a base that was out of copyright. This was then updated from aerial photographs and then by the surveyors walking, drawing their reports, re-walking and then checking their paths yet again. In the event the map was more accurate than the current Ordnance Survey, and after its publication was even used in planning enquiries. Because the drawing of the legal paths was copyright HMSO were paid their minimum fee for it.

The Steering Committee comprised Patrick Holden as publisher and organiser of finance, advertising and copyright; Dudley Drake as cartographer; Terry Brand, who dealt through Fairplan with the computer and graphics layout, and is a local artist; Howard

Jenkins who liaised with the printers; and Alan Guilford who contributed his local knowledge of the flora and fauna. The other artist was Michael Clark, the well known local wildlife expert, (illustrations on this page and on map). We were lucky to find a local printer, Goads of Hatfield, owned by two nearby villagers who gave us a competitive quotation.

The other major problem was that of finance. Having started with the prize of £250 from the Hertfordshire Society, Tewin Parish Council were good enough to give £200. While village maps following the Tewin map have been largely funded by councils, this was the first and there was an obvious shortfall between the money available and the quotation of £1,000 for the printing. It was resolved to cover this by advertising and 11 advertisements for the reverse of the map at £50 each were sold.

The 'Catch 22' situation, between not having a product to sell to advertisers and not having a product without advertisers, by promising to repay their cheques if the map did not proceed!

The quotation included £200 for the folding costs. This was avoided by having a team of villagers fold the maps themselves. Finally there was a technical problem with the colours on the map which increased the quotation somewhat, so there was a further shortfall. This second shortfall was covered by getting agreement to advance sales from the various outlets, Tewin Stores, Tebbutts Stores, Goads of Hatfield and *The Tewin Society* direct.

The sales in fact have gone remarkably well, with well over 3,000 copies being sold - not bad for a village with only 600 households! Copies have been sent to friends and relations as far away as Papua New Guinea as well as Australia and New Zealand. There have been visiting delegations from Japan and China. In each case they have taken copies of the map back to their home countries. The Tewin map is thus truly international!

In addition to the Steering Committee and the 10 or so surveyors who walked and re-walked the paths there were a considerable number of other local people involved in the map: well over 50 in all. This truly concerted village effort has been recognised and rewarded by a number of awards, both countywide and national.

The objectives of producing an attractive walkers' and riders' map at an affordable price had been achieved. As a result of its accuracy it has been used in planning cases and is attractive enough to be a village map. An updated (2008) version can still be purchased from Tewin Stores.

The Flora and Fauna

The countryside within the Parish of Tewin comprises three main categories, arable farmland, semi-natural woodland and riverside meadows.

Even though many of the old hedgerows and coppices have disappeared during the last few decades a wide diversity of wildlife remains in the area. The rambler may still encounter such interesting bird species as Kingfisher, Grey Wagtail and Green Sandpiper along the Mimram valley in addition to a wide variety of wild flowers including Marsh Marigold, Ragged Robin, Red Bartsia and Marsh Orchid. The freshwater crayfish inhabits the gravel and stones of the riverbed.

A walk through the chalk valley, situated along the South-Western boundary of the Parish, will reveal small areas of unimproved grassland where many interesting chalk loving plants may still be found. These include Cowslip, Primrose, Yellow-wort, Carline Thistle, Hairy Violet, Common Rockrose, Salad Burnet and Orchid species. The large Roman Snail also inhabits these chalkland areas.

Within the woodlands Muntjac deer are common residents and several active badger setts are known. Foxes may be encountered especially at dawn and dusk. The Sparrowhawk has made a noticeable and welcome recovery.

The Map

This map was originally published for the Tewin Society by Patrick Holden, in 1991. Updated and republished by the Tewin Society in 2007.

It is based upon the 1935 Ordnance Survey Sheet 96 and the Rights of Way are reproduced with the permission both of the Controller of Her Majesty's Stationery Office © Crown Copyright, and Hertfordshire County Council from their 1988 1:10,000 Definitive Map and Definitive Statement as at June 1988, with additions to July 1989.

Cartography is by Dudley Drake with amendments and additions from the Tewin Society. Layout is by Terry Brand of Flairplan Ltd and the additional drawings are by Michael Clark and Terry Brand.

Thanks are also given to the Tewin Parish Council, the Countryside Management Services, and the HCC Information Management Unit for their support.

Chapter 17

Tewin Village Events

V.E. Commemoration 1945 - 1995

'V.E. Day' on the 8th May 1945 marked the ending of the War in Europe when World War II Allies formally accepted the unconditional surrender of the armed forces.

In May 1995, the 50th Anniversary of this historic day, Tewin marked the occasion with a number of commemorative events, including an Exhibition of 'Tewin at War' during the years 1939 to 1945. Residents of Tewin produced some amazing nostalgic souvenirs which included items ranging from Air Raid Precautions (ARP) equipment, a portable air-raid warning siren, a stirrup pump for dousing incendiary bomb fires, Wardens' warning rattles and whistles, gas masks, an unexploded bomb warning and official notices.

There were also Service uniforms, photographs of war-time weddings, Home Guard platoons, local anti-tank obstacles, weapon pits and gun emplacements, and details of local enemy bomb incidents and downed enemy aircraft.

The 'Home Front' memorabilia also included exhibits and records of women recruited into local factories working on war production, *'Dig For Victory'* campaigns, War Savings Bonds, Ration Cards, and many other associated items which illustrated how people coped with rationing and the many other restrictions of war.

Further events included a commemorative ball in the Memorial Hall. The main hall, corridor and a marquee in the car park were decorated with flags and bunting. Nostalgia was the theme as more than 200 people dined and danced to an old style 'big band' with the poignant tunes of the 1940s bringing back memories. People dressed in the style of the period and as well as 1940s suits and dresses, there were Land Army girls and many men and women wearing Service uniforms. It was pointed out that one lady in ATS (Auxiliary Territorial Service) uniform, would not have passed inspection during the war - her long hair would have been cut since regulations stated that hair had to be clear of the shirt collar!

At midnight, the evening was brought to a close by the sound of the air-raid siren signalling the 'All Clear' – time for people to return safely home.

The younger people of the village were not left out of the VE commemorations. Children from Tewin Cowper School provided colourful entertainment with maypole dances on Lower Green, (see the picture on page 257).

A party for children was held in the Memorial Hall, and a disco for the teenagers. Every child in the village received a commemorative £2 coin in a presentation box - a memento of a major world event which may not have directly affected their lives, but would have had a significant influence on those of their grandparents and older members of their families. Those people would have had their own personal recollections of World War II and the part it played in their lives, which is why a large number of them gathered on Lower Green on the 7th May to hear the Reverend Paul Betts conduct a service of remembrance for all those who had lost their lives and to celebrate the 50th Anniversary of its cessation.

Golden Jubilee Celebrations

The Golden Jubilee of Queen Elizabeth II in 2002 was celebrated in Tewin with community events held over the weekend of 1st and 2nd June.

On the Saturday evening a dance was held in the Memorial Hall, the outside of which was adorned with red, white and blue bunting and hanging baskets, whilst on the inside, gold and purple coloured decorations enhanced the Royal theme. A large framed photograph of HM The Queen overlooked the proceedings as a full house enjoyed supper and danced the night away to the music of a live band.

The following day, the St Peter's Church morning service was transferred to Lower Green where a large congregation took part in a service of worship lead by the Reverend Robert Eardley.

In the afternoon, a Pensioners' Tea Party was held in Tewin Memorial Hall where guests enjoyed an excellent tea and listened to a lively local banjo band. At the end of the party, every pensioner present was presented with a commemorative tea towel.

The weekend had been financed by a grant from the East Herts District Council and sponsorship from Greene King Breweries, via their two local hostelries, *The Rose & Crown* and *The Plume of Feathers*. Many local organisations and individuals donated equipment, food and other items, and provided manpower for the events. The result was a memorable and fitting celebration of The Queen's Golden Jubilee.

Village Fête

The Village Fête has been a central part of summer activities in Tewin for many years. Now the event is held on Lower Green. In the past it was held in the gardens of local residents. For several years a fête was held at the Cottage Rectory, Lower Green, when the Revd. Stebbings was the Rector. Later Dickie and Joan Dunn held the fête in their garden at 39 Upper Green Road and there are memories of a fête being held at Keepers Cottage in Desborough Drive. Upper Green has also been the venue for similar events.

However, the current Lower Green location has allowed activities to be extended and presents a colourful tableau of decorated craft stalls and other attractions. In recent years there have been fancy-dress competitions, martial arts and dance displays, jazz bands, and even a Wild West shoot-out.

With multi-coloured bunting decorating the village green and lively music accompanying the activities, the Tewin Fête is a significant day in the village calendar and one which attracts not only local people, but also many visitors.

Tewin village fête, the proceeds of which are put towards the running of the Memorial Hall. (See also pp 256-257)

Celebrating the Millennium in Tewin

In 1998 a committee was formed to celebrate the Millennium in Tewin. Wyn Carlton, who had done much for the village over the years, including helping with the 1995 VE Day commemorations, took on the Chairmanship. The committee began raising funds and planning events. The following projects were completed:

The family celebration Pig Roast on Upper Green.

The Millennium kneelers in St Peter's Church and shown at the school .

The History of Tewin by the People of Tewin exhibition.

The planting of the Oak tree on Lower Green and three Oaks at Tewin Cowper School.

The Tewin Millennium Orchard (three sites at Tewin Orchard, on Paddy Loughrey's land off Back Lane, and at 106 Orchard Road, Sewell's Orchard).

Floodlighting the Church on special occasions.

The Village sign on Lower Green.

The Tewin Millennium Register.

The Tewin village website.

Open air church service on Lower Green.

Senior Citizens' lunch in the old Victorian School house.

Bell ringing to see out the old year and bring in the New Year.

New Year's Eve party.

Open Gardens in the village.

Many of these activities continue today such as the flood lighting of the Church, the annual New Year's Eve party, and (now two) annual events for Senior citizens, (a lunch in the winter and tea party in the autumn), the village sign, the Millennium orchards, and the oak trees, which continue to give pleasure to us all. Other activities mentioned above have spawned *The Friends of Tewin*, (which run barn dances, scarecrow competitions, a Classic Car rally, and events for young and old) and the Tewin Horticultural Arts and Crafts Society (**THACS**), which puts on twice yearly village shows, organises art and garden excursions and still runs Open Gardens in the village every other year.

After nearly ten years the last of the kneelers for the church are just being finished. This began as a project to make one long kneeler for one pew, and has ended by making them for all the pews.

All of them can be seen on the village website which has become very useful to many who search the web for information about Tewin.

The Tewin Millennium Register is a unique record,

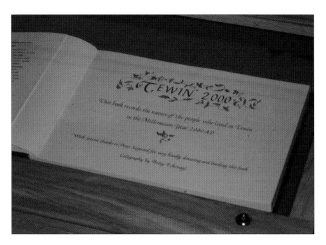

Above: **The Millennium register which is kept in St. Peter's Church.**
Below: **Betty Eskenazi with her beautifully calligraphed Millennium register of all residents of Tewin arranged by road in 2000.**

of the people resident in the village in 2000 and their occupations. The last Millennium project was a specially crafted display case for the Register, made by Ken Feakes for the Church, in memory of Sue Bushell, a lifelong resident of Tewin who died suddenly in 2004.

The original idea for *The History of Tewin by the People of Tewin* exhibition came from Elizabeth Wilson and Ben Roberts. They had put together a small display in 1995 for the VE Day commemorations and were keen to do something similar for the Millennium. They drew up a list of ideas for research and began to encourage others to come forward with information.

People loaned display panels and by careful planning of the exhibits, by a small sub committee, composed of Elizabeth and Ben, Peter Leigh, Lilian Southgate and Linda Adams, everything came together, was well advertised, and looked extremely professional. The exhibition was very successful and was staged again in 2003 and 2008. The exhibition has now evolved into this book as a more permanent record of the village history.

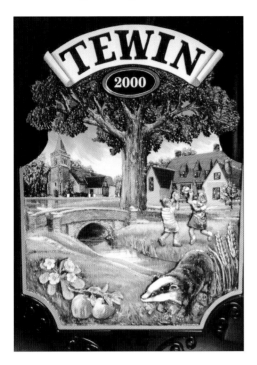

Above right **Dennis and Wyn Carlton unveil the village sign on Lower Green. It was one of the Millennium projects, designed by Michael Clark and cast in metal in Suffolk. The base includes Tewin flints donated by Ivor and Vaughan Williams from their farm and was constructed by Ronald Brand.**
Below: **The planting of one of the Millennium Oaks on Lower Green with Basil Kirkham (left) and Jack Bird (right).**

Tewin Village Awards

Dickie Dunn, in 1984, ready to put in place on Lower Green the Best Kept Village Sign which he had just renovated.

Over the years Tewin has won many village awards and, in particular, featured prominently in the Hertfordshire Best Kept Village competitions, reaching the finals in most of them and becoming winners on a number of occasions.

1967 was the first occasion on which Tewin won the Best Kept Large Village competition and between then and 1988 has won the award five times, culminating in the most coveted prize of all, the Mercury Rosebowl, which was first awarded to Tewin in 1987. The Rosebowl is given to the village with the highest overall marks among all the area finalists in East Hertfordshire's Best Kept Village competition which, in this particular year, started with 81 entries.

This success was achieved through the enthusiasm and industry of the villagers. Not least among these was Dickie Dunn, who became involved in the competitions from the late 1950s and fronted many Tewin entries during the forthcoming years. He was responsible for co-ordinating the efforts of the villagers, who tended gardens, cleared paths,

trimmed hedges, picked up litter, and generally ensured that the whole village was presented at its best. He was ably assisted by Dave Pullen, who spent many hours strimming from one end of the village to the other, as well as carrying out numerous other jobs. They in turn were supported by Mrs Brenda James, Vice Chairman of Tewin Parish Council.

Mrs James was subsequently presented with the Rosebowl at County Hall, and in July 1987 she, Dickie Dunn and Dave Pullen were joined on Lower Green by hundreds of villagers who gathered to see the unveiling of 'Hertfordshire's Best Kept Village' sign by the High Sheriff, Mr Harry Bott, accompanied by East Herts Council Chairman, Councillor Frank Clay. In addition, rose bushes were presented to Mr Dunn and Mr Pullen by Mrs James.

Tewin's winning streak continued the following year, 1988, when it again won the Mercury Rosebowl, tying with Westmill - both being awarded 98% of the marks. Since Tewin were winners the previous year, it was decided that Westmill should take possession of the trophy but Tewin retained the

248

Dickie Dunn, Brenda James, (Chairman of the Parish Council), and Dave Pullen celebrate Tewin winning the Best Kept Large Village contest in July 1987.

sign. This had been refurbished by Dickie Dunn and was unveiled on Lower Green by Mr John Wood, High Sheriff of Hertfordshire. Mr Dunn, who was due to retire as Tewin's co-ordinator, was then presented with a tie and made an honorary member of *The Hertfordshire Society*.

Over the years Tewin has won many additional awards and grants in a variety of categories and these are a testimony to the hard work of the residents and their pride in the village. Details of awards are shown below:

1967 Winner - Best Kept Large Village.
1973 Winner - Best Kept Large Village.
1984 Winner - Best Kept Large Village.
1985 Runner up - Best Kept Large Village.
1987 Winner - Best Kept Large Village.
   Winner - Mercury Rosebowl.
   Winner - Hertfordshire Society's Jubilee.
   Conservation Award -
   Footpaths. (Cup, Shield, Certificate, £250.)
1988 Winner - Best Kept Large Village.
   Winner - Mercury Rosebowl,
   (tied with Westmill.)
   Winner - Hertfordshire Tree Scheme -
   Parish Category, (Tewin Society tree planting). (Certificate and Grant).
1991 Runner Up - Calor Best Kept Large Village.
   Village Ventures Competition Preservation of Rural Community Life
   in Hertfordshire - Footpaths and
   Conservation. (Certificate.)
   ATCO Fine Garden Medal - Best Kept Village - for Upper Green.
1992 British Trust for Conservation Volunteers. Footpaths and Conservation. (Grant £50).

Hertfordshire Conservation Society:
Countryside Man Section - (Certificate of Merit) for the Footpaths and Parish Map - (£250.)
Nature Conservation - (Certificate) for the Pond and Back Lane.
1993 Esso Community Footpath 1992 Award Scheme –
   Second Prize, Nationally - Footpaths and Map. (Certificate and £500).
1994 Shell Better Britain Campaign Grant - Footpaths and Pond. (£325).
1995 Runner Up - Calor Best Kept Large Village.
2001 Calor Gas and Daily Telegraph, Hertfordshire Village of Year:
   Winner - Environment Category.
   (Certificate, Plaque, £50).
2002 Hertfordshire Society Village of Year:
   Winner - Business Category.
   (Certificate, £50).
2003 Calor Gas and Daily Telegraph, Hertfordshire Village of Year:
   Winner - Environment Category.
   (Certificate, Plaque, £100).
2004 Hertfordshire Society Village of Year:
   Highly Commended -
   Business Category (Certificate).

September 5th 2002: Linda Adams, Secretary of *The Tewin Society* receives the Tewin Commendation for Business Category from the Honorary Director, Kevin Fitzgerald.

Appendix 1

The Cowpers of Panshanger			
Sir William Cowper Baronet 1st Earl Cowper 1665 - 1723.	Created Earl Cowper and Viscount Fordwich in 1718.	1706 1707 1714 1718 1723	Married Judith Booth. Married to Mary Clavering. Appointed Lord Chancellor by Queen Anne. Created Baron Cowper of Wingham, Kent. Appointed Lord Chancellor to George I Created Earl Cowper. Died at Cole Green House.
William 2nd Earl Cowper 1709 - 1764.	1723 - Inherited title at the age of 14.	1733/47 1764	Married to Henrietta Grantham, the daughter of the Earl Grantham. Lord of the Bedchamber to King George II Lord Lieutenant of Hertfordshire. Died at Cole Green House.
George 3rd Earl Cowper 1738 - 1789.	1764 - Inherited title.	1759/61 1764 1785 1789	Married Anne Gore. Member of Parliament for Hertford. After he inherited the title, he lived mainly in Italy. Created Prince of the Holy Roman Empire by Josef II. Died in Florence.
George 4th Earl Cowper 1776 - 1799.	1789 - Inherited title.	1799	Died unmarried aged 22 years following a riding accident.
Francis 5th Earl Cowper 1778 - 1837.	1799 - Inherited title. – (He was the 2nd son of the 3rd Earl).	1805 1801 1801/21 1807 1837	Married Emily Lamb, daughter of the 1st Viscount Melbourne. Pulled down Cole Green House. Building of Panshanger House and Art Gallery. Pulled down Tewin House. Died at Panshanger.
George 6th Earl Cowper 1806 - 1856.	1837 - Inherited title.	1855 1856	Married to Lady Anne Florence de Grey (formerly Robinson). There was a serious fire at Panshanger House during the ownership of the 6th Earl. Died.
Francis 7th Earl Cowper 1834 -1905.	1856 - Inherited title.	1870 1880/82 1905	Married Lady Katrine Cecilia Compton. Lord Lieutenant of Ireland. Built many houses in the villages around Panshanger in pale yellow brick. Died without heirs. The earldom became extinct.
Katrine Countess Cowper 1845 - 1913.		1913	Died at Panshanger.
Ethel Ann Priscilla Lady Desborough 1867 - 1952.	1913 - Niece of the 7th Earl Cowper inherited the estate bequeathed to her by the 7th Earl on the death of his widow Katrine.	1887 1913 1952	Married Mr William Henry Grenfell, later Lord Desborough. Lady of the Bedchamber to Queen Mary. Died at Panshanger. There were no direct heirs to the estate as all three of her sons had died as young men. It was left to her grandson, Julian Salmond, who subsequently sold the house and estate. Panshanger House was demolished in 1954.

250

Appendix 2
**Militia Lists &
Early Occupations**

Constables
1758-1786 John Ward
1762-1798 Theophilus
          Thurrowgood
Glass Grinders
1762-1763 John Parker

Militia List 1758-1801
Glass Grinders (Cont.)
1778-1801 John Hinder
1778-1787 Henry Rose
Tailors
1773-?? Benjamin Nash
1784-?? George Little
1787-1798 James Ambrus
(Pcrhaps at Grubbs Barn)
Wheelwrights or Wheelers
1758-1786 William Watson
1775-1778 John Watson
1792-1796 Richard Watson
1792-?? Thomas Watson
Other Professions & Trades
1801-?? William Daws Sawyer
1758-1761 James Muns Snr.
          Weaver
1783-1792 James Ray *Lathe
Render, Hurdle Maker*
1781-1783 William Ray *Lathe
Render, Hurdle Maker*
1801-?? Robert Ray
Hurdle Maker
1761-1762 Daniel Winch
Tallow Chandler
1763-?? John Wollos
*Reben Rider (Possibly a
travelling Haberdasher)*
1784-?? John Smith *Rockbuck
(Possibly A Stonebreaker)*
Cordwainer Or Shoemaker
1758-1768 Thomas Culver
1763-1768 Samuel Daniel
1778-1786 William Bray
1781-1792 Edward Culver
1772-?? John Spiser
1801-?? John Ephgrave
1794-1801 Thomas Sheath
1801-?? James Hall

Militia List 1758-1801
Household Richard Warren
(Esquire) 1758
1758-1762 John Carrington
          Gardener
1763 Jonas Bush *Horsekeeper*
      John Carrington *Gardener*
      Simon Warby *Footman*
1764 John Carrington *Gardener*
1765 Jonas Bush *Servant*
      Simon Warby *Servant*
1773 James Webster *Servant*
Household The Lord Olevent
(0lliphant) 1758
1758 John Cooper *Footman*
      John Sute *Butler*
1759 Thomas Body *Butler*
      John Cooper *Coachman*
Household Thomas Blindel
(*Farmer*) 1763
1765 James Glearsbrock *Servant*
1769 John Parsel *Ploughman*
1772 William Ollen *Servant*
      John Parsel *Labourer*
      William Emington *Servant*
1773 William Handley *Servant*
      John Parsel *Labourer*
Household John Ward (*Farmer
& Constable*) 1759
Household William Ewington
(*Farmer*) 1760-1792
(*Overseer of the Poor 1762*)
Household William Toovey
(*Farmer*) 1764
1765 William Moobry *Servant*
Household Jonathon Darlin
(*Farmer*) 1768
Household Mr Gutters 1760
James ? *Shepherd*

Militia List 1758-1801
Household Edward Kent
(*Farmer*) 1758
(*Overseer to the Poor 1762*)
1759 John Penn *Servant*
1760 John Penn *Ploughman*
Household Widow Valentine 1758
1759 John Gooses *Servant*
      Thomas Tyler *Servant*
1772 Thomas Tyler *Servant*
1773 Thomas Tyler *Labourer*
Household John Warby

(*Butcher*) 1759
    Churchwarden 1759-1762
1759 William Wrenn *Servant*
1760 William Ward *Ploughman*
1761
1762
1763) William Ammerus
Ploughman
1764
1765
1768 William Ammerus
Labourer
1769 William Ammerus
Labourer
1778 William Ward *Servant*
Household Benjamin
Whittenbury (*Farmer*) 1759
1759 Thomas Hall *Servant*
      Robert Whittenbury *Servant*
1772-1793 John North *Labourer*
Household William Senior Esq.
1768 John Williamson *Gardener*
      John Carter *Butler*
      John?? *Coachman*
1769 John Hollis *Butler*
Militia List 1758-1801
Household Mr Cahuac 1772
1772 Stephen Lewis *Servant*
      Isaac Puddingfoot *Servant*
1773 John Hughes *Servant*
      Joseph Porter *Servant*
1778 Joseph Porter *Servant*
Household Robert Smith 1769
1769 William Walker *Ploughman*
1772 William Garner *Servant*
      Richard Shuffel *Servant*
1773 Richard Shuffel *Servant*
      William Garner *Servant*
      Thomas Darys *Servant*
      Thomas Dymmerks
Servant
1775 Thomas Dymmerks
Servant
1778 William Parsel *Ploughman*
Household Francis Dean
(*Farmer*) 1786
1796 Francis Dean *Farmers Son*
      Richard Dean *Farmers Son*
1797 Richard Dean *Farmers Son*
1798 Richard Dean *Farmers Son*
1801 Richard Dean Jnr. *Farmer*

Militia List 1758-1801
Household Richard Clark
    (*Farmer*)
1758 *Assessor Of Land Tax*
1758 John Gillburd *Ploughman*
    Richard Mash *Ploughman*
    Joseph Milton *Ploughman*
    John Wicks *Ploughman*
1759 Richard Clark (*Farmer*)
    Overseer of the poor
    John Milton *Servant*
    James Pond *Servant*
    Thomas Wacket *Servant*
    John Wicks *Ploughman*
1760 William Burges *Shepherd*
    William Clark *Horsekeeper*
    Richard Mash *Ploughman*
    William Wacket
    Horsekeeper
    John Wicks *Ploughman*
1761 Robert Crawley *Tasker*
    John Surry *Ploughman*
1762 Joseph Whittenbury
    Shepherd
    John Wicks *Ploughman*
1764 Jonathon Darlin
    Ploughman
    James Deller *Ploughman*
    William Moobry *Odman*
    Adam Ward *Odman*
    Joseph Whittenbury
    Shepherd
1765 John Wicks *Ploughman*
    William Moobry *Odman*
    Henry Burges *Servant*
1768 William Burges *Labourer*
1769 George Garner *Blacksmith*
    George Norman
    Ploughman
    John Reed *Horsekeeper*

Militia List 1758-1801
Household Col. John Sabine.
(*Described as Deputy Lieutenant*)
1758
1758 Richard Boor *Steward*
    Stephen Oakley *Butler*
    Edward Warde *Footman*
    William Wood *Coachman*
1759 Richard Boor *Steward*
    Thomas Covey *Butler*
    James Preston *Coachman*

1760 Thomas Boor *Steward*
1761 Thomas Boor *Steward*
    Thomas Covey *Butler*
1762 Thomas Covey *Butler*
    James Preston *Coachman*
    Hugh Watson *Gardener*
1763 Richard Cartwright *Butler*
    James Cooper *Groom*
    Thomas Ensom *Postillion*
1764 Richard Cartwright *Butler*
    James Cooper *Footman*
    Thomas Ensom *Coachman*
1765 Richard Cartwright *Servant*
1768 John Carter *Butler*
1769 James Smith *Butler*

Militia List 1758-1801
Household George Archer
    (*Farmer*) 1759
1759 James Warby *Servant*
1765 William Gaylor *Servant*
1768 William Gaylor *Labourer*
1773 William Kent
    Servant & Publican
1778 William Kent
    Alehouse Keeper
1781 James Warby *Labourer*
Publicans
1765-1772 William Kent
1769-1775 John Williamson
1778 Joseph Whittenbury
1792-1801 John Carrington
Bakers
1763-1775 William Dolling
1765 John Underwood *Servant*
1781-1783 James Ward
1792-1794 Benjamin Burton
Blacksmiths
1758-1768 John Squire
1768-1798 Theophilus
Thurrowgood
1773-1775 William Izard
1775-1801 Benjamin Squire
1778-1787 William Canfield
Butchers
1759-1765 John Warby
(*Church Warden* 1758-1762)
1768-1787 Simon Warby
Joseph Row *Shepherd*

Militia Lists 1758-1801
Household Richard Clark (named
previously as *Farmer*)

1769 William Wilcher
    Tasker
1772 William Burges *Labourer*
    George Garner *Blacksmith*
    Hosea Hanchant *Tasker*
    John Ilitt *Cowman*
    William Wilcher *Labourer*
1773 Francis Dean *Servant*
    George Garner *Labourer*
    Hosea Hanchant *Servant*
    William Wilcher *Labourer*
1775 Hosea Hanchant Tasker
1778 Hosea Hanchant
    Ploughman
    Joseph Row *Shepherd*
1781 William Smith *Ploughman*
    William Burges *Ploughman*
1782 Hosea Hanchant *Tasker*
    Thomas Hanchant *Tasker*
    William Smith *Ploughman*
1783 William Smith *Tasker*

Militia List 1758-1801
Household Lady Cathcart 1768
1768 Thomas Ansell *Coachman*
    Patrick Colly *Butler*
    Philip Cosgrave *Footman*
    John Edwards *Gardener*
1769 Patrick Colly *Butler*
    John Edwards *Gardener*
    James Reilly
    Under Gardener
    George Warby *Servant*
1772 Thomas Main *Servant*
    John Godfrey *Servant*
1773 John Crouch *Coachman*
    John Godfrey *Footman*
    James Reilly *Gardener* ?
    Father
    James Reilly *Servant* ?
    & Son
1775 James Reilly *Gardener*
    James Reilly *Servant*
1778 James Reilly *Gardener*
    James Reilly *Labourer*
    Philip Reilly *Labourer*
    George Warby *Servant*
1781 James Reilly *Gardener*
    Philip Reilly *Labourer*
1782-1787 James & Philip Reilly
    both appear as
    Gardener

252

Appendix 3

Charitable Tewin

Charitable giving has played a big part in the life of the village particularly in the days before high taxation and the welfare state. Bequests were either land and buildings or money. They were for four main strands: the Church, relieving the poor, education and the village as a whole.

In *1334 Sir Philip Pelytot* gave lands to the Prior of Wymondley to build a chantry at Tewin Church, in *1610 Thomas Pigot* left monies in his will for the poor.

In *1710 Rev Charles Layfield DD* left the interest of some South Sea annuities for the poor, particularly in apprenticing poor boys of Tewin, where he was born.

In *1678 Sir Francis Botelers* conveyed a farm called Clarkes to trustees for the benefit of 5 poor widows, 4 belonging to the parish of Hatfield and 1 to Tewin.

The Almshouses were built on Lower Green in 1717. A parish register records *'the parishioners built almshouses consisting of 4 partitions out of the poor's money by consent of the whole parish poor and rich. The interest of the remaining £50 is to be used to be distributed among the poor about Christmas'.* Later the almshouses were converted into the parish workhouse and it is recorded later in the 19th century that there were *'at present 6 paupers in the workhouse but the numbers fluctuate'.* The buildings were demolished in the 20th century.

In *1748 Margritta Sabine* of Tewin House gave to the rector of Tewin and his successors the sum of £200 to be invested to give interest to be applied in keeping up the tomb of her husband (which now fills the south porch) and the surplus to be expended in yellow serge for clothing poor boys of Tewin. A later record shows that the rector tried to apply yellow serge but none of the poor that he approached would accept it! Mr Sabine therefore adopted a variation by clothing 6 poor boys of the parish of Tewin in a complete set of apparel consisting of a blue cloth coat, blue and yellow toilinet waistcoat, cord breeches, hat, shoes, 2 shirts, 2 pairs of stockings and a coloured neck handkerchief at an expense of £21. The same thing happened in *1818* and in *1831*.

In *1735 Henry Cowper* set up a Sunday Savings Bank. It paid a good rate of interest particularly for regular savers. This was an inducement for the savers to go to church where the money was collected and interest paid!

The establishment of the *Schools* covered by the bequests of *Dr Henry Yarborough, Lady Cathcart, and Henry Cowper in 1773, 1783 and 1835* respectively are recorded elsewhere.

The buildings demised by *Dr Yarborough,* the house currently known as The Old School House, and 3 cottages on the site of 22 to 26 Lower Green, Tewin, together with the orchards and appurtenances thereunto appear to have been annexed by the Cowper family after the generous donation by Henry Cowper of the new schoolhouse in 1845 now known as Cowper Hall also on Lower Green, Tewin.

The position was rectified by the Charity Commission on *3 January 1896* when it was agreed that *'a piece of copyhold land containing 1 r, 3p or thereabouts situate near Tewin Lower Green with the 3 old cottages and an old school house (let as 3 tenements) erected thereon'* was to be passed to the Cowper family as purchasers in return for a rent charge of 8 guineas per annum on Holwell Farm. One of the anomalies in the record of these charities is the amount of land covered by the Charity Commission's ruling. 1 rod and 3 perches or thereabouts is not a sufficient piece of land even to cover the current Old School House and the Lower Green houses. It is certainly not enough for the *'gardens, orchards and other appurtenances'* which later became the village allotments and in more recent times Godfries and Harwood Closes which appear to have been kept by the Desborough Estate.

The Yarborough and the Cathcart bequests were subsumed into the then Board of Education, (now the Ministry of Education and Skills) in 1926. At that time the capital in Consols and cash amounted to some £700.

It is interesting to note that the lands covered by these bequests are worth in the 21st century several million pounds!

In *1975 Florence Picton* left money worth £1500 for the poor.

This charity together with the Piggott, the Layfield and the Henry Cowper have all now been subsumed into *'Tewin Charities'* which superseded the 1938 scheme in a Charity Commission Scheme in 1995. Its objective is to help those in need, hardship or distress, resident in Tewin, with priority to disadvantaged children, and the elderly. Trustees include the Vicar, two appointed by the Parish Council and two co-opted. The present (2006) Clerk to the Trustees is David Little FCA.

One of the buildings for the benefit of the entire village is the *Memorial Hall,* (see pp. 109 -115).

Appendix 4

Plotlands

Early in 2002, a local farmer sold Green Belt farm land to a property developer. It is likely that the developer paid the market rate of £1000 to £2000 pounds an acre.

The first area of land was between Marden Hill and the village. The developer designed a brochure showing one acre plots in areas bound by potential roads. He offered each plot for sale to the public for £30,000. He claimed that although no planning permission had been granted for house building, there was a long term potential for planning permission to be granted, perhaps after 10 years.

Many people, particularly people from other countries, put down a non-returnable deposit with the option of completing the purchase later. East Herts District Council were alerted by *The Tewin Society* and the Council issued an order to prevent the erection of fencing or other changes on this land.

However, very soon a further 180 acres or thereabouts were being offered. The developer bordered each plot with fences before the council could serve a notice to prevent this happening. The fencing can be seen on the land from the B1000 road. The land is part of the Mimram Valley and includes water meadows with many rich habitats for wildlife.

The developer tried to get permission to increase the size of access to these plots, but this was turned down by the Council. As this behaviour has been occurring elsewhere in the south east, Parliament have taken an interest and issued guidelines.

It is highly unlikely that planning permission will ever be granted to the owners for housing, but it is impossible to farm the land here productively now.

Appendix 5

The Tewin Society

The Society was formed in 1969 by a group of people who had concern for the preservation of the village of Tewin and the surrounding area.

The Reverend K. R. Blamire Brown and Mr C. G. Kemp were soon joined by others, including Dilys Applegate, Arthur Edwards, Harry Munn, Keith Sykes and John Lee.

The timing of the formation of the Society was due in part to strong local feeling that people in Tewin had not been adequately consulted on the approval process of the Brosnan Estates' development of Harwood Close and Godfries Close.

From 1971-1979, the Society was heavily involved with a traffic survey and two major planning applications for the extraction of gravel at Marden Hill and Panshanger Park. A considerable amount of time was spent on this by members, and was followed by possible planning proposals for a golf course, which was finally considered unacceptable.

The Society has been responsible for the preparation and printing of the Tewin Map on which all the footpaths are clearly marked and numbered. Two editions of the Tewin Trail were printed over the years and regular copies of the Newsletter have been distributed to all members. Tree and bulb planting in the Parish of Tewin is ongoing and, in the winter months, there have been many lectures and talks for people in Tewin to enjoy. To date *The Tewin Society* has over 300 household members.

Aims of the Society:
- To preserve the environment and character of the Parish and to monitor planning.
- To enhance the environment by the planting of bulbs and trees.
- To monitor the state of the footpaths and by-ways (in conjunction with the Parish Council), and take action to maintain and improve them.
- To promote activities of a cultural and artistic nature by way of meetings, lectures and outings.
- To raise funds by way of subscription and donation.

The Tewin Road Study

The Tewin Road Study was published in the autumn of 1972 by Arthur Edwards for *The Tewin Society*. Monitoring of the traffic in Tewin has been carried out at intervals since then.

Appendix 6

Friends of Tewin

Following the successful achievements of the Millennium Committee it was decided in February 2001 to continue the good will and community spirit by forming the *Friends of Tewin*. Since that time, the committee, chaired by Linda Crawford, has been responsible for arranging numerous projects which have now become standard events in the village.

Amongst the most popular are the well attended free annual Senior Citizens lunches and teas in the Memorial Hall. The bi-annual barn dance also attracts a good crowd, as does the classic car show on Upper Green which draws people from surrounding areas and has become an annual event.

The committee arranges outings during the year and the scarecrow weekends see the creative abilities of villagers given full rein as very imaginative scarecrows appear all over the village. The Christmas carols service round the brightly lit tree on Lower Green has become an important part of the festive season.

As a result of funds raised through some of these activities, the *Friends of Tewin* have been able to help finance many village projects. Donations have been made towards the installation of electricity on

Programme cover for the first of the *Friends of Tewin's* summer events which has since become a **THACS** bi-annual feature in the village.

Lower Green, the purchase of a freezer for the community shop, chairs for the Memorial Hall, music equipment for St Peter's Church, notice boards for the Brownies and a donation to the cost of the Tewin History book.

Help has been given to renovate the bus shelter, to apply for and receive a grant for the children's playground on Upper Green, to help run the village fête and sponsor a book sale twice a year. As a result of all this enterprise, the *Friends of Tewin* is now a central organisation for the village.

Appendix 7
An Outdoor Scrapbook

Left: **Watercolour of Lower Green from Vine Cottage, c1918, (before the Hall was built in 1922; unknown artist, collection of Roger & Elizabeth Temple).**Top right: **1ˢᵗ Tewin Girl Guides, April 1980.** Middle right: **Finals day at Tewin Tennis Club on 12ᵗʰ September 1987: Charlotte St Pier, winner of the Girls' Singles, Doubles and Junior Mixed Doubles.** Below right: **The great all-rounder Derek Randall (Notts & England) with Bridget Petherbridge, August 1991, during the match on Upper Green between Nottinghamshire CC and Tewin CC. Tewin lost narrowly after 'dismissing Notts for a paltry 845'. Trent Bridge now has a stand named after Derek Randall.**

255

Life on Lower Green in the 1920s, inset left, with children in 'Sunday best' holding hoops to play with; main picture: Alf Fulford's village fête scene of 2008; inset right: the 8th May 1995 VE Commemorations; inset below: one of Tewin's jumble sales in the Memorial Hall, where Todd Canton, who has helped plan local events for many years, is seen as a figure of calm amongst the crowds.

Sponsors

The following have sponsored this book by supporting the publication with advanced payments of £50 or more towards its production. For this generous help, the Tewin Society Book Group and the Publishers are most grateful.

K Adams
Dilys Aileen Applegate, Jane Wesley Berridge (née Applegate), Juliet Ann Smith (née Applegate)
Pat Ashman
Joy Barker
Ian & Mari Barton-Jones, Seimon, Robin & Oliver Barton-Jones
Michael & Cheryl Cook
Pauline Cooper
Angela Crawford-Ingle
Mr & Mrs A W Davis
Reverend Tom & Janet Gladwin
Patrick Holden
Stuart James, Douglas James
Michael & Gloria Kersey
Rob Killingback
Dr Richard & Margaret Knight
Brenda Langton
John & Ann Lee
Paddy & Valerie Loughrey
Tricia & Edward Lyons
Jenny & Roger Malec
Anne & Arthur Mead
Marian Meads
Alan & Dorothy Mole,
Clare & David Holley,
Lucy & Johnny Horstead
Ann & Jim Moon
Gerry, Jackie,
Andrew & Laura Murphy
Lia Parkinson
Paul Phillips, Lynne Haley (née Phillips), Carol Phillips,
Gary Phillips
David Plews
Martin & Christine Sharpe
Eric Sherriff
Kate & Steve Stott
Roland & Jo Swift
Hilary Tipping & Terry Brand
Ivor & Linda Williams
Elizabeth Wilson
Kenneth J Wilson JP
Ruth Woodroff
Chris Zaidi

Subscribers

The following have subscribed to this book in advance of its publication. For this generous support, the Tewin Society Book Group and the Publishers are most grateful. Our thanks, too, to several doners who wish to remain anonymous.

Mrs Abbot
Karin White & David Adams
Linda Adams
Peter Addison
Jill & John Allen
Terry Archer & Eileen Orton (née Archer)
Philip Arnold
Bertha Banks
Brenda Barber
The Barker Family
David & Anna Bateson
Peter and Anne Beale
Graham & Helen Bennell
Alison Benton
Tony Berry
Brigitte Bevan
Mr E Bird
Dr & Mrs W Boardman
David Bond
Patrick, Gillian & Guy Bonwick
Karin Borg
Charles & Lena Bowden
Kelvin & Brenda Bowen
Henry & Janet Bowrey
John & Georgina Brace
Di & Keith Bradley
Richard and Jay Briers
Kevin & Beverley Brazier
Dagmar, Phillip, Julian, Daniel, Dominic & Olivia Brook
Raymond Brown
Dr & Mrs Tom Brown
Sylvia & Tom Brown
Alistair & Elisabeth Buchanan
Fran Buckley
Derek & Pamela Bucknall
Susan Burgess
Miles & Suzanne Bullivant
Peter & Alison Burleigh
Carl & Mary Burnside
Todd & Jean Canton
Esther, Bruce and May Carley
Wyn & Dennis Carlton
Mike & Gay Cates, Roddy Cates, Mary Lisa Webb née Cates
Joan Chalkley
Anna & Michael Clark
Barbara Clarke
Paula Collins
Denis & Marian Compton
Ivan & Joan Cosgrove
Keith & Amy Cox

Linda & Richard Crawford
John & Karen Crowe
Christa & Robert Cullen
Mrs M Dawson
A J T D'arcy
Margaret Davies
A Day
John & Rosaline Downes
Jenny Doxey & Family
Eileen Doyle
Marius & Lizanne Du Plessis
Barbara Eavis
Gail & Peter Elliott
Bryan & Jennie Evans
Jim, Lynn & Rebecca Farr
Ken & Sheila Feakes
Stephanie & Don Fisher
Janet Fitzpatrick, Nick Fitzpatrick
Anthony & Sue Flind
Pat & Alf Fulford
Elizabeth Gardner
Michael Gibbons
Alasdair & Joy Gillies
Jan & Alan Guilford
Mr & Mrs Martin Gouldstone
Dave & Felix Green
Bob & Tess Greener
David & Mary Gregg
Wayne Griggs, Vicki Griggs
Gaye Grimmond
Mr & Mrs Grimmond
Julie Grimwade
Robert Guilbert
Chris & Sue Haden
Hector Hadley
Nicky Hadley
Mavis & Tony Haggar
Diane & Paul Hagger
Mrs I Hall
Janet & Tony Hall
John & Sheila Hampson
Graeme Harman
Peggy Harris
Pamela Haughton
Kim & Helen Hawkey
Anne & David Henson
Pauline Hay
Oliver Heald MP
Roe & Adrian Hill
Susan Hobart
Nigel & Alison Hollingsworth
R & M Horgan
Mike and Anne Horsman
Roger & Margaret Huggins
Mr & Mrs J Hughes
Jean & Steve Hughes
Jennifer Hume
The Humphreys family
Colin & Tove Nisson Huntley
Jenny Izzard
Trevor J James
M & T Jepson
R H and J M Judkins
Shirley Ashby & Peter Kent

Bridget & Ray Keppler
Ann Kevis
Brian King
Stuart & Julie Kirkham
Pat Klijn
Lord Laming of Tewin
David and Sharon Laming
Colleen M Large
Joy C Lawson & Kristina Lawson
Peter and Rene Leigh
Liz Lewinton
Daisy Lewis
Rose Lind
Doreen & Mick Lloyd
Paul & Eleanor Lohr
Nicholas Maddex
Anne McCloy
Caroline McCloy
Sally McCloy
Caroline & Jeff Mcfarlane
Michael McMullen
Maria & Noel Mcquaid
Geof Malin
Linda Joyce Mandall
Geraldine & David Marshall
Pauline Marshall
Diane & Malcolm Meeson
Gillian Alexander & Rowland Minos
R Morgan
Olly Morrisroe
Victor Murray
Barry & Julie Nash (née Bridgman)
Valerie Newman
Deborah & Simon Newton
Rosemary Nodder
Nigel & Stephanie North
Elizabeth Nutting
Carole Oliver
Betty Osborn
Jude O'Sullivan
Freda Owen
Geof Malin
Roy A Meads, Tim Peacock
Hazel Paul
Karol Perley
Mr & Mrs J Perry
Grace & Gill Petty
Jonathan, Julie, Lucy & William Pickworth
Mike & Viv Pilbeam
Janet E Pitman, Randolf Pitman
Lesley & Richard Poole
Lynne & Antony Powell
Judy Puddefoot
David Rawlins
Dave Reavill
Joan Reynolds
Brian & Rita Robbins
Ben, Kirsten & David Roberts
Albert Robinson
Lesley S Robinson
Jane & David Room
Keith & Marie St Pier
Sam Sadler

Merralyn Sandison
Peter Saywood
Geoffrey & Jennifer Schoon
Menna & Geoff Searle
Ted and Ruth Sharp
James Shaw
J Shepley
John & Christine Sheridan
Barbie Short
Warren, Tracey, Maximilian and Tobias Shirvell
Brenda Smith
Gwyneth O Smith
Helen & Gerry Smith
Don and Lilian Southgate
Christine & Roger Spendley
Graham & Pauline Spring
Liz Staddon
Tim Stephens
Richard & Susanne Stevens
Michael & Ann Sullivan
A D Swift
Richard & Sue Tebbutt
Roger and Elizabeth Temple
Jules Thelwell
Jeff and Heidi Tipper
Julia Tizard
Barbara and Roger Toms
The Trevarthen family
Jill Turner
Elisabeth Tyers
Natalie & Christopher Wade
Marion Walby (née Cole)
Peter and Audrey Walters
Thomas & Pauline Warehand
The Watts Family
Katie and Russell Westwood
Chrissy and Andrew Whawell
Edna Whisker
Susan Whitbourn
Margaret Wilson
Maureen Woolne
Maureen & Alf Yates

David Temple and the successful Tewin band *The Roosters* performed at the Millennium celebrations on Upper Green in the summer of 2000. David is shown here playing at *The Rose and Crown*.

There are a number of musicians living in the village and several members of both the Hertford Choral Society and the Hertfordshire Chorus. Their many performances in Hertford and elsewhere have been critically acclaimed and their concerts are well supported by residents of Tewin. Hilary Jones (cello) and Gerry Ruddock (trumpet) both play in the London Symphony Orchestra.

Paul Griggs entertains the village each New Year's Eve in the Memorial Hall, as here in 2005. Since the days of performing and recording at home and abroad with Guys n' Dolls he has continued with a very successful solo career and has recently published the diary he has kept during the years of his life singing and playing the guitar, (see his *Diary of a Musician* featured on page 240).

259

Acknowledgements, Bibliographic Notes, Sources and General References

The Book Group members, (see page 2), prepared the text for the chapters and many other people have provided information. We wish to thank Roger Temple for his substantial input as well as the following who have made invaluable contributions:

Dilys Applegate, Tina Baker, Joy Barker, Brian, Andrew and Maria Bennett, Tom and Sylvia Brown, Barbara Clarke, Ivan Cosgrove, Richard Crawford, Reg Davis, Gerry Edwards, Peter Ephgrave, Graham Fish, Revd. Tom and Janet Gladwin, Mavis Hagger, Mike Horsman, Roger Huggins, Ann Kevis, Margaret Knight, Paul and Eleanor Lohr, Tricia Lyons, Weston Marchant, Alan McNab, Marian Meads, Betty Osborne, Tony Rook, Frank Shadbolt, Jill Sinclair, Bruce Tyler, Susan Tyler, Jean Scottow, Peter and Audrey Walters, Ivor and Linda Williams, Evelyn Wright.

The Book Group is indebted to all these people and apologises to anyone inadvertently omitted from its thanks.

The following notes on references, permissions and sources are from lists provided by the authors and are not intended to form an ordered bibliography.

Translation of Aethelgifu's Will Letchworth Museum & Art Gallery.
Artefacts Hertford and Mill Green Museums.
The History and Antiquities of the County of Hertford. R. Clutterbuck.
A History of Hertfordshire. R. Cussans.
A History of Hertfordshire. Tony Rook (1984, 1997).
North Mymms: Parish and People. D. Colville.
Edward Sabine of Tewin. Tom and Janet Gladwin.
Tewin House, Tewin. Report for the Hertfordshire Garden Trust by Margaret and Harold Smith (2005).
A foreign view of England in the reigns of George I and George II. The letters of Monsieur César de Saussure to his family, 1725 edited by Madame Van Muyden; *Census Returns, Panshanger Archives, Grenfell family material, Repton Red Books and maps:* References and pictures by kind permission of Hertfordshire Archives & Local Studies, County Hall, Hertford and Viscount Gage.
Julian Grenfell Nicholas Mosley, (1976) Holt, Rinehart & Winston, New York
Julian Grenfell, soldier & poet. Letters & diaries

1910-1915. Edited by Kate Thompson. Hertfordshire Record Society.
Lord Desborough. Monica Salmond.
Ettie. Richard Davenport-Hines. Weidenfeld & Nicholson.
Firle Place, Sussex. Tim Knox. Trustees of the Firle Estate, Firle Place, Lewes, East Sussex BN8 6LP *A Deep Cry - First World War Soldier Poets killed in France and Flanders.* Anne Powell. *The Tewin William Cowper: 1st Earl Cowper.* Wikipedia.
Millennium Exhibition.
The Book of Welwyn. Richard J Busby, Barracuda Books Chesham Buckinghamshire. (With additional facts researched on the Welwyn Rifle Range).
Parks in Hertfordshire since 1500. Hugh Prince. University of Hertfordshire Press.
Country Life. March 1889, January 1936, June 1999
The Ice Houses of Britain. 1990 Sylvia P Beamon & Susan Roaf. Routledge.
Some Ancestral Estates & Interesting Castles. 1894 *Hertfordshire Civic Society Newsletter.* Oct 1976: 'When I worked for Lady Desborough'.
Hertfordshire: Some Ancestral Estates & Interesting Careers. (1884) Hertfordshire Standard, Watford Times, Barnet & Southgate Times & Finchley Telegraph.
Hertfordshire Countryside. Jean Gardner article on Alfred Beit.
A Brief History of Tewin Water Robert Lee.
British History Online.
Tewin Church. Revd. A.C. Vidler M A, Rector of Tewin 1912 - 1930.
A Hertfordshire Family. 1555 - 1923. Evelyn Wright.
The Tomb of Lady Anne Grimston. Published by Anthony Knight.
The NADFAS* record of Church furnishings in St. Peter's Church 1985 and *addendum.*
*(National Association of Decorative and Fine Art Societies).
A Survey of Burial Registers between 1810 and 1990 and the headstones of the churchyard. Peter Walters. (Church Warden 1985 - 2003).
Jesus College Archives via Susan Sneddon, Records Manager: Jesus College, Cambridge.
The Diocesan Archive, at County Hall, Hertford. www.beittrust.org.
The extracts from *Nicholas Nickleby.* Charles Dickens by kind permission of Wordsworth Editions.
The extracts from *'Memorandoms for... the Carrington Diaries'.* W Branch Johnson (1973) by kind permission of Phillimore & Co.

Other sources include:
The Old School House, Tewin, A Dickensian School. Patrick Holden, (1999). Training Publications Limited, Watford.
'The Gentleman at Muspatts' a biographical essay on Joseph Strutt. W E Hughes (1932).
The Carrington Diary. W Branch-Johnson (1956).
Kelly's Directories 1838-1937.
The Modern House in England. F.R.S. Yorke.
The Modern House today. Nick Dawe.
We are grateful to the Governors and Head Teacher for consent to quote from both: *Two hundred years of Tewin School.* Stephen James, and *March 2006 School Report.* Eileen King.
Tewin Militia list 1758-1810. HALS.
A Hertfordshire family 1555-1923.
The story of Tewin. K N Brettel.
Twentieth Century Hangings. Peter Wilson.
The Story of My Life. Henry Gullet.
Highways and Byways in Hertfordshire. Herbert W. Tompkins.
A Survey of Agriculture in Hertfordshire. H.W. Gardener. *Royal Agriculture Society of England.*
Yesterday's Farm. Valerie Porter.
The place names of Hertfordshire. J.E.B. Gover, (1938). Cambridge University Press.
The Origins of Hertfordshire. Tom Williamson. Manchester University Press.
The Folklore of Hertfordshire. Doris Baker-Jones. B.T. Batsford.
Old Hertfordshire. Doris Baker-Jones. Phillimore.
Welwyn Garden City Past. Tony Rook.
Deserted Mediaeval Villages in Hertfordshire. K. Rutherford Davis. Phillimore.
Hertfordshire Murders. Nicholas Connell and Ruth Stratton. Sutton Publishing, (2003).
Barrow's Boys. Fergus Fleming. Granta Books.
'The Arctic Council planning a search for Sir John Franklin' courtesy of the National Portrait Gallery.
Queen Hoo: The Story of the Manor and the Hall based on research by W.H.H. Van Sickle. Frank Cox.

Photographs and illustrations

Special mention must be made of the great help that the staff of **HALS** - *Hertfordshire Archives & Local Studies,* at Hertfordshire County Council, County Hall, Hertford, have given to the committee for the research for pictures as well as all the general history enquiries over many years. This wonderful source of history, which allows studies of all kinds, is a credit to the county.

The pictures have come from a mixture of sources and the old postcards used rarely named the photographer. Susan Tebbutt very kindly gave special help from her extensive collection. Michael Creasey helped with early family pictures related to *The Plume of Feathers.* Anne and Arthur Mead gave generous access to Queen Hoo Hall for research on this chapter. Many of the houses were photographed by Ben Roberts. Others were mostly by members of the Book Group, but three of the wild bird photographs were by the late Les Borg, by kind permission of Karin Borg.

We have sought permission to reproduce all the material, but we apologise to any copyright owners we have not been able to contact or who have not responded to our attempts to verify picture use.

Just as the writers have made no charge for their work, all the permissions for pictures used have been given freely, at no charge. For this we are very grateful indeed.

All profits from the sale of this book are to be given to the *Tewin Memorial Hall Committee* to assist in its work in the maintenance of Sir Herbert Baker's splendid 87 year old building which is a focal point for the activities of the village community.

The Hundred Year Wood, (featured on page 93, when the children helped to plant the trees), has been a great success. It is hard to believe now that the wood and wild flower meadow was once just the corner of the arable field next to Upper Green.
This was the scene in 1995 when it was first being planted out. Growth was initially slow due to the dry summers which followed. A detailed, well illustrated account of the planting and management was kept by Alan Guilford which he has kindly donated to the village archive.

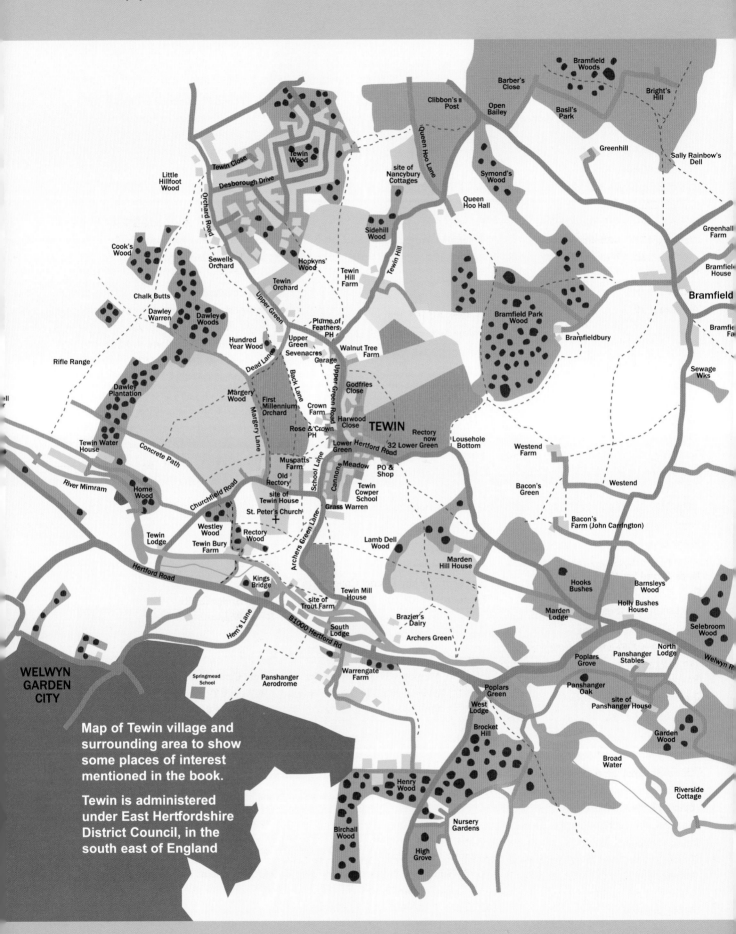

Map of Tewin village and
surrounding area to show
some places of interest
mentioned in the book.

Tewin is administered
under East Hertfordshire
District Council, in the
south east of England

Index

Tewin continues to welcome visitors and new residents to the village. Above: **Wyn Carlton was presented in 2003 with a bouquet, in recognition for all she had done for the Millennium projects, by Rosie and Florence Christian-Cox who had moved to the village that year.**